ROUTLEDGE LIBRARY EDITIONS:
THE ECONOMICS AND BUSINESS OF
TECHNOLOGY

Volume 23

THE BRITISH
COMPUTER INDUSTRY

THE BRITISH COMPUTER INDUSTRY

Crisis and Development

TIM KELLY

Routledge
Taylor & Francis Group

LONDON AND NEW YORK

First published in 1987 by Croom Helm

This edition first published in 2018
by Routledge
2 Park Square, Milton Park, Abingdon, Oxon OX14 4RN

and by Routledge
711 Third Avenue, New York, NY 10017

Routledge is an imprint of the Taylor & Francis Group, an informa business

British Library Cataloguing in Publication Data
A catalogue record for this book is available from the British Library

ISBN: 978-1-138-50336-6 (Set)
ISBN: 978-1-351-06690-7 (Set) (ebk)
ISBN: 978-0-8153-8440-3 (Volume 23) (hbk)
ISBN: 978-1-351-20439-2 (Volume 23) (ebk)

Publisher's Note
The publisher has gone to great lengths to ensure the quality of this reprint but
points out that some imperfections in the original copies may be apparent.

Disclaimer
The publisher has made every effort to trace copyright holders and would welcome
correspondence from those they have been unable to trace.

THE BRITISH COMPUTER INDUSTRY
CRISIS AND DEVELOPMENT

TIM KELLY

CROOM HELM
London ● New York ● Sydney

© 1987 Tim Kelly
Croom Helm Ltd, Provident House, Burrell Row,
Beckenham, Kent, BR3 1AT
Croom Helm Australia, 44-50 Waterloo Road,
North Ryde, 2113, New South Wales

Published in the USA by
Croom Helm
in association with Methuen, Inc.
29 West 35th Street
New York, NY 10001

British Library Cataloguing in Publication Data

Kelly, Tim
    The British computer industry: crisis
    and development.
    1. Computer industry — Great Britain
    I. Title
    338.4'7004'0941   HD9696.C63G7
    ISBN 0-7099-3123-9

Library of Congress Cataloging-in-Publication Data

Kelly, Tim

    The British computer industry.
    Bibliography: p.
    Includes index.
    1. Computer industry — Great Britain. I. Title.
HD9696.C63G765 1987   338.4'7004'0941   87-569
ISBN 0-7099-3123-9

Printed and bound in Great Britain by
Biddles Ltd, Guildford and King's Lynn

CONTENTS

List of tables
List of figures
Acknowledgements

Contents

LIST OF TABLES

List of tables

List of tables

List of tables

LIST OF FIGURES

List of figures

Acknowledgements

This book is based on three years of Ph.D research funded by the Economic and Social Research Council (ESRC) between 1982 and 1985 with fieldwork funded by the Philip Lake Fund. During the course of research I have been helped by countless individuals and organisations of which it is possible here to acknowledge only a few.

The book would have been impossible without the time and effort of the business executives and entrepreneurs who filled in postal questionnaires and gave personal interviews. I am particularly grateful to Mr J.G.Bates and Mr M.D.Stott of STC ICL and IBM (UK) respectively. In addition I have received valuable assistance from the Scottish Development Agency, the Scottish Council, the DTI, the EITB, Hertis, Cambs County Council and Logica Consultancy. To my colleagues at St. Catharine's and the Dept. of Geography at Cambridge University I am grateful for the help they gave me in penetrating the complexities of the University Computer Service. For the maps and diagrams in the book, I owe a debt to Ian Gulley, Mike Young, Jeff Mander and Carol Kelly. For data entry and typing I was assisted by Ron Mander and Carol Kelly whose accuracy and speed far surpassed my own. My parents have supported and encouraged me throughout the research and long before it and I am especially thankful for the help they gave me while I was carrying out the fieldwork. To all the above, I can only offer my most sincere thanks.

Two people above all others have provided inspiration over the last three years and to them I owe a debt which I will never be fully able to repay. The first is my supervisor, Dr David Keeble who has proved to be everything a research student could hope for. He provided direction when it was needed and gently steered me away from the cul-de-sacs I was intent on exploring. I have benefitted greatly from his wealth of experience in industrial geography and it has been a privilege to work with him. Finally I must thank my wife Carol who has given me the motivation, patience and encouragement to see this book

Acknowledgements

through to a conclusion. Without her, it may never
have been finished and would certainly have been
riddled with errors of spelling, grammar, logic
and jargon. As it is, I must accept full
responsibility for the errors which remain.

Dr Tim Kelly,
Logica Consultancy,
64, Newman St.,
London,
W1A 4SE

Chapter One

INTRODUCTION

1.1 Crisis or Development?

High technology industry, and particularly the
technology-based new firm has, in the last few years, emerged
as an increasing focus for government policy. In November
1981, Norman Lamont MP spoke on behalf of the Department of
Industry when he declared that, along with regional policy,
high technology industry is "the sector to which we now devote
the greatest resources in aid to private industry". Concern is
founded on the potential of high technology industry to
create wealth, employment and, in the long term, to generate
industrial revival. It is clear too that the consequences for
British industry of failing to adopt new technology may be a
loss of international competitiveness.

High technology industry may be defined according to a
variety of criteria, such as the level of innovation, the
occupational composition of the workforce or the dynamics of
production and employment growth (Kelly, 1986, chapter 4). By
whatever definition chosen, one industrial sector stands out
as exemplifying the popular conception of 'high tech', and that
is computer electronics. Between 1975 and 1983, when
production in British manufacturing industry as a whole
declined at a rate of 1.1% p.a. compound, the computers and
office machinery sector (AH 330) grew by 12.3% p.a. Similarly,
while manufacturing employment was falling by 4% p.a. over the
same period, employment in computer manufacturing grew by
almost 4% p.a. In both indices of production and employment,
the computer industry has been the top performer in the
British economy over the last decade.

In the light of this apparent success it may seem strange
to talk of a 'crisis' in the British computer industry, and yet
that is precisely the title of a recently published NEDO
report on the state of the industry (NEDO IT SWP, 1983). The
crisis reflects the crucial point that the growth which has
occurred has not matched that of Britain's international

competitors. The short-term outlook in the electronics sector is for market rationalisation, job loss in the older-established firms, and for a permanent trade imbalance due to the failure to maintain sufficient productive capacity. The software industry is not immune from this crisis. A recent report from ACARD (1986) concludes that "if the UK industry does not more vigourously compete in the world market .... then within 10 years only MoD-supported firms will remain". The report goes on to predict that by 1990 the UK will have a trade deficit of £9 billion in Information Technology of which £2 billion will come from trade in software products. Only the new firms sector offers prospects for a brighter future, and even here there is evidence that the growth firms of the early 1980s are struggling. The two shining lights of the microcomputer revolution, Acorn Computers and Sinclair Research, have both experienced highly publicised financial crises and have both been taken over, by Olivetti and Amstrad respectively.

This book takes the computer industry as an example of a high technology sector and explore its recent development in Britain. In chapter two the emphasis is on technological development and the way this has shaped the competitive structure of the computer industry. The chapter also uses statistics from the government and other sources to provide a background to the evolution and present structure of the industry.

In chapter three, the origins of the computer industry are traced with reference to specific firms, focussing on the two market leaders in the UK, IBM (UK) and STC International Computers Ltd. The chapter covers the period from 1948, when a stored-program computer was used successfully for the first time in the world at the University of Manchester, until 1979. Chapter four covers the period from 1979 to the present day and charts the growing crisis in the British computer industry and the government's response to it.

The choice of the year 1979 is significant for several reasons. In political terms it marked a shift in government away from the industrial interventionism of the Wilson-Heath-Callaghan years to the free market Conservatism of the Thatcher Government. In economic terms 1979 saw the onset of a global industrial recession which paralleled that of the 1930s in its severity. In the specific case of the computer industry, 1979 marked the start of job-shedding and ultimately financial collapse of Britain's only major indigenous computer manufacturer, ICL.

Introduction

The year 1979 was significant too because it was the high-water mark of the wave of new firm formation which had been apparent in the computer industry since 1975. In chapter five it is argued that higher rates of new firm formation are intimately connected with the advent of microelectronics and the subsequent development of the microcomputer. It is shown that between 1975 and 1984 more than 300 independent and currently surviving new firms were created and their impact on the industry is assessed.

The themes of the historical development of the computer industry, the rationalisation of ICL and new firm formation are brought together in chapter six which surveys the current 'geography' of the industry. This chapter uses national employment data from the EITB, the Department of Employment and original survey research carried out at the University of Cambridge to examine recent changes in employment. The contrasting fortunes of two areas of computer industry concentration, in Scotland and around Cambridge, are examined in more detail.

Finally chapter seven returns to the title of the book and asks whether 'crisis' or 'development' depicts more accurately the current state of the computer industry in Britain. The answer varies according to what part of the industry, and what part of the country is under consideration. However, the conclusions which are drawn are highly critical of the neglect for industrial policy which has characterised recent governments. It is argued that the growth of high technology industry in Britain has been hampered by a defence sector which is out of all proportion to Britain's current status, and which has 'crowded out' commercial research and development.

1.2 A functional definition of the computer industry

Under the 1968 Revised Standard Industrial Classification, the manufacture of computers is classified to MLH 366 which is defined thus:

Manufacture of digital, analogue and hybrid electronic computer equipment and systems (except those which are not separable from industrial process control systems). This heading includes the manufacture of computer sub-assemblies and peripheral equipment.

Introduction

Under the 1980 revised Standard Industrial Classification,
MLH 366 is combined with MLH 338 (Office Machinery) to create
a new classification, AH 330, for the 'Manufacture of Office
Machinery and Data Processing equipment'. This is divided into
two sections:

3301 Office Machinery - Manufacture of typewriters,
      duplicating machines, adding machines, calculating
      machines, cash registers, electronic desk calculators,
      non-electronic data-processing and handling equipment,
      mail-handling machines, ticket-issuing machines and
      other machines for office use.

3302 Electronic Data-processing equipment - same definition
      as MLH 366 (see above).

Further clarification of this definition is provided in the
'Indexes to the Standard Industrial Classification Revised
1980' (CSO, 1981) which provides a list of industries covered
by AH 3302:

      Analogue computer, manufacturing
      Central processor unit, computer, manufacturing
      Computer, electronic, manufacturing
      Computer, peripheral equipment, manufacturing
      Computer system, manufacturing
      Converter (for computers), manufacturing
      Data-processing equipment, electronic (other than
            electronic calculators) manufacturing
      Digital computer, manufacturing
      Hybrid computer, manufacturing
      Memory store, computer, manufacturing
      Peripheral equipment, (including card punches and
            verifiers) for computer uses, manufacturing
      Printer, computer, manufacturing
      Store, computer, manufacturing
      Tape reader, computer, manufacturing
      Terminal unit, computer, manufacturing
      Visual display unit, computer, manufacturing

In the compilation of the company database which was used as
the basis for the national postal questionnaire, an attempt
was made to include all identified establishments in these
categories. However, those firms involved only in the
marketing, installing, retailing and repairing of computers,
in the process of which no manufacture is carried out and

4

little value is added to the product, were excluded. The Computer Services sector was formerly classified to MLH 865:

> Typewriting, duplicating, document copying, translating, employment agencies (not government), computer services and other similar business services.

Under the 1980 revised classification, this becomes AH 839 with computer services represented by AH 8394. The 'Index to the SIC revised 1980' shows that this includes:

> Computer Services
> Computer consultancy
> Software house
> Time hire (computer)

In the Cambridge University survey, a slightly narrower definition of computer services was used. This definition includes firms which might be said to 'generate wealth' and therefore contribute to the local industrial base, but excludes firms which purely offer business services. Thus companies involved in software development for 'package programs' and for custom or 'turnkey' projects are included, but computer bureaux (time sharing), recruitment agencies and retail/distribution outlets are excluded. A fuller description of the computer industry and the format of the Cambridge University survey can be found in Kelly, T. (1986) 'The location and spatial organisation of high technology industry in Great Britain: Computer electronics', unpublished Ph.D thesis, Cambridge University library.

Chapter Two

TECHNOLOGICAL CHANGE AND MARKET STRUCTURE

2.1 Technology cycles

This chapter provides a general background to the history of the computer industry in Britain which is presented in later chapters. In section 2.2 there is a short review of technical change in the electronics sector and in sections 2.3 and 2.4 a description of the market structure and general characteristics of the British computer industry.

The precise connection between technology and the evolution of market structure is complex, but in general terms it is hypothesised that technological change will impact market structure in three particular ways. Firstly, technical change may alter the competitive structure of an industry. For instance, the optimal size of operating units may increase or decrease and the 'barriers to entry' for new firms or market entrants may be lowered or raised during the course of a product cycle. The tendency towards structural concentration or deconcentration will typically be marked by a parallel change in the level of spatial concentration of the firms in that industry. Secondly, technological advances may change the labour input required for successful development, manufacture and sale of a competitive product range. Thus the balance of skills available in a particular labour market and the level of wages that workers command may no longer be appropriate to the particular stage of the product cycle. Thirdly, technological change may alter the physical requirements for raw materials and energy consumption in the production process, for the size and layout of premises, and for transport, communications and accessibility.

Technological change is also frequently cyclical and may be seen to be occurring in two distinct time scales. In the short-term (3 to 7 years) there is a 'product life-cycle' associated with the stage of design, development, pilot production and volume production of a new product. In recent years, the expected life span of products has generally

6

diminished, though product segmentation – customising the same basic product to a variety of niche markets – has increased. Over the longer term (40 to 60 years) technological change induces more fundamental shifts brought about by basic research rather than incremental development. Thus the age of microelectronics has superceded the technology of electronics, which, in turn, grew out of electrical product technology. This long-wave cycle is often associated with the name of the Russian economist, Nikolai Kondratiev, who popularised the notion of long waves in economic life.

Clearly however, technological change does not operate in a vacuum, and at every stage its effects are tempered or directed by the requirements of the marketplace. Short-term or long-term fluctuations in demand may also affect the competitive structure of an industry. New markets may appear where new consumer demands are generated while older markets may reach saturation. The evolution of the computer industry has reflected the impress of both changing technology and changing markets.

A key distinction may be drawn between 'product innovations' and 'process innovations' and the changing balance between these two over the course of the technology cycle. Product innovation creates new markets, and even new industries, and will generally provide employment opportunities. Most new and improved products come from within the R&D departments of the largest firms, for instance videos and compact discs. However, some new product markets, such as microcomputers and biotechnology, have been associated with the emergence of new firms and decreasing industrial concentration. Markusen (1985, p38-42) has argued that the rate of firm formation and the level of industrial concentration can be used as key variables to determine the competitive structure and hence the stage of the profit-cycle (or product life-cycle) of a particular industry. In the biotechnology industry in the US, Feldman (1985 p74) identifies 113 competing firms of which the great majority employ less than 50 staff. In the information technology industry in the UK for instance, Preston et al (1985 p41), show how the level of industrial concentration (sales of top 5 firms as a percentage of total output) has decreased from 69% in 1968 to 54% in 1979. This has occurred because the technology of microelectronics has allowed new entrants and other high growth firms to challenge the established market oligopoly.

7

By contrast to product innovation, process innovation or 'embodied technical change', tends to increase the level of concentration by raising the threshold of investment needed for market entry. The use of volume production techniques will typically reduce prices and profit margins and force firms with small market share out of the market. While those firms which are able to adopt process innovations and to compete effectively may maintain employment, jobs will inevitably be displaced elsewhere in the industry as profits are competed away and market rationalisation proceeds. Hannah (1976) has shown that acquisition and merger activity appears to have long wave characteristics with the peak periods during the 1920s and the late 1960s immediately preceding phases of slower growth and higher unemployment.

Freeman et al (1982 p44-63) use a dataset assembled by the Science Policy Research Unit (SPRU) of 195 basic innovations in the UK between 1920-80. Distinguishing between product and process innovations, they show that the former are bunched in the immediate post-war years and continue to provide the bulk of all innovations until the late 1950s. In the 1960s however, process innovations became dominant and there is a general decline in all innovations in the 1970s. Thus product innovations are characteristic of the early stages of the long cycle and process innovations of the later stages. However, the two are not mutually exclusive and may occur simultaneously even within the same industry. Freeman (1979) comments on the way that product innovations from one sector such as microelectronics may 'colonise' other industries as process innovations.

Product and process innovations also vary in their implications for employment. In the popular perception, technical change is seen as a destroyer of jobs because of the productivity gains which generally result from the introduction of new process machinery (Freeman et al, 1982). It is often the case that the employment displacement effects and the employment creation effects of technological change are geographically removed (Sayer, 1983). This spatial dislocation is particularly apparent when the qualitative as well as quantitative aspects of employment change are considered. Technological change may alter the skills balance required in the production process. If the new proportions in which these skills are required are different to the proportions in which they are available in the local labour market, then the resulting 'mismatch' will result in unemployment amongst the displaced skill categories.

8

Technologically-induced 'structural unemployment' may therefore overlap with 'demand deficient' unemployment thus explaining the apparent paradox of skill shortages co-incident with 14% national unemployment in the UK (Butcher Committee, 1985).

The following sections examine the effects of technical change on market structure in the particular case of the computer industry. The theme of technical change creating new market opportunities is returned to in chapter five which charts the effect of microelectronics in creating a new firms boom in the computer industry. The spatial dislocation between the employment creation and employment dislocation effects of technical change is the theme of chapter six which considers the changing geography of the British computer industry.

2.2 Technical change in the electronics sector

Throughout the brief history of the computer industry, it has been technical change in the basic electronic components which has provided the spur to commercial diffusion (Braun & MacDonald, 1978). It is commonplace to define this evolution in terms of successive 'generations' of components, though there is only partial agreement over the timing of generation shifts. The first 'generation', which was based on thermionic valves, was superceded by transistorised computers such as the IBM 7090 and the Elliott 803 around 1958/9. The space race and the demand for increasingly sophisticated guided weapons systems greatly increased the pace of miniaturisation of electronic circuitry and the introduction of integrated circuits in the mid-1960s and microprocessors in the mid-1970s heralded the third and fourth generations of computers. The term 'fifth generation' has been coined to describe research currently being undertaken to develop computers for the 1990s using VLSI microchips, parallel processing and artificial intelligence techniques. The term comes from a much-publicised Japanese government-sponsored research project which aims to leapfrog current, more conventional, technical evolution in the USA and Western Europe.

The diffusion of computer usage in the UK was relatively slow at first. Sales of computers did not exceed 50 per annum until 1957 and 1000 p.a. until 1965. Thereafter however sales increased rapidly with 31% p.a. compound growth in shipments between 1965 and 1970 (Stoneman, 1976, p122). Since 1965 there has been a doubling in the level of miniaturisation of electronic circuitry approximately every two years, and since

1970 the development of Random Access Memory (RAM)
semiconductor chips from 1K (1000) bits capacity to 64K in
1979 and 256K in 1984. This has been associated with a decline
in the cost per bit of 35% (Soete & Dosi, 1983, p12). The one
megabyte chip is now in production and has been used in the
latest generation of IBM mainframes introduced in mid-1985;
the so-called 'Sierra' 3090 range. Further research is
proceeding into the use of alternative materials to Silicon,
such as Gallium Arsenide.

Whereas the gap between the invention of the transistor
at Bell Labs in 1947 and implementation in computer design was
10/12 years, the gap between laboratory advances in Very
Large-Scale Integration (VLSI) technology and implementation
is now typically only 2/3 years. While it may not be possible
to reduce this gap any further, there is no reason to suppose
that the rate of technological change will slow down.
Price/performance ratios are continually improving. For
instance, cost of storing one million characters of data on
current IBM high speed disc storage devices is around a tenth
of what it was in 1976 in constant prices. The improvement in
price/performance ratios is fundamental to the broadening of
the market for computers which has taken place since the
introduction of personal computing. However, it has also meant
a reduction in profit margins which has implied a shift
towards selling cheaper computers as commodity products
through distributorships and franchises rather than by a
direct sales force.

Table 2.1: Physical characteristics of three generations
            of ICL mainframe computers of similar power

Year	Mainframe Model	Power consumption (Kilowatts)	Weight (Kg.)	Volume (Cu. Metres)
1975	2980	57.0	4,364	14.0
1980	2966	17.0	855	2.7
1985	3930	0.4	140	1.0

Source: Dace (1982, p7)

One consequence of the progress in electronics miniaturisation is that the dimensions and power requirements of the central processor units have been drastically reduced. Some idea of the extent of these changes can be gained by consideration of the physical characteristics of three generations of ICL mainframe computers of similar power levels; the 2980, the 2966 and the series 39 level 30 (Table 2.1). These were introduced at five year intervals since 1975. When this miniaturisation is coupled with the trend towards automated production lines and 'volume' rather than 'customised' production, it can be seen that the requirement for manual labour input in the production process has been substantially reduced. Consequently, the focus of development has now shifted to networking of computers and to software where the lack of standardisation and a poor perception of market requirements has hindered further diffusion of computer usage. Recent developments have attempted to improve the efficiency of existing hardware, such as ICL's Content Addressable File Store (CAFS) software; to enable the interrogation of large databases through expert systems; and to develop 'packages' for non-specialists in middle-management and clerical work including word processing, spreadsheets, database management systems and graphics applications

2.3 Market structure

2.3.1 Product life-cycle evolution

Drawing upon Kuhn's (1962) work on revolutions in the practice of Science and Schumpeterian (1939) notions of technology-induced long wave cycles, Dosi (1983) has developed a model of technological paradigm change relating technological change to market structure. The birth of the electrical industry at the start of the 19th century and to a lesser extent the development of the electronics industry in the post-war period are both taken to represent 'paradigm shifts' marked by the emergence of new firms exploiting product niches in a competitive market. The intervening years are described by a 'technological trajectory' - "the 'normal' problem-solving activity determined by the paradigm" (Dosi, 1983 p85). During these phases, the structure of competition within the industry moves towards 'oligopolistic maturity' through mergers, takeovers and liquidation of unsuccessful competitors.

Technological change and market structure

The birth of computing in the immediate post-war period did not however constitute a fundamental shift in the technological paradigm. The early entrants to the emerging computer industry such as IBM, Remington Rand, Burroughs and NCR in the US and English Electric, Ferranti, ICT and Elliott Bros. in the UK, were largely long-established multinationals already involved in electrical engineering, telecommunications and the manufacture of electro-mechanical business machines. The initial growth of the market was hindered by poor perception of the commercial potential of computers, even in IBM (Katz & Phillips, 1982, p426-32). In the UK too it was widely believed that computers would be limited to scientific and military applications and the ACE machine constructed at the NPL was expected to be the 'British national computer' sufficient to serve most scientific needs (Lavington, 1980, p23). The first generation computers were thus mainly restricted to small production runs, with the exception of the IBM 650 which, first introduced in 1954, eventually sold 1,800 machines.

The transition to transistorised computers 1958-60 did allow some new entrants in the US including Honeywell and several new start-up companies, including Control Data (1957) a spin-off from Sperry Rand, Digital Equipment Corp. (1958) and Scientific Data Systems (1961). Three other companies, General Electric, Philco and RCA, all of which had been involved in transistor manufacture, also entered the market at this stage but later pulled out of computer manufacture following fierce price competition from IBM. In the UK however, neither of the new entrants at this stage, Metropolitan-Vickers and EMI, prospered in the computer industry. Table 2.2 shows the distribution of the installed base of computers between manufacturers in the UK and the US at the start of the period of widespread diffusion in 1963. Interestingly, the 'Snow White and the Seven Dwarfs' structure which has characterised the US computer industry had already emerged by 1963 with IBM dominant, whereas the UK market was much more competitive until the formation of ICL in 1968. This brought together Ferranti, English Electric, ICT and Leo Computers.

New entrants in the UK were largely restricted throughout the 1960s and early 1970s to the peripherals market. An example is Data Recording Instruments (1956) acquired by ICT in 1962. More significantly, most of the current market leaders in software were established during

Table 2.2:   Computer manufacturers' market share in the UK
             and USA, 1963, by value of installed base

UK		USA	
Ferranti Ltd.	25%	IBM	69.8%
ICT	25%	Sperry Rand	11.2%
English Electric Co.	13%	Control Data	4.0%
Elliot Bros.	12%	RCA	3.5%
NCR	11%	General Electric	3.5%
Leo Computers Ltd.	7%	NCR	2.7%
Others	7%	Others	5.3%

Source: Lavington (1980, p84) derived from National
          Computing Index, NCC
          Brock (1975, p21-2) derived from Honeywell vs.
          Sperry Rand Decision (1973, p15)

the 1960s and early 1970s including F International (1962),
CAP (1962), Datasolve (1964), BIS (1964), Data Logic (1968),
Logica (1969), Dataskil (1970), Baric (1970) and Software
Sciences (1970). Several of these have passed through the
hands of different corporate owners with ICL absorbing
Dataskil and Baric while Thorn-EMI re-entered the information
technology market after 1982 with the acquisition of
Datasolve, Software Sciences and EPS Consultants.

The adoption of integrated circuitry into the 'third
generation' of computers after 1966 similarly produced few new
entrants in the UK all of which have remained relatively small
and specialised. These include Computer Technology Ltd. (1966
- now Information Technology Ltd.), Kode International Ltd.
(1968), Computer Machinery Co. (1968 - now part of Microdata,
US) and Systime (1972 - now split between Control Data and
Digital Equipment Co., both of the US). During this period US
market penetration grew substantially from 10% in 1960 to 50%
of the installed base by 1970, especially after the
introduction of the IBM 360/370 series in 1964. This was the

first true 'range' of machines stretching across the spectrum from small business machines to large-scale scientific mainframes. Furthermore the innovation by IBM of software that was 'upwards compatible' throughout the range and which was planned to be 'forwards compatible' with future machines made IBM a formidable competitor. Thus by 1968 the structure of the industry in the US was monopolistic and in the UK fully duopolistic (Table 2.3) with ICL and IBM (UK) competing for dominance of the domestic market.

Table 2.3:   Computer manufacturers' market share in the UK and USA, 1968, of the installed base by value

UK		USA	
ICL	41.0%	IBM	73.8-74.6%
IBM	23.4%	Sperry Rand	5.6%
NCR/Elliott	10.7%	Honeywell	4.7%
Sperry Rand	8.8%	Control Data	3.9%
Burroughs	6.4%	General Electric	3.2%
Honeywell	5.4%	RCA	2.4%
Other Non-UK	3.4%	NCR	2.2%
Other UK	0.9%	Other	3.6-4.2%

Source: Moonman (ed. 1971, p88) derived from 'Appendices' of the Select Committee on Science & Technology, Sub-Committee D vol. H.C. 272
Brock (1975, p21-2) derived from IBM internal figures, Computers & Automation and Automatic Data Processing Newsletter.

2.3.2 Mainframes and minicomputers
     The duopolistic structure of the mainframe market in Britain has persisted since 1968 though increasingly IBM has exerted its dominance at the expense of ICL. Figures from the International Data Corporation (IDC - Table 2.4) show that in

Technological change and market structure

Table 2.4: Large-scale multi-user processors, manufacturer's market
share in the UK, 1985

Vendor	Year End 1985 Installed Base		1985 Shipments			
	Units	(%)	Units	(%)	Value (£m)	(%)
IBM	565	(41%)	140	(44%)	491	(63%)
ICL	425	(31%)	85	(27%)	119	(15%)
Honeywell	85	(6%)	17	(5%)	30	(4%)
Burroughs	80	(6%)	20	(6%)	36	(5%)
Amdahl	71	(5%)	16	(5%)	31	(4%)
NAS	55	(4%)	18	(6%)	28	(4%)
Sperry	40	(3%)	6	(2%)	12	(2%)
Control Data	22	(2%)	2	(1%)	3	(0.3%)
BASF	17	(1%)	7	(2%)	6	(0.8%)
Others	32	(2%)	6	(2%)	25	(3%)
TOTAL	1,392	(100%)	317	(100%)	781	(100%)

Source: Adapted from IDC (1986)

1985 IBM and STC ICL shared almost three-quarters of the UK installed base of large-scale multi-user processors (costing more than $1 million). However, two trends are evident from this table: First, it is apparent that IBM is continuing to gain market share particularly in value terms. IBM mainframe shipments accounted for 63% of the total UK mainframe market in 1985. It seems likely that over time the duopoly will tend towards a monopoly in the absence of nationalistic protectionism towards STC ICL. Second, the rise of the Japanese manufacturers is disguised by the fact that several companies either sell Japanese-built computers (Amdahl - Fujitsu; NAS and BASF - Hitachi; Honeywell - NEC) or have technology-sharing agreements with Japanese firms (STC ICL - Fujitsu).

IBM is also market leader in Britain in the minicomputer market (Table 2.5) for systems costing between $100,000 and $1 million, but here the market is more open. Two British companies, STC ICL and Ferranti, together with the US-acquired formerly-British company, Microdata, compete with the Americans for dominance. While IBM has not traditionally done well in this market, it has made recent gains in the financial sector where the System 34/36/38 is popular. DEC is IBM's nearest rival and has gained market share recently. DEC (UK) was the best-performing subsidiary of DEC worldwide during 1985. DEC sells well in the engineering, research and education fields. STC ICL's medium-scale systems have benefitted from strong sales in the retail sector, as well as its traditional markets of local government, universities, health care and defence. Ferranti holds fourth place in the listing by virtue of a strong presence in the defence sector.

2.3.3 Microcomputers

The market for computer systems costing less than $100,000 has recently been the fastest growing segment of the computer market worldwide. The impact of microelectronics, and in particular the microprocessor, since the mid-1970s has transformed the industry and in Dosi's terms represents a 'technological paradigm shift' - a major discontinuity in the development of the industry. The first valve computers emerged from the liaison between long established electrical engineering companies, universities and the military. However, the first commercially available micros such as the Altair, the Apple, the PET and the ZX80 surprisingly did not come from within the multi-million dollar R&D budgets of the large American multinationals, but from spare-time enthusiasts and

Technological change and market structure

Table 2.5: Medium-scale multi-user processors, manufacturer's market
share in the UK, 1985

Vendor	Year End 1985 Installed Base		1985 Shipments			
	Units	(%)	Units	(%)	Value (£m)	(%)
IBM	3,330	(15%)	795	(15%)	249	(26%)
DEC	3,180	(15%)	800	(15%)	132	(14%)
ICL	2,520	(12%)	435	(8%)	139	(14%)
Ferranti	1,740	(8%)	600	(11%)	61	(6%)
Honeywell	1,717	(8%)	295	(6%)	54	(6%)
Hewlett-Packard	900	(4%)	250	(5%)	33	(3%)
Prime	860	(4%)	315	(6%)	48	(5%)
Wang	840	(4%)	295	(6%)	38	(4%)
Microdata (McDonnell Douglas)	800	(4%)	295	(6%)	37	(4%)
Data General	592	(3%)	212	(4%)	28	(3%)
Other	5,246	(24%)	1,028	(19%)	143	(15%)
TOTAL	21,725	(100%)	5,320	(100%)	963	(100%)

Source: Adapted from IDC

17

disaffected graduate students. Technological change allowed new entrants into this previously oligopolistic market and small, new firms played a major part in the development of microcomputers, associated peripherals and software on both sides of the Atlantic. Firms such as Apple, Microsoft, Sinclair Research and Microvitec had already grown to a considerable size by the time the established multinationals began to move into this emerging market in the early 1980s. Behind these market leaders came a myriad of smaller firms exploiting new market niches in micros for small businesses, educational or scientific applications and in the home. In software too the multiplicity of programming languages and operating systems used by manufacturers encouraged new firm formation as did the demand for a range of peripheral devices and data communications equipment.

Recent market growth has been concentrated at the two extremes of the computer spectrum: one million dollar plus supercomputer systems for use in defence, weather forecasting, banking etc; and single-user microcomputer systems typically costing less than £10,000. This latter sector accounted for 9% of the UK computer market by value in 1984, but is predicted to rise to 29% by 1989 (Smith 1985, quoting a BIS-Pedder report). The National Computing Centre (1985) enumerated 434 different brands of single-user system currently available in the UK including 80 portables and 44 programmable Word Processors. This number will inevitable fall and market rationalisation through takeovers and liquidation is already taking place following a slump in microcomputer sales and overstocking in the first half of 1985. Comparisons are frequently drawn with the automobile industry in which there were more than 300 competing companies in the US in the early 1920s but only four left by 1960. America again seems to be leading the way in rationalisation of the microcomputer industry with a 25% fall in the number of manufacturers and a 75% fall in computer software houses between 1983 and 1985 (Reed, 1985)

The microelectronics revolution has produced a number of fast growth new entrants in the UK who have challenged the existing oligopoly including Apricot (formerly ACT), founded in 1966 as a distributorship which became involved in manufacturing in 1983, Acorn (1978 - now part of Olivetti) and Sinclair Research Ltd. (1979 - now part of Amstrad). Other new entrants have prospered in peripherals - Rodime (1979), Microvitec (1979), software - Micro Focus (1976), CIS (1977) and CAD/CAM systems - Pafec (1976), Telemetrix (1978). This

18

theme of new firm growth is taken up in chapter five.

Table 2.6: Major software and service vendors in the UK, 1985

Vendor	Country	Revenue (£m)	Share
Thorn-EMI	UK	50.6	3.5%
Logica	UK	43.0	2.9%
Hoskyns	US	39.8	2.8%
Geisco	US	26.0	1.8%
Scicon	UK	25.2	1.7%
Systems Designers	UK	24.9	1.7%
Centre-File	UK	23.0	1.6%
CAP Group	UK	21.8	1.5%
CMG	UK	20.4	1.4%
BIS	UK	17.9	1.2%
Other	-	1,127.5	79.5%
TOTAL	-	1,409.2	100%

Source: Adapted from IDC

2.3.4 Computer software

The distribution of market shares in the UK software and services industry (Table 2.6) is different from that of computer hardware in two important respects: First, the level of overseas control is much lower. Only 9 of the top 20 firms are US-owned, the rest are British. Even this though is higher than in the French software and services market, the largest in Europe, in which only one of the top twenty firms is non-French. The level of overseas ownership in the UK market is increasing through acquisitions, notably the takeover of

Technological change and market structure

Table 2.7: Change in the index of production in selected
            industries and all manufacturing in Great Britain, 1975-83

Rank	Sector	AH (1980 SIC)	Index of Production (1980=100) 1975	1983	% Change p.a.
1	Computers & Office Machinery	330	57.7	146.4	+12.3%
2	Ordnance, small arms & ammunition	329	71.4	120.4	+6.7%
3	Telecommunications equipment etc.	344	78.6	108.4	+4.1%
4	Soft drinks	428	80.5	107.8	+3.7%
5	Pharmaceutical products	257	88.4	113.3	+3.2%
6	Preparations of milk & milk products	413	84.1	106.3	+3.0%
7	Animal feedstuffs	422	87.1	107.1	+2.6%
8	Soap & toilet preparations	258	88.9	107.1	+2.4%
All manufacturing		SIC 2-4	104.9	95.9	-1.1%

Note The Index of Production for all manufacturing is not strictly
      compatible with the sum of its component parts (see Annual
      Abstract of Statistics, 1985, p244-5).

Source: Annual Abstract of Statistics (1985, tables 8.2 & 14.6)

20

Technological change and market structure

Figure 2.1:   Time-series trends for output, employment and
              productivity in the electronics and computer
              manufacturing sectors, 1959–82

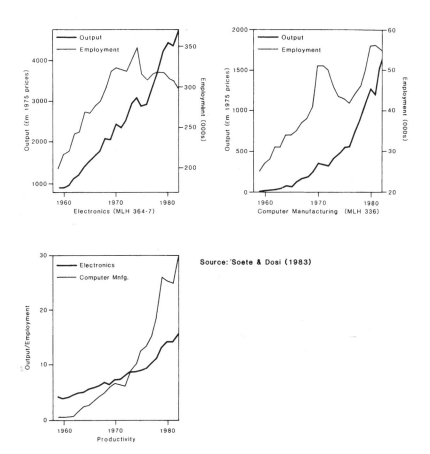

Source: Soete & Dosi (1983)

Hoskyns by Martin Marietta Data Systems, Unilever Computer Services by EDS, and Data Logic by Raytheon Corp. Second, competition between computer services firms is more open than among hardware firms with the top ten firms having barely 20% of the total market. Only Thorn-EMI has a share greater than 3%, and this has been gained through an active acquisition policy which has taken in Datasolve, Software Sciences, Altergo and EPS Consultants. The largest independent computer systems company in the UK is Logica which was founded in 1969 and in 1985 had a turnover of £80m, around half of which comes from outside the UK, and employment of 2,400.

2.4 Computer hardware

2.4.1 Time-series trends in production and employment

Over the last decade the computer electronics industry has exhibited the fastest rate of growth in production and employment of all manufacturing industry sectors in the UK. Table 2.7 shows that between 1975 and 1983 the computers and office machinery sector grew by 12% p.a. compound during a period when manufacturing industry as a whole fell by 1% p.a. The growth in output is also reflected in employment. Computer electronics was one of only six UK manufacturing sectors which grew in employment between 1975 and 1983 (Table 2.8) and indeed showed the greatest percentage gain (+34%) compared with a decline in total manufacturing employment (-27%).

The particularly rapid rate of technological change in the electronics sector compounded with changes in the standard industrial classification means that it is difficult to construct accurate time-series data. Recent work on the electronics industry in the UK by Soete & Dosi (1983) has however yielded a time-series dataset for employment and output in the electronics industry since the late 1950s which can be used with some confidence. Figure 2.1 shows time-series trends between 1959 and 1982 for output, employment and productivity for the computer hardware and electronics sectors (defined as MLH 364-367 under the 1968 SIC). Output in the computer hardware sector grew by 25.3% p.a. compound in real terms, 1959-82 compared with just 7.7% for the electronics sector as a whole.

The rate of employment growth in the computer hardware sector also outstripped the rest of the electronics sector where employment has been in decline since 1974. Interestingly, the time-series trend for employment in the

22

Technological change and market structure

Table 2.8: Manufacturing industries which expanded employment
between 1975 and 1983 in Great Britain

Rank	Sector	MLH (1968 SIC)	Employment (thousands)			% Change p.a.
			1975	1983	Change	
1	Electronic Computers	366	43.4	58.1	+14.8	+3.7%
2	Printing & publishing of newspapers	485	73.6	96.8	+23.2	+3.5%
3	Radio & electronic capital goods	367	89.3	105.3	+16.0	+2.1%
4	Ordnance, small arms & ammunition	342	20.3	23.9	+3.6	+2.1%
5	Food industries not elsewhere specified	229	33.4	37.6	+4.2	+1.5%
6	Cement	464	13.9	15.0	+1.1	'+1.0%
	All manufacturing		7,333.8	5,346.0	-1,987.8	-4.0%

Source: Annual Abstract of Statistics (1985, tables 8.2 & 14.6)

computer hardware sector shows a peak of 51,000 in 1970 and
thereafter a decline to a trough of just under 43,000 in 1977.
However, since 1977 employment growth has resumed though it is
difficult to determine the extent of this growth because of
changes in the collection of official statistics. Following
the Rayner review (Rayner, 1980) of government statistical
services, the frequency of the census of employment has been
reduced after 1978 to a triennial basis and a further census
was carried out in September 1981 using the 1980 SIC.

Quarterly estimates based on the 1978 census and sample
returns from the larger establishments predicted an
employment level of around 40,000 for the computer industry by
1981. However, the census in that year actually showed a level
of 56,064 indicating a margin of error of 40% between
predicted and actual employment levels which was the highest
for all manufacturing AH codes. This error is unlikely to have
arisen due to misclassification of establishments because
employment estimates for other electronics AHs were similarly
upgraded following the 1981 census. It is more likely that the
error arose due to an underestimate of the importance of new
and small firms. Quarterly estimates subsequent to September
1981 have been based on the 1980 SIC and do not subdivide AH
330 between office machinery and electronic computers. The
figures for the combined AH indicate a fall of about 2,000
jobs to 1984 but this may well be due to continued decline in
the office machinery sector which fell from 24,000 in 1976 to
17,000 in 1981 (-29%). Furthermore, because the final results
of the September 1984 census will not become available until
at least 1987, it seems inevitable that the period since 1978
which has experienced intense recession, technical change and,
it is argued later, a fundamental shift in market power
between large and small firms, will remain poorly documented
by official statistics.

    An alternative source of employment data is the
statutory returns by engineering establishments to the
Engineering Industry Training Board (EITB) which are
available on the basis of the 1980 SIC from 1978 onwards.
There are certain problems of compatibility with the Annual
Census of Employment (ACE) but nevertheless the EITB data
gives an invaluable and unique insight into recent employment
change in the industry during a period of traumatic national
recession and industrial decline (Table 2.9). Between 1978 and
1981 total employment grew by 4,000 jobs (+5.8%), but then
declined slightly to 1984 (-240 jobs: -0.3%). This is
consistent with the trend, but not the scale, of employment
change in the ACE data suggesting that a large part of the
employment gain recorded in the latter was due either to
reclassification of establishments or to new firms, which are
poorly represented in the EITB data. These hypotheses are
confirmed by the survey data. Between 1978 and 1984,
employment in other electronics sectors fell by 86,300 jobs (-
25.5%) masking a slight increase in electronic capital goods,
but declines in telecommunications, components and electronic
consumer goods. The manufacturing sector as a whole shed 1.7m

Technological change and market structure

Table 2.9: Employment estimates for the computers, electronics,
manufacturing and services sectors in Great Britain, 1978-84

Sector	Employment (Thousands)			
	1978	1984	Change	% Change
Computer Mnfg. [1]	68.4	72.2	+3.8	+5.5%
Other electronics [1]	338.0	251.7 [a]	-86.3	-25.5%
All Manufacturing [2]	7,147	5,415	-1,732	-24.2%
Computer Software [3]	23.4	33.8	+10.4	+44.4%
All Services [2]	12,877	13,363	+488	+3.6%

Notes: [a] April 1983

Sources: 1 EITB statutory returns
2 Dept. of Employment Gazette, Historical Supp. No. 1,
April 1985
3 Business Monitor SDQ 9

jobs, almost a quarter of the manufacturing workforce, between
1978 and 1984 in an unparalleled period of labour 'shake-out'
and rationalisation (Keeble, 1986a; Martin, 1986).

The graph in Figure 2.1 showing growth in productivity
1959-82 (defined as output/employment) demonstrates that,
from a smaller base, the rate of growth of productivity in
computer hardware manufacturing (19.1% p.a. compound) has
exceeded that for the electronics industry as a whole (7.0%
p.a.). Clearly productivity is a complex variable dependent

not only on technical change but also on the level of capital investment, economies of scale and short-term labour-hoarding. However, in both series a steepening of the upwards trend in productivity is discernible in the middle and late 1970s. This would be consistent with the impact of technological change through the diffusion of microelectronics in the industry in line with arguments advanced earlier (Soete & Dosi, 1983, p52-6).

2.4.2 Employment composition

The EITB data also enables a consideration of employment change by skill categories and gender. The raw data defines eight separate occupational categories, but these can be combined into four divisions which are used in the survey data. These are: Managerial/Administrative/Sales (MAS); Research & Development (R&D); technicians and skilled manual incorporating supervisors and craftsmen; and semi-skilled and unskilled manual occupations.

Figure 2.2 shows that in the electronics sector between 1978 and 1984 there was a markedly different experience of demand for skilled and non-skilled jobs. Indeed there is a spectrum, graded by occupational composition, which ranges from very high demand for scientists and technologists, whose numbers rose by more than 60%, through to low demand for unskilled manual labour grades which fell by around a third. The returns for the computer industry (AH 330) illustrate even more graphically the high priority placed on skilled labour (Table 2.10). Research & Development employment (defined by the EITB as "Scientists and Engineers .... for which the normal qualification is a university degree in engineering, science or technology") recorded the highest, and remarkable, increase of 5,831 jobs (+92.7%). However, over the same period almost a fifth of unskilled manual jobs were lost in the computer industry and a similar proportion from the electronics sector as a whole. There is little evidence therefore of any 'deskilling' within the electronics sector, as has been postulated by some economists (Braverman, 1974), at least at this level of disaggregation. Indeed, on the contrary, the need for qualified scientists and engineers is clearly increasing (Brayshaw & Lawson, 1982; Fidgett, 1984) and this would tend to suggest that the availability of highly skilled personnel is likely to exercise more of a locational pull in the electronics industry than 'pools' of semi-skilled or unskilled labour.

26

Figure 2.2:   Employment change by occupation in the
electronics industry, 1978–84

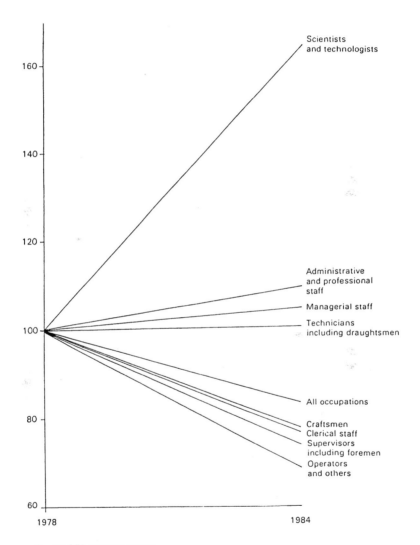

Source: EITB statutory returns

27

Table 2.10: Employment change by occupation in the computer
hardware sector, 1978-1984

Occupation	1978	(%)	1984	(%)	Change	% Change
Managerial/Admin./						
Sales	25,761	(37.7%)	27,638	(38.3%)	+1,877	+7.3%
Research and						
Development	6,288	(9.2%)	12,119	(16.8%)	+5,831	+92.7%
Technicians/Skilled						
Manual	16,573	(24.2%)	16,453	(22.8%)	−120	−0.7%
Unskilled						
Manual	19,779	(28.9%)	15,950	(22.1%)	−3,289	−19.4%
Total	68,401	(100.0%)	72,160	(100.0%)	+3,759	+5.5%

Source: Unpublished EITB data

The increase in the level of R&D jobs in the computer industry is even more remarkable in the light of the already percentage of skilled jobs in the industry. Table 2.11 shows estimates from the EITB and the Census of Production of the ratio of administrative, technical and sales staff as a percentage of all employees. In both data sources the list is headed by the computers and office machinery industry.

Employment change by occupational category shows a significant degree of overlap with employment change by gender. Whereas recent work on labour market trends stresses the increasing importance of female participation and part-time working in the labour force (Frost & Spence, 1981; Martin, 1985), computer manufacturing and the electronics sector

Technological change and market structure

Table 2.11: Ratios of administrative, technical and sales staff
             to all employees in selected manufacturing sectors

			Administrative, technical & sales staff as percentage of all employees	
Rank	Sector	AH (1980 SIC)	EITB (1983)	Cen. of Prod. (1981)
1	Computers & office machinery	330	69.8%	58.8%
2	Process machinery for food, chemical inds. etc	324	43.7%	58.8%
3	Pharmaceutical products	257	n.a.	50.0%
4	Paints, varnishes & printing ink	255	n.a.	50.0%
5	Telecommunications equipment etc	344	49.7%	47.6%
6	Aerospace Equipment	364	48.3%	47.6%
7	Specialised chemicals for domestic use	259	n.a.	47.6%
8	Measuring, checking & precision instruments	371	53.9%	40.0%
All Engineering			36.5%	n.a.

Note: n.a. — not available

Sources: Annual Abstract of Statistics (1985, table 6.3)
          Report on the Census of Production, 1981 (Business Monitor
          PA 1002, table 10)

29

Table 2.12: Employment by tenure and gender in the computer industry,
manufacturing and services in Great Britain, Sept. 1981

	Employment (Thousands)						
	Computer Mnfg.		All Mnfg.		Computer Services		All Services	
Full-Time								
Male	41.7	(73.4%)	4,242.0	(70.0%)	35.8	(65.3%)	5,592.0	(41.7%)
Female	13.2	(23.2%)	1,351.5	(22.3%)	14.7	(26.8%)	2,855.2	(21.3%)
Part-Time								
Male	0.2	(0.3%)	68.9	(1.1%)	0.5	(0.9%)	615.3	(4.6%)
Female	1.7	(3.0%)	395.0	(6.5%)	4.0	(7.3%)	3,358.3	(25.0%)
All emp.	56.8	(100.0%)	6,057.5	(100.0%)	54.8	(100.0%)	13,421.3	(100.0%)

Source: Dept. of Employment Gazette, Occasional Supplement No. 2,
Dec. 1983, 'Report on the 1981 Census of Employment', Table 3

generally exhibits a different pattern. Table 2.12 shows the
1981 composition of the workforce by gender and tenure
divisions. Both part-time working and female employment are
less important in the computer hardware sector than for
manufacturing as a whole. Furthermore, from examination of
employment trends over time, there is no reason to suppose
that these forms of employment are increasing in importance.
EITB returns show that female employment within the computer
sector is more concentrated in unskilled manual categories
(35.4%) than male employment (16.9%). This is the sector which
has experienced the greatest job loss. All other sectors,
particularly the growth sectors of management and R&D, exhibit
relatively low proportions of female employment indicating

30

that longstanding barriers to entry for females in the engineering profession still remain. For the electronics industry as a whole, there has been a significant loss of female jobs during the 1970s corresponding to the reduced requirement for unskilled manual labour (Soete & Dosi, 1983 p69-73). During the period 1978-84, male electronics employment declined by 11% but female employment fell by almost a third. Thus it is more accurate to talk of 'defeminisation' in the electronics sector, whether or not any 'feminisation' trend is apparent in other sectors.

2.4.3 Production

Two main indices of output for the computer manufacturing sector are available from published government statistics. The index of production is an estimation of the average rate of change of 'value added' in different industries (Central Statistical Office, 1976). The index for AH 330 is calculated from the measurement of production in terms of value of sales. Table 2.7 shows that when the index is standardised so that 1980=100, then by 1983 it had risen to 146.4 making computers and office machinery the fastest growing manufacturing sector in the UK. Accurate figures for the actual value of output are more difficult to obtain. Sales of data-processing equipment manufactured in the UK by manufacturers contributing to the PQ 366 (now PQ 3302) Business Monitor series amounted to £2,533.7m in 1984. However, this is likely to be an underestimate as the survey accounts for firms employing less than 36,000 workers whereas September 1981 Census of Employment figures indicate that the total employment in the industry is over 56,000. Furthermore, according to company reports, the turnover attributable to UK production of just two firms, ICL and IBM (UK) Ltd. amounted to over £2,100m in 1984.

Table 2.13 presents an analysis of output under six different product headings for 1973 and 1984. Between 1973 and 1983, the percentage of sales of Central Processor Units (CPUs) declined from 40.1% to 33.7%, but in 1984 a new category of 'Compact Processing Units' was introduced, defined as "comprising in the same housing, at least a central processor unit and an input/output unit". This heading therefore contains mainly microcomputers and the value of sales rose from £393m in 1983 to £813m in 1984 (+107%) when 2.1 million units were sold, produced by 35 separate establishments. The rise in microcomputer production accounted for almost half of the total rise in output in the hardware manufacturing sector.

Table 2.13:   Sales of electronic computers by UK
              manufacturers, 1973 and 1984, (Actual prices)

Product	1973 Output (£m)	%	1984 Output (£m)	%
Compact Processing Units (Microcomputers)	-	-	813.3	32.1%
Central Processor Units (Mini/Mainframes)	141.3	40.1%	158.6	6.2%
Peripheral Equipment:				
Storage Units	45.0	12.7%	171.0	6.7%
Input and/or Output units	107.2	30.4%	567.0	22.4%
Other peripherals and Services	17.4	4.9%	395.3	15.5%
Subassemblies, accessories, software and unclassified	41.8	11.8%	428.4	16.9%
Total Sales	352.6	100.0%	2,533.7	100.0%

Source: Business Monitor PQ 366 Fourth Quarter 1974
        published May 1975 (HMSO)
        Business Monitor PQ 3302 Fourth Quarter 1984
        published April 1985 (HMSO)

By contrast, the value of the market for low volume, high value minicomputer/mainframes has remained fairly static since 1973 and has declined in real terms. This is partly explained by reductions in the price of CPUs now that basic components (microchips and printed circuit boards) are both cheaper and more efficient through large-scale integration. However, between 1983 and 1984 there was also a 10% drop in the number of units sold as market interest switched to microcomputers, which can be networked together or used as intelligent terminals in multi-user systems.

The value of peripheral sales currently accounts for 45% of total output in the computer hardware sector, but since 1973 a more diverse range of peripherals has been manufactured with Visual Display Units (VDUs) and data communications equipment growing in relative importance. Subassembly production, principally through subcontracting, has increased particularly since 1981. This again reflects technological change leading to greater standardisation of components which has encouraged firms, especially new entrants, to subcontract routine production to utilise spare capacity elsewhere in the electronics industry.

2.5 Computer Software

2.5.1 Time-series trends in production and employment

The Computer Services sector was not classified as a separate entity in official statistics until the 1980 Standard Industrial Classification which defined AH 8394 as being 'The provision of computer services on a fee or contract basis to other enterprises'. Thus it is not possible to construct accurate time-series data for the software sector on the basis of the Census of Employment before 1981 and as a service rather than a manufacturing activity it is excluded from the Census of Production. The total employment recorded in the Census of Employment in 1981 (54,739) was only marginally less than for the hardware sector (56,064). Department of Employment quarterly estimates indicate a rise of around 4,400 jobs (+8%) to December 1984. By comparison, quarterly estimates for computers and office machinery (AH 330) and EITB data for computer manufacturing both suggest a fall in employment since 1981. Thus it is likely that UK employment in computer services firms is now greater than in computer manufacturing.

The Business Monitor series SDQ9, which has been published quarterly since 1969, does however provide some basis for consideration of the development of the sector. Several problems exist with this data source. Chief amongst these is that figures are based on returns from a voluntary panel of contributors which, in 1984, numbered 172 firms, data processing departments and other organisations. This was less than 10% of the firms listed as computer consultancies, systems and software houses and computer bureaux in the 'Computer Users Yearbook, 1984'. The Business Statistics Office estimate that the 172 firms cover 54% of the output of the sector in that year. Provisional figures for employment in 1984 are 33,809 which is just under 60% of the Dept. of

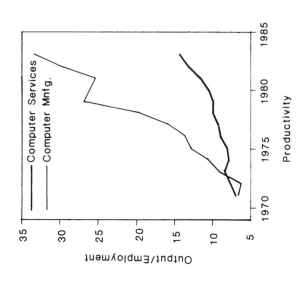

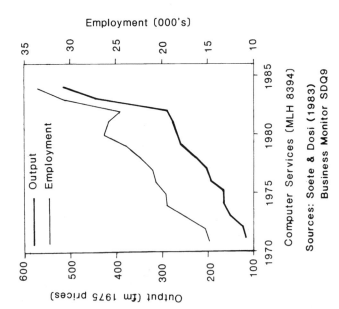

Figure 2.3: Time-series trends for output, employment and productivity in the computer services sector, 1971-84

Computer Services (MLH 8394)

Sources: Soete & Dosi (1983)
Business Monitor SDQ9

34

Employment estimate of total employment in the sector in June 1984. Figure 2.3 shows that since 1971 the SDQ returns indicate a rise of 17,900 jobs (+112%) or 8.6% p.a. for the computer services sector. This compares with an increase of only 13.7% (1.0% p.a.) for computer hardware employment over the same period. Employment in computer services rose every year between 1972 and 1980 but thereafter declined slightly, reflecting the effects of national recession and therefore reduced demand. Between 1982 and 1984 however, employment growth resumed and an extra 8,200 jobs have been added. If this were projected to total employment in the sector, then it would imply as many as 13,000 new jobs in the computer services sector since 1982.

In the production time-series too (standardised at 1975 prices) growth averaged 10.8% p.a. 1971-82, but since 1982 has been 23.2% p.a. suggesting a considerable upturn in business since the recession. Productivity has shown a much slower rate of increase (6.4% p.a. compound, 1975 prices) than for computer hardware (15.8%) which is to be expected given the more labour intensive nature of services activity. However, this has important implications for future employment change in the computer industry. For instance, suppose that during 1984-5 both hardware and software production increased by 10%. At current levels of increase in productivity, this would produce a loss of 2,760 jobs in hardware, but a gain of 1,970 in software. Thus it can be seen that future employment growth is likely to be concentrated in the services sector. A pronounced upward trend is apparent in the rate of productivity increase in computer services since 1980. This may be due to the effects of recession forcing some of the less efficient firms to restructure their activities or face liquidation. Alternatively, it may reflect a genuine increase in the productivity of services activity through the application of improved package programs, expert systems and other software engineering tools. If the latter is the case, then it may reduce future employment prospects in this field.

2.5.2 Employment composition

The 1981 Census of Employment shows that both part-time working (8.2%) and female participation (34.1%) are more important components in the computer services workforce than in computer hardware (3.3% part-time; 26.2% female: Table 2.12). However, in the Services sector generally (SIC 6-9; 1980) part-time working (29.6%) and female participation (53.7%) are much more prevalent than in manufacturing. The SDQ 9 Business

35

Monitor Series suggests that since 1971 part-time working has increased marginally in importance (from 4.8% to 5.6% of total employment in the voluntary sample) but the data does not differentiate between male and female employment.

Table 2.14: Employment change by occupation in the
             computer services sector, 1974-1984

Occupation	1974	(%)	1984	(%)
Consultancy	1,294	(6.5%)	3,796	(11.2%)
Programming/Analysis	5,487	(27.5%)	12,531	(37.0%)
Computer Operators	2,902	(14.5%)	3,113	(9.2%)
Data Control	1,105	(5.5%)	1,161	(3.4%)
Data Preparation	4,983	(25.0%)	2,110	(6.2%)
Administration	2,004	(10.0%)	4,426	(13.1%)
Sales	807	(4.0%)	2,476	(7.3%)
Others	1,369	(6.9%)	4,216	(12.5%)
Total	19,951	(100.0%)	33,629	(100.0%)

Source: Business Monitor SDQ 9 - Fourth Quarter, 1975
         published April 1976 (HMSO). Fourth Quarter, 1984
         published April 1985 (HMSO).

Table 2.14 shows employment change by occupation in the computer services sector between 1974 and 1984, using figures derived from SDQ 9. Interestingly, the trend towards employment gains in the more skilled professions observed for the hardware sector (Table 2.10) is also apparent here. Consultancy and programming/analysis both grew in importance while less-skilled grades of computer operators, data preparation and data control all declined. Non-specialist professions (administration, sales and others) increased their share of the workforce from 20% to 33% paralleling the trend in hardware manufacture to non-production occupations.

36

2.5.3 Production

Output in the computer services sector is more difficult to measure than for the computer hardware sector because the firms involved are much more numerous and because many large firms, primarily engaged in other activities, have a 'data processing department' which may do contract work outside the parent firm. Thus if an 'index of specialisation' (computer-related sales as a percentage of total sales) were calculated for computer services, it would be much lower than the figure of 94% for the computer hardware and office machinery sector (1981, Census of Production). Furthermore, Business Monitor SDQ 9 shows that more than a quarter of 'billings' recorded are to clients within the same organisation.

Table 2.15: Value of 'billings' by product headings for the computer services industry, 1971-84 (actual prices)

Service	1971 Value (£m) (%)	1984 Value (£m) (%)
Computer processing	40.2 (58.0%)	357.3 (30.8%)
Professional Services:		
Turnkey Systems		277.5 (23.9%)
	17.7 (25.5%)	
Systems/Software		263.9 (22.8%)
Services/Consultancy	4.8 (6.9%)	254.6 (22.1%)
Data Preparation	6.6 (10.0%)	6.0 (0.5%)
Total	69.2 (100.0%)	1,159.5m (100.0%)

Source: Business Monitor SDQ 9 Fourth Quarter 1974 published April 1975 (HMSO), Fourth Quarter 1984 published April 1985 (HMSO)

Five separate product headings within the software sector are shown in Table 2.15. Over the period from 1971 to 1984 computer processing and data preparation operations have decreased in relative importance while consultancy and sale of software/systems have increased. These changes are consistent with the more widespread availability of computer power. The microcomputer in particular has enabled even small businesses to acquire their own computer rather than renting time from, or subcontracting work to, computer bureaux. The bureaux sector has experienced much slower growth than the software industry as a whole and most bureaux have attempted to diversify into other areas of business. The use of typewriter-like keyboards and data acquisition devices rather than punched card equipment has virtually eliminated the market for data preparation.

When these figures are taken in conjunction with those in Table 2.13 showing occupational change they underline the need for software firms to upgrade the balance of the skills composition of their workforce in order to be able to offer clients services which are not available in their own data processing departments.

2.6 Long-term trends in the computer industry - a review

The arguments advanced thus far have been centred on the primary role of technical progress in electronic circuitry in shaping the evolution of the computer electronics industry. Successive 'generations' of electronic components, from thermionic valves to VLSI microchips have effectively determined market structure through the creation of opportunities for new entrants but also the incitement of fierce price competition as a particular 'generation' matures. It has been argued that the changing labour requirements implicit in the shift from manual to non-manual occupations has been underwritten by electronics miniaturisation in making the production process less labour-intensive and far more capital-intensive through product standardisation and trends towards volume production. Furthermore, the pace of technological change has made an effective corporate research and development programme an essential prerequisite for market competitiveness.

However, this crude technological determinism must be tempered by other considerations. Firstly, over the past decade as technical progress has facilitated much wider access to computer power, market considerations have become more important. The market domination of IBM has forced other firms to co-operate in joint agreements on their R&D and marketing programmes in order to be able to compete. International agreement on interface protocols has also increased the openness of international markets. Greater market orientation has also been expressed in the growing importance in employment and revenue terms of the software, services and consultancy sector. As profit margins in hardware supply have been squeezed, firms have become more dependent on the labour-intensive services sector where the sale of expertise and repeat business guarantees higher returns. As a result, market segregation and specialisation has increased. In tightly-defined market sectors, supply and demand considerations have become paramount. For instance, a severe downturn in demand for home computers in 1985 followed pre-Christmas overproduction and led to overstocking and financial crises in the two UK market leaders in this field, Acorn and Sinclair Research. During 1985, the crisis in the UK electronics sector worsened substantially. Warnings of losses from Racal, reduced profits from STC, Logica and Thorn-EMI, and job-shedding by Plessey, STC, Ferguson, Logica VTS and INMOS have all precipitated a loss of confidence in share prices in the electronics sector. It is likely that the downturn in the electronics sector is preceding a more general business-cycle downturn in the economy. However, further market rationalisation through mergers and firm failure, particularly in the overcrowded microcomputer and software sectors, seems inevitable. Hence it can be seen that the recent period has witnessed unparalleled technological, occupational and structural change within the computer industry in the UK and thus provides a fascinating topic for study.

Chapter Three

THE ORIGINS OF THE BRITISH COMPUTER INDUSTRY

3.1 Introduction

In discussing the origins of computing, it is necessary to acknowledge the role of both the 'visionaries'; those whose insight into the potential of an automatic computational machine pointed the way for others to follow but whose contribution remained largely theoretical; and of the incremental improvement in the efficiency of conventional calculators and tabulators which preceded the birth of the true computer. Amongst the former were Charles Babbage (1791-1871), the Cambridge mathematician, who planned a mechanical analytical engine to be controlled by punched cards; and Alan Turing (1912-54), the mathematician and logician, whose original ideas for a stored-program computer contained in a 1936 paper finally became reality in the Pilot Automatic Computing Engine (ACE) built at the National Physical Laboratory (NPL) in 1950. Among the latter were electro-mechanical hand calculators, punched card sorters and tabulators and differential analysers which had been available since the turn of the century. The 'stored-program digital computer' differs from these forerunners in its ability to hold an internal store or 'memory' which can be selectively altered during computation and to vary its actions according to the value of data items encountered during computation (Lavington, 1980 p1).

The actual question of 'who invented the computer?' may never be satisfactorily answered because much of the original research during the war years on cipher-breaking (e.g. the COLOSSUS machine in the UK) and ballistics calculations (e.g. ENIAC in the US) was carried out in secrecy. In the immediate post-war years there were several centres of activity in America and Germany, and at Manchester University, Cambridge University, Birkbeck College and the NPL at Teddington in Britain. However, it is generally agreed that a prototype machine at Manchester University which on 21 June 1948 ran a

52 minute factoring program, was the world's first operational stored-program computer. The Manchester research had close links with Ferranti which led to the development of large mainframe computers for scientific and military applications. Ferranti's ATLAS machine was to form the basis for ICT's 1900 series following the sale of its main civilian computer interests in 1963. By contrast, research in other centres such as Dr. Booth's work at Birkbeck and Dr. Wilkes' team in Cambridge developed commercial links with more market-driven companies including British Tabulating Machines (BTM - based in Letchworth, Herts) and J. Lyons & Co., a catering company who, with remarkable foresight, sponsored the original Cambridge research (Lavington, 1980, p33). The split between development of mainframes in the North West and smaller business machines in the South East was inherited by ICL (now STC ICL) and is still apparent in its current structure.

3.2 STC International Computers Ltd.

3.2.1 The formation of ICL

ICL was founded in 1968 under the Wilson Labour Government in the Industrial Expansion Act as part of its industrial rationalisation programme in order to create a large internationally-competitive presence in the computer industry (Hague & Wilkinson, 1985). The formation of ICL was the culmination of a series of mergers and acquisitions during the late 1950s and 1960s which brought together the two strands of punched-card equipment manufacturers and general electrical equipment manufacturers both of which were diversifying their interests into computer manufacture (Figs. 3.1 & 3.2). The immediate merger brought together International Computers and Tabulators Ltd. (ICT) and English Electric Computers. ICT had been formed in 1959 through the merger of Powers-Samas Accounting Machines Ltd. which had been founded in 1915 from the same American parentage that was to produce Univac Corporation, and the British Tabulating Machine Company (BTM). BTM had been founded in 1907 to market the tabulating machines of Hollerith's Tabulating Machines Company, one of the American forerunners of IBM. BTM's interest in computers originated in research work carried out at Birkbeck College, London by A.D.Booth under the sponsorship of the British Rayon Research Association. The first BTM computer, the 1200 series, was launched in 1954 followed by the 1201 series in 1956. ICT grew further through the

The origins of the British computer industry

Figure 3.1: The origins of IBM (UK), STC and STC ICL

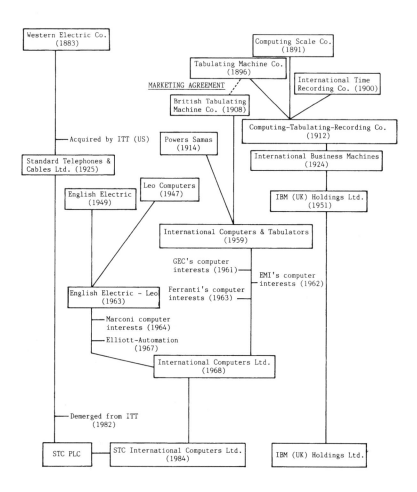

Figure 3.2: The origin companies and successive
rationalisations of ICL

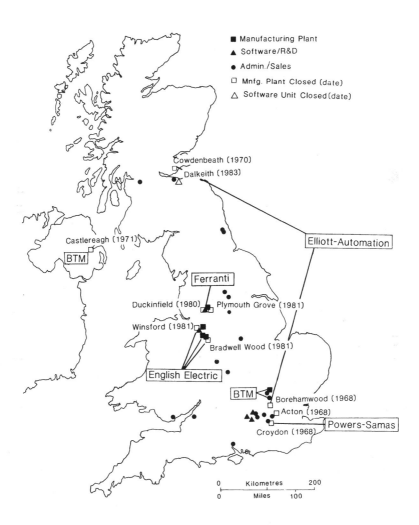

acquisition of the civilian computer interests of the General Electric Company Ltd. (GEC) in 1961, those of the Electrical and Musical Industries Ltd. (EMI) in 1962 and of Ferranti Ltd. in 1963. Interestingly, each of these companies have now developed new computer services or information technology sections. ICT developed the 1300 series jointly with Computer Developments Ltd. (part-owned by GEC), and bought the 1500 series directly from RCA of America. But the main ICT development lay in the 1900 series, originally introduced in 1964 and drawing upon the research carried out by Ferranti in conjunction with Manchester University.

The English Electric Company Ltd., a long-established manufacturer of electrical machinery and electronic equipment, first became interested in digital computers in 1952 through contact with the National Physical Laboratory where a pilot version of the Automatic Computing Engine (ACE) had been constructed according to specifications set out by Dr. Alan Turing. Research continued at EEC's Nelson Research Labs in Stafford and later at a special factory in Kidsgrove. The development work led to the launch of the DEUCE Computer in 1955. Further work in conjunction with RCA in America led to the KDP10 in 1961 and the innovative KDF9 in 1963. In 1963, English Electric Computers merged with Lyons Electronic Office (LEO) Computers Ltd., a firm founded in 1954 as the computing interests of J.Lyons and Co. who had sponsored the development of the EDSAC computer, 1947-9, under the team lead by Prof. Wilkes at Cambridge University.

In 1964, English Electric Leo Computers acquired the Marconi Company's commercial and scientific interests and in 1967 merged with Elliott-Automation. The history of Elliott Brothers, a London-based manufacturer of scientific instruments, goes back to 1801 but their involvement with computers dates from 1947 when their research laboratory at Borehamwood was established. Their first two commercial computers, the NICHOLAS and the 401 series, were developed under contracts from the Royal Navy and the NRDC respectively. In 1958 Elliott launched the 800 series of transistorised computers, forerunners of modern minicomputers. By the time English Electric joined ICL, its future development plans were based around the IBM-compatible System 4 range which, despite early design problems, appeared to offer significant potential.

The formation of ICL in 1968 thus brought together nine formerly independent computer manufacturers along with the expertise acquired from contacts with the Universities of

Cambridge, Manchester, Birkbeck and the NPL amongst others. According to records kept at the National Computer Centre, 220 commercially-produced computers had been installed in the UK by 1960 and 90% of these had been produced by the constituent members of ICL, then independent, plus Standard Telephones and Cables Ltd. (STC), now the parent company of ICL. By 1970 however, of 6500 installations, only about half were designed and manufactured in the UK, a figure which has continued to decline under international competition despite the formation of ICL. The two partners in the ICL marriage, ICT and English Electric, had shown an initial reluctance to come together, but negotiations were encouraged by the intervention of Plessey in trying to acquire first ICT and later English Electric. Technical problems which emerged with English Electric's System 4 meant that it only acquired an 18% shareholding compared with the 40% it had originally hoped for. This shareholding later passed to GEC when it took over English Electric. Other shareholdings were split between Plessey (18%), the Government (10.5%), in exchange for a £17m cash injection, and ICT's shareholders (53.5%) (Moralee, 1981, p790).

3.2.2 Product range

The diverse origins of ICL produced a company which in 1968 was spread both geographically in the organisation of its activities and sectorally across its product range. Despite rationalisation, both these generalisations remain broadly true. In terms of the product range, ICL inherited two incompatible mainframe computer ranges: The ICT/Ferranti 1900 series and the English Electric System 4 IBM-compatible series. Worse still, the company inherited partisan loyalty divided between the two original companies amongst management and employees (Moralee, 1981, p792). Faced with this two-range dilemma, the company opted for an unhappy compromise – to continue marketing both ranges while developing a new range which was to be incompatible with both its predecessors. Instead the 2900 series, which was first released in 1975, was to have a totally new operating system designed to cope better with communications between machines. This was the technologically-advanced Virtual Machine Environment (VME) system which ICL still uses today. In retrospect this brave decision was more technology-led than market-led and in the short term at least many users chose to change to IBM rather than rewrite all their software for the new range. Ironically, the best selling part of the range has been the low-end 2903/4 and its successor the ME29 which were basically 1900 series upgrades. The performance of ICL's mainframes has been greatly enhanced by the introduction of Content Addressable File Store (CAFS) software which is now a general feature on all the larger machines.

The acquisition of Singer Business Machines in 1976 took ICL back into the field of IBM-compatible machines with the System 10 and its successor the System 25. However it raised again the problem of trying to compete with IBM on too many fronts. The new management, appointed in 1981, were highly critical of this policy and following Sir Michael Edwardes' strategy at BL, decided to focus on selected market sectors rather than trying to cover the entire product spectrum. This has been achieved by splitting activities into product groups or 'business centres' each with its own profit and loss account. The policy involved concentrating on company strengths, in particular public administration, including local government, retailing, financial services other than banking, manufacturing and defence (Crisp, 1985, p8). Beyond this ICL has sought to make alliances and collaborative agreements with other manufacturers to supply skills and products in which ICL are deficient, or which it would not be cost-effective for them to develop themselves (de Jonquieres, 1981). In common too with BL, the company quickly put together a five-year product strategy, with long lead-times on the announcement of new products currently in the development stage.

The general strategy is shown well in a series of public advertisements launched in May 1983. It is based upon a 'networked product line' - the ability of different strata of computing facilities offered by ICL to intercommunicate with each other and with products from other leading manufacturers, particularly IBM. The campaign has been promoted with the slogan "We should be talking to each other". The trend towards networking is necessitated by applications such as office automation and electronic funds transfer which is opening up new markets. The campaign aimed to promote particularly the Distributed Resource System (DRS) series of office systems, covering workstations, word processors, electronic filing systems, electronic mailing systems, videotex and the network systems (MicroLan and OSLAN) which join them. Whereas the decision taken to develop a completely new operating system for the 2900 series was undoubtedly 'technology-led', the new management team have stressed the importance of being 'market-led'. While shying away from becoming merely another IBM-compatible manufacturer, ICL products have been designed to 'surround' IBM mainframe hardware. So much so that at a recent IBM user show, ICL occupied the largest stand. A higher volume of sales has been achieved by selling through independent dealers and computer systems houses, as well as through marketing agreements with Logica and British Telecom's Business Systems subsidiary. In addition, ICL have established the 'Traderpoint' network of franchised dealers to achieve a higher profile in the high street.

ICL's collaborative deals were settled in a remarkably short time after the new management took over, despite their resolution to break off talks over possible takeover with foreign manufacturers. The chief collaboration is with the Japanese manufacturer, Fujitsu, to take advantage of its semiconductor technology at an early stage in its development; what ICL has termed 'intercept technology'. In particular Fujitsu's CMOS (complementary metal oxide semiconductor) and ECL (emitter coupled logic) microchips. The new technology is used in the Series 39 mainframe range launched in April 1985. The level 30 machine (previously codenamed DM1) and the level 80 machine (Estriel) machine both use the same VME operating system as the 2900 range and incorporate optical fibres (Heaford, 1985). In turn, ICL have agreed to market the Fujitsu Atlas 10 Series powerful IBM compatible mainframes in the UK, though this particular agreement was terminated in 1984 following a sluggish sales record. In 1984 the Fujitsu collaboration agreement was extended until the end of 1991. ICL have been collaborating too with Mitel, the Canadian telecommunications manufacturer recently taken over by British Telecom, to market the DNX 2000 digital exchange system. This was ICL's first foray into telecommunications. In November 1984 ICL also launched the 'One-per-desk' (OPD) voice/data workstation terminal jointly developed with Sinclair Research and Psion at Bracknell.

ICL was slow to move into the market for microcomputers – perhaps for fear of undercutting profitability of established lines. ICL was originally involved in manufacturing and marketing a business micro based on the 'Black Box' micro designed by Rair, a small British company, but have recently launched the PC Quattro. One of the most successful deals was in the field of computer-aided engineering with the PERQ professional workstation. The machine is based on a design from the US PERQ Systems Corporation (formerly Three Rivers Computer Corporation) in which ICL now has a minority shareholding. However, in this increasingly competitive product market, ICL has now adopted a workstation from Sun Microsystems of America rather than develop the PERQ further.

3.2.3 Geographical location of activities

Geographically too the diverse origins of ICL produced a disparate company in need of rationalisation. The HQ of the organisation is in Putney, South London; manufacturing is split between sites in Letchworth, Stevenage, Stoke-on-Trent, Kidsgrove and Manchester; software, sales support services and marketing are concentrated in Bracknell and Reading and Research and Development activities are carried out at no less than four centres in the UK at Bracknell, Reading, Kidsgrove and Manchester (Fig. 3.3). From BTM the ICL inherited manufacturing plants in Hertfordshire at Letchworth (opened 1921) and Stevenage (1955). Both of these sites were originally involved in manufacturing calculators, tabulators and associated peripherals and subsequently have manufactured principally high volume/low value products from the ICL range. The Letchworth site formerly produced peripherals for the 1900 range (phased out during the mid-1970s) and the ME29 range (transferred to Ashton in the early 1980s). Now the Letchworth site is involved in volume manufacture of the 'One-per-desk' voice/data workstation which is currently being produced at around 50,000 units p.a. with potential capacity of 100,000 units p.a. Letchworth also manufactures the DRS range of office automation equipment which is central to ICL's new emphasis on a 'networked product line'. At its peak in the mid-1970s, the Letchworth site employed around 3,500 people, but this has been progressively reduced to 1,700 in January 1985 when a further round of redundancies were announced bringing the total down to 1,230.

The Stevenage site formerly manufactured a range of printers and other peripherals but in 1975 these were transferred to Computer Peripherals Inc. (CPI), a joint venture with Control Data and NCR of the US. In 1981 manufacturing operations of CPI in Stevenage were closed down. Similarly, the office supplies and accessories division, Dataset, which was based in Letchworth, was sold to Control Data in 1976. Other manufacturing operations were transferred from Stevenage to Letchworth in the mid-1970s and in 1985 the advanced R&D centre was transferred to Bracknell. Thus the function of the Stevenage site is now mainly administrative including the worldwide spares and supplies division, customer services/support, and legal and patents division. Employment in Stevenage in three sites is now around 900, down

The origins of the British computer industry

Figure 3.3: Functional division of activities by site
for STC ICL, 1985

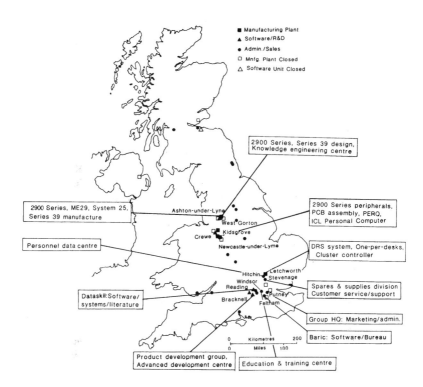

from a peak of 2,000 in the early 1970s.

From Ferranti, ICL inherited the West Gorton complex in Manchester (opened in 1956) and the expertise associated with large mainframe computers. The Ferranti Atlas series, co-developed with Manchester University, formed the basis for ICT's 1900 series in the early 1960s. The 2900 series was developed at West Gorton and is manufactured there and at a new plant opened nearby at Ashton-under-Lyne in 1978. In the confident atmosphere of the later 1970s a third, but short-lived, manufacturing facility in Manchester was opened at Plymouth Grove, and an extension was added to the West Gorton site for VLSI microchip design and production. These new facilities replaced a site at Dukinfield, a six floor mill opened in 1890. The series 39 mainframe computers, introduced to the market in April 1985, were developed at West Gorton utilising Fujitsu's microchip technology (Crisp, 1985) and are manufactured at Ashton-under-Lyne where the company has a Flexible Manufacturing System (FMS) automated production line for assembly and test (Heaford, 1985).

From English Electric ICL inherited the North Midlands complex of sites at Kidsgrove/Stoke-on-Trent plus Winsford and Bradwell Wood in Cheshire which were closed down during the 1981 rationalisation. The Kidsgrove site was opened in the 1950s close to English Electric's research establishment in Stafford, and became the main manufacturing site for the System 4. In 1974 the headquarters of manufacturing operations moved to Kidsgrove from Letchworth and as the System 4 was phased out, Kidsgrove moved into manufacture of peripherals for the 2900 series. Now the Kidsgrove site has responsibility for the ICL Personal Computer and the PERQ professional workstation, including software development which was transferred from Dalkeith, Scotland in 1983. Kidsgrove also possesses a Printed Circuit Board (PCB) assembly facility for all ICL's manufacturing activities.

From Elliott-Automation, ICL inherited a development and production facility at Borehamwood which had been opened in 1946 and had manufactured part of NCR's product range during the 1960s. Elliott had also opened a manufacturing site at Cowdenbeath, Fife in 1965. Both of these sites were closed down following the 1968 rationalisation as was the former Powers-Samas site at Croydon. A controlling share in the former BTM site at Castlereagh, Northern Ireland was sold to the Northern Ireland Development Corporation in 1971 in an attempt to safeguard the jobs there.

The origins of the British computer industry

Figure 3.4:   ICL employment by skill division, 1985

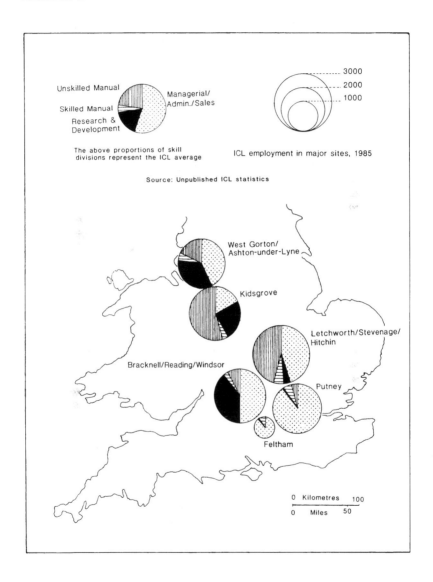

Consequently, after the 1968-71 rationalisation ICL was left with three main R&D/manufacturing complexes amongst which it split its product range. In general terms, Manchester took responsibility for high value mainframes; Kidsgrove/Stoke-on-Trent developed the capability for manufacturing the medium range computers, peripherals and PCB assembly while Letchworth specialised in volume production at the bottom end of the range. However, when ICL came to choose sites for new facilities for its new advanced research and development centre, and its software subsidiary Dataskil, it chose instead to initiate a fourth complex in Berkshire. The R&D plant at Bracknell and the Dataskil offices at Reading were both opened in 1970. An internal ICL training and education centre was opened in the same year at Beaumont Park, Windsor, and a residential centre for training courses and other activities was acquired in 1969 at Hedsor Park in South Buckinghamshire. Figure 3.4 shows that more than 90% of the current staff in the Berkshire complex are involved in non-manual occupations and the availability of highly qualified manpower in the area was the key locational factor. Ferranti Computer Systems Ltd. had located a software/R&D unit in Bracknell in 1956, and the area was already showing signs of becoming Britain's 'silicon valley'. The decision by ICL to locate their new facilities in Berkshire was not seen to favour too overtly either ICT or English Electric. Furthermore, Bracknell Development Corporation offered excellent financial assistance terms.

In 1971, for the first time, ICL's expenditure on software research and development exceeded that on hardware. Thus the decision to locate the new investment in software and R&D facilities in Berkshire has proved to be highly influential in shaping the present geography of the company. Berkshire now has the greatest single concentration of ICL employees anywhere in the country.

Around 24% of ICL staff in the UK are female, which is slightly less than the industry average, but higher than for IBM. Figure 3.5 shows the balance between job functions in ICL. The major difference from IBM is a higher percentage involved in R&D at ICL. IBM by comparison have a higher percentage of the workforce involved in manufacturing and in Information Services Ltd., a subsidiary company. The differences between the two firms are explained by the continental-scale integration of IBM activities in Europe whereas ICL has all its manufacturing and R&D in the UK. Outside the UK, ICL has marketing subsidiaries in 27 other countries, chiefly in

Figure 3.5: Functional division of employment in IBM
and STC ICL, 1985

IBM (UK)

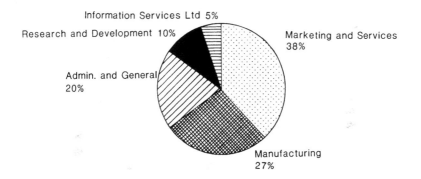

Information Services Ltd 5%

Research and Development 10%

Marketing and Services
38%

Admin. and General
20%

Manufacturing
27%

STC ICL

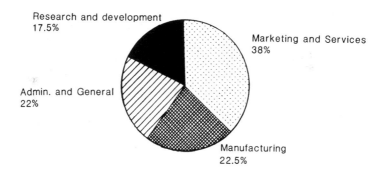

Research and development
17.5%

Marketing and Services
38%

Admin. and General
22%

Manufacturing
22.5%

Europe and the Commonwealth, and minority stakes in manufacture and marketing organisations in India. Overseas sales in 1985 comprised 40% of turnover, down from 45% in 1981. It is the stated intention of the company to expand its interests abroad to 60% of turnover. Profitability has been under pressure in Europe recently due to heavy losses in France, but these have now been turned round.

In the UK, ICL's chief subsidiary was formerly Baric computing services, with branches in Feltham, West London and Crewe. The company was set up in 1968 jointly by ICL and Barclays Bank, mainly to provide a computer bureau service, but was fully acquired by ICL in 1984 with the bureau activities being sold off to CMG in 1985. ICL also has a 40% stake in CADCentre Ltd., the Computer Aided Design Centre at Madingley, Cambridge, which was sold off by the Government in April 1983 to a consortium which included ICL, W.S.Atkins Ltd., the French SIA Group, Cambridge University and two Cambridge colleges. The Centre was set up in 1969 by the Ministry of Technology and was supplied with technicians and management by ICL. The centre now employs around 150 people. In 1982 ICL also acquired Computer Leasings Ltd., which it has subsequently absorbed into the group. Also in 1982 ICL acquired, jointly with Logica, the word-processing division of Nexos, the ill-fated NEB subsidiary which was set up by the Government to gain a foothold in the office automation market.

3.3 International Business Machines Corp.

3.3.1 IBM in Europe
IBM was formed as the Computing-Tabulating-Recording Company in 1911 by a merger of the International Time Recording Company, the Computing Scale Company and Hollerith's Tabulating Machine Company. The name was changed to International Business Machines in 1924 and the company joined the commercial market for electronic stored-memory computer in 1953 with the 700 series. Its present world headquarters is at Armonk, New York State. It operates in more than 100 countries throughout the world with nearly 405,000 full-time employees of which around 108,000 are in Europe. Its worldwide operations are split into three divisions: IBM Corporation, which covers the US; IBM World Trade Americas/Far East Corporation; and IBM World Trade Europe/Middle East/Africa Corporation which is the intermediate parent of IBM (UK). Within this structure, functional operations are

organised on a three-tier basis: IBM's research and development laboratories, of which there are 26, including 9 in Europe, operate on a global basis. Manufacturing is carried out at a continental scale with most products being manufactured in at least three plants worldwide. For example, virtually the the whole of IBM's product line is manufactured in Europe with activities split between 15 sites. Marketing, at the bottom level of the hierarchy, is carried out at a national level.

Figures 3.6 and 3.7 show the location of IBM's manufacturing and R&D activities in Europe. Germany is the major European IBM employer with 27,500 employees in December 1982 (IBM Europe, 1983, p4). German links with IBM stretch back to 1910 when the company Dehomag was formed to market Hollerith machines from the Tabulating Machine Company in continental Europe (Connolly, 1968, p E2). In 1923 90% of the stock of the company was acquired by the Computing-Tabulating-Recording (CTR) company, one of the predecessors of IBM. There are four manufacturing plants in Germany involved mainly in the manufacture of peripherals, including disc files, power supplies and memory products. The main German site is at Sindelfingen near Stuttgart, opened by Dehomag in 1924. Together with the nearby Boblingen site, it is chiefly involved in the manufacture of semiconductor components, and has R&D responsibilities for VLSI semiconductors, medium range computer systems and software products.

France too has a long association with IBM since offices of the CTR company were established in Paris in 1914 (IBM Europe, n.d.). The first manufacturing plant in France was established eleven years later in Vincennes. Now IBM has four manufacturing plants including the Montpellier site opened in 1965 in a development region. This is the European production site for large systems (308X and 3090 series). A second major site is at Corbeil-Essones, near Paris, opened in 1941, which manufactures components and has production links with the Havant site in the UK. IBM France also has R&D facilities at Corbeil-Essones for VLSI logic microchips and at La Gaude, near Nice, opened in 1963, with special responsibilities for telecommunications systems. IBM employed a total of 20,778 employees in December 1982 plus a further 2,016 at IBM's European HQ in Paris, which moved there from Geneva, Switzerland in 1946.

The UK is the third largest IBM employment base in Europe followed by Italy (12,439) which has responsibility for small

Figure 3.6:   IBM's manufacturing facilities in Europe, 1984

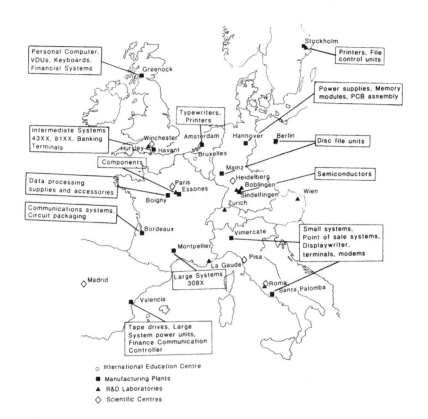

The origins of the British computer industry

Figure 3.7: IBM's research and development facilities in
Europe, 1984

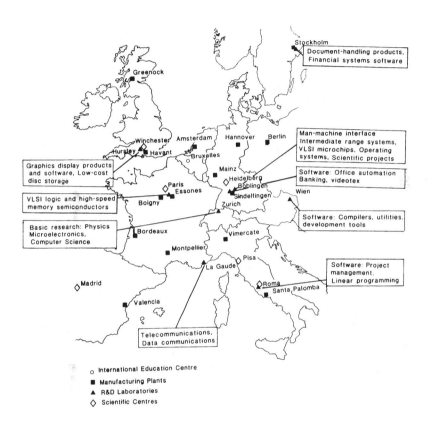

systems, point-of-sale terminals and office automation equipment. In the Netherlands, an IBM manufacturing site was opened at Amsterdam in 1952 shortly after the Greenock site opened in the UK. This plant now has responsibility for typewriters and printers. Total IBM employment in the Netherlands is just over 5,000. Elsewhere in Europe IBM has one of its three research division laboratories involved in basic research at Ruschlikon, near Zurich (opened in 1956), plus smaller R&D centres in Austria and Sweden. IBM employs over 5,000 scientists and engineers in R&D work in Europe. There are also manufacturing plants in Spain and Sweden and an international education centre in Belgium at La Hulpe near Brussels (IBM Europe, 1984a).

Table 3.1 shows IBM's main European markets in 1985. The position of the UK is interesting because it was IBM's fastest growing national market in Europe in 1985 apart from Spain. Furthermore, the UK is IBM's greatest net exporter in Europe and is the only country in which net exports exceed local sales. The reason for this is the high level of demand for personal computers manufactured in Greenock which were one of the fastest growing parts of IBM's product line. In addition, the UK is a relatively low wage country compared to the rest of Europe.

IBM has been heavily involved in promoting an image of contribution to national economies and communities within Europe through corporate advertising, sponsorship, secondments, work with charities and through its science centres of which there are ten in Europe and the Middle East. Altogether IBM's corporate responsibility budget was around $30m in 1985 in Europe/Middle East/Africa (IBM Europe, 1984b). In the UK, the corporate advertising budget was reintroduced in 1978 and the Saatchi and Saatchi advertising campaign has stressed the 'Britishness' of IBM's activities: "as British as Marks and Spencers". More recently, playing on concern about high unemployment, corporate advertising has used the slogan 'Just the job for Britain'. Similar campaigns have been carried out in other European countries and one of the tangible consequences of the campaign is that IBM has been included in the EEC Esprit research programme despite widespread criticism that IBM's research programme does not need to be subsidised by European tax-payers.

Table 3.1:   IBM's major markets in Europe, 1985

Country	Revenue, 1985 ($m)	% Change 1984-5[a]	Inter-Co. Transfer ($m)	Local Sales ($m)	Income ($m)
W. Germany	4,500	+17%	1,693	2,806	290
France	4,183	+13%	1,920	2,263	322
UK	3,901	+30%	2,028	1,873	395
Italy	2,241	+17%	707	1,534	250
Spain	1,129	+38%	520	609	129
Netherlands	1,032	+26%	356	676	101
Sweden	846	+25%	354	492	66
W. Europe[b]	14,065	+18%	n.a.	n.a.	2,104

Notes: a – % Change calculated in actual accounting currency
        b – Includes a small contribution from Middle East
           and Africa

Sources: Datamation magazine, Aug 1, 1986, p35-9
           IBM Corp. Annual Report, 1985

3.3.2 IBM (UK) Ltd.

The International Time Recording Company (a forerunner of IBM) was registered as a private company in the UK in 1912. However, while manufacturing plants to build tabulators were established in France and Germany in the 1920s, US-produced IBM products in the UK were marketed by the British Tabulating Machine Company under an agreement signed in 1908, and later manufactured by BTM under licence from IBM. In 1949 these agreements were terminated and in 1951 IBM (United Kingdom) Ltd. was established with six employees on assignment from other IBM companies around the world in a small office in Wigmore Street, London. Since then, the headquarters facilities has twice moved to larger premises, and finally in

1976 out of London altogether to a new purpose-built office complex on an extensive site in the north-east corner of Portsmouth harbour. The site, initiated in 1970, was reclaimed by the Dutch polder method utilising dykes formed by the M27 motorway embankment, and creating a freshwater lake of 15 acres to give a parkland setting. In addition to being close to manufacturing facilities at Havant and R&D at Hursley, the Portsmouth site also has excellent motorway, train and port facilities and good access to international airports. Administrative facilities have continued to expand within Portsmouth and two other sites have been acquired for particular HQ functions.

IBM's manufacturing operations in the UK are carried out at two locations though the division of products is structured on a European basis. The first site to be opened was at Battery Park in Greenock in 1951. This plant transferred to the current site in Spango Valley in 1954. The Greenock area has been designated a Development Area since 1934 and a Special Development Area since 1967, and in 1984 had an unemployment rate of 24% (Goddard, Coombes and Owen, 1984). Choosing a site at Greenock was thus in line with IBM's stated policy

> "to locate plants where they will help achieve
> regional development plans, wherever possible" 'IBM
> in Europe' (not dated)

IBM was one of a group of US multinationals, including Burroughs, Honeywell, and NCR, which located plants in Scotland in the 1940s and 1950s to manufacture electro-mechanical business machines. These firms were attracted by government assistance, labour availability and the support of the Scottish Industrial Estates Corporation (SIEC). The plant originally employed just over 100 people to make typewriters and mechanical accounting machines. Later the plant specialised in assembling and testing Optical Character Recognition (OCR) equipment, Information Display Systems, data entry systems and banking terminals.

While other US multinationals experienced job loss during the early 1970s as they made the transition from electro-mechanical to microprocessor-based products, IBM has maintained its full employment policy. Following major investment in automated production equipment, Greenock is now geared up for high volume assembly and testing of monochrome and colour visual display units, keyboards, power supplies and logic cards. In 1982 Greenock was chosen to become the

European base for the manufacture of the highly successful
IBM Personal Computer. Since its launch in the US in 1981 the
IBM PC has effectively set an industry standard in this
emerging market. Two new sites at Larkfield and Dalrymple
Street in Greenock have been opened housing new production
lines for the Personal Computer. Further development work on
the PC range has introduced a portable version, the expanded
memory PC AT, and graphics workstations, PC/G, developed at
Hursley. These are all manufactured at Greenock. Marketing of
the PC in the UK however is carried out by a special unit set
up at Basingstoke, Hants in 1983.

Some 150 engineers are employed in process technology
R&D at Greenock where robots are used extensively on the
automated assembly line. Despite the fact that Greenock has no
product R&D or marketing functions, only a third of its
workforce is taken up directly in manufacturing. The rest are
in managerial and administrative support roles, with between
one quarter and one third being graduates. This serves to
emphasise the way in which technological change has eroded
many of the formerly labour-intensive functions in the
production process. The plant formerly had an extensive
machine shop for instance, but latterly has moved towards
final assembly and test facilities only. The Greenock plant
has received considerable aid from the British government in
return for guarantees on the British-supplied component
content of products. Between 1975 and 1980 for instance, the
Greenock plant received £2.8m in Regional Development Grants
alone, amounting to nearly 30% of the total received by US
electronics companies in Scotland.

The Greenock site was also chosen for a £22.7m project to
construct an automated materials distribution Centre. The
recently completed complex is one of the most advanced
warehouse systems in Europe and represents a major investment.
IBM now has over 1 million square feet of floorspace in the
Greenock area and employs 2,700 people in the three plants. It
is now one of the major employers in the area. Employment at
the Greenock site has risen steadily from 2,150 in 1977
following a slight decline in the workforce in the mid-1970s.
The plant has enjoyed an excellent productivity record (it is
claimed by the Scottish Development Agency to be the most
productive IBM plant in Europe) and good working relations
(no working days lost over 30 years). The firm is closely
integrated in backward linkages with the local economy with,
for instance, £103.5m being spent in contracts for parts and
services with over 4,200 firms in 1983. IBM estimates that 40%

of this is currently spent in Scotland. Work subcontracted out includes electrical (£28.0m), metalwork (£12.5m), cards/cables (£11.5m) and plastics (£11.0m). With forward linkages however, 85% of IBM's production from the UK manufacturing plants is exported or transferred internally within IBM's European operations.

IBM's other manufacturing plant in the UK was established in 1966 at Millbrook in Southampton and transferred to Havant near Portsmouth when manufacturing commenced in 1967. The present building was occupied in 1971. The Havant plant has assembled and tested some of IBM's largest computers for the European, Middle Eastern and African markets including the System/370 Model 168 and the 3033 processor but in the later 1970s the large systems 'mission' was transferred to the Montpellier plant in France. More recently the Havant plant has concentrated on intermediate range systems, principally the 8100 Information System which is designed for distributed data processing, the 4300 series and communication controllers. Havant now also manufactures all IBM's European banking products except for printers and has moved towards high volume manufacture with disc files for the 8100 series, and for the IBM Personal Computer AT. It has worked in close co-operation with the R&D laboratories at Hursley and has manufactured computer systems and disc files developed there. In September 1982, IBM announced a £20m investment programme at Havant for equipment and buildings to produce semiconductor substrates (Crisp, 1982). Havant will eventually become the sole European source of substrates which are, at present, made at Corbeil-Essones outside Paris and Sindelfingen in Germany. Production is expected to reach 40m per annum and products will be shipped to Corbeil-Essones where memory and logic microchips are manufactured to be mounded on the substrates. Though 300 people will eventually be employed in the manufacture of substrates, the overall employment of the plant of around 2,000 will not increase as this is to be achieved through internal staff transfers facilitated by a reduction of the workforce needed in assembling and testing computers due to increasing miniaturisation.

IBM UK's Development Laboratories at Hursley near Winchester were opened in 1958 after planning permission to locate near to Cambridge had been refused. It is now one of the biggest of the 9 R&D labs in Europe and employs around 1,700 people. The complex is set in parkland and is based around the eighteenth century Hursley House. Development work there covers a broad spectrum but with a special 'mission' for graphics hardware and software. Developments originating from Hursley include the 3279 Colour Display System, the 8775 Display Terminal, the Customer Information Control System (CICS) package programme and the Personal Computer Graphics Workstation announced in 1984. A further 30 people work in IBM UK's Science centre in Winchester which seeks to develop more general computer applications which benefit society particularly in medical research. This Science centre had originally been located in the science park at Peterlee in County Durham in 1969 but moved to Winchester around 1978 mainly due to the desire to be closer to the main R&D labs but also because of difficulties in recruiting high-calibre personnel in Peterlee.

Beyond the sites already mentioned, IBM has over 30 sales and support sites throughout the country including 15 in London and the rest of the South East. There are education centres, intended primarily for customers, in Arundel in West Sussex and at Sudbury in Greater London though the education function is increasingly being decentralised to customer locations. A major new, and architectural award-winning, site was opened at Warwick in 1980 variously described in IBM literature as the 'Midlands marketing centre' or the 'Advanced industrial applications centre'. However, it is widely speculated that it was designed to be the location for the proposed joint project with British Telecom codenamed Jove which was intended to set up a joint Value-Added Network (VAN) service. This proposal was turned down by the Government in October 1984 (Computer News, 18/10/84).

In 1983, IBM launched the IBM Institute as part of a programme of building bridges between industry and education. The first project is at Cambridge where IBM is working in conjunction with the Department of Engineering to explore new ways of using information technology in curriculum development and increasing sales to academic institutions. The Cambridge operation has taken premises in the Science park. The second project of the IBM Institute was initiated in November 1984 with the Dept. of Chemical Engineering at Imperial College, London. A final function, fulfilled by a subsidiary - IBM Information Services Ltd. - which employs around 900 people, is to develop computer systems for use in internal administration, and to manage IBM's internal telecommunications network.

IBM has a stated worldwide policy of full employment, and the UK subsidiary has a compound annual growth rate of 3% per annum since 1973. Employment turnover is exceptionally low at just 2.7% in 1985 down from 3.4% in 1981. This compares with an industry average for computer electronics of between 10% and 15%. The approximate breakdown of IBM staff by function (1984) is given in Fig. 3.5. Some 6,500 employees are involved in marketing and after-sales support services which has traditionally been one of IBM's strongest selling points. It is a popular legend of the data-processing industry that no dp manager ever lost his job by buying IBM. IBM salespeople build on this reputation by employing sales techniques intended to induce fear, uncertainty and doubt (FUD) in the minds of users with non-IBM equipment. IBM also has a reputation for selling over the heads of dp managers at the level of Board management. With the Personal Computer however, IBM is increasingly moving towards high volume sales and has started selling through an authorised dealer network. In addition IBM has recently signed contracts with UK software houses for the supply of package programs for the PC, including Micro Focus for Professional COBOL, Compsoft for the Delta database management program (Cane, 1983) and Torus of Cambridge for its user-friendly Tapestry software for Local Area Networks (LANs).

In 1985, women held 19.4% of all company jobs. This is below the industry average of 26.2% but the female content has risen recently. No trade unions are recognised in IBM plants in the UK, or in the rest of the world, but in 1977 in the context of an ACAS enquiry, some 96% of the British workers responded that they did not want union negotiation of pay and conditions.

IBM (UK) spent £834m in business with outside suppliers in 1985 which the firm claims created or sustained an estimated 12,500 jobs. Altogether 7,780 firms did business with IBM in 1984 and two-thirds of this expenditure went to UK firms in addition to contracts from other IBM plants in Europe. This marked a decline from the 83% UK supply achieved in 1982, but a considerable increase in the amount spent. Problems were experienced in finding domestic suppliers of the right price and quality in certain products, for instance cathode ray tubes which have to be imported from Japan.

3.4 Other indigenous computer manufacturers

The electronics industry as a whole is notable for a
relatively high level of spatial concentration within the
South East of the UK (Keeble, 1976, p191-9; McDermott & Taylor,
1982, p87-92). This reflects the presence in the South East of
several interlocking locational factors which affected the
growth of the new industry in the inter-war and immediate
post-war period. These factors include the availability of
skilled   labour,   the   location   of   research
facilities/universities, the importance of the BBC in radio,
television and broadcasting, the location of Heathrow and
Gatwick airports, and the pull of the south eastern market for
consumers and above all for defence contracts.

The distribution of the major indigenous computer firms
reflects these locational attractions of the South East. Those
firms with manufacturing facilities in the UK are shown in
Figure 3.8. Most of the major firms, including STC ICL, Thorn-
EMI, Logica and GEC have their HQ in London or elsewhere in
the South East. The major exceptions to this rule are
Ferranti,   a   long-established   Manchester-based
electronics/electrical   engineering   firm,   and   Apricot
(formerly ACT) which was set up in Birmingham as a
distributorship in 1966 but has subsequently moved into
manufacturing. There are also two other firms, Fortronic and
Rodime, both spin-offs from US multinationals, which started
up in Fife during the 1970s and have grown rapidly. Like HQ
functions, software and R&D facilities are located almost
exclusively in the south of the country, the major exceptions
again being Ferranti and Apricot together with STC ICL which
has an R&D establishment at West Gorton in Manchester.
Manufacturing facilities are however more widely spread with
concentrations in the 'M4 corridor area' of Berks/Hants, in
Hertfordshire, and in the North Midlands/North West.

In comparison to the overseas firms (Fig. 3.9), which have
invested heavily in manufacturing facilities in Scotland, UK
firms have few branch plants in assisted areas. Apart from the
two Scottish firms, only Apricot and Ferranti have
manufacturing plants outside England at Glenrothes in Fife
and Cwmbran in Gwent. This could be explained in terms of the
efforts of the regional development agencies such as the
Scottish Development Agency (SDA), the Welsh Development
Agency (WDA) and the Invest in Britain Bureau (IBB) to attract
overseas multinationals to the neglect of indigenous firms
(Hillier, 1985). However, apart from STC ICL and Ferranti, few

The origins of the British computer industry

Figure 3.8: The location of major indigenous computer firms
in Great Britain, 1985

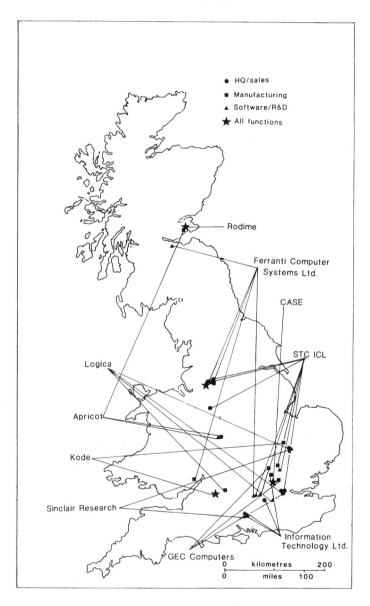

The origins of the British computer industry

Figure 3.9:   The location of the major foreign-owned
             computer firms in Great Britain, 1985

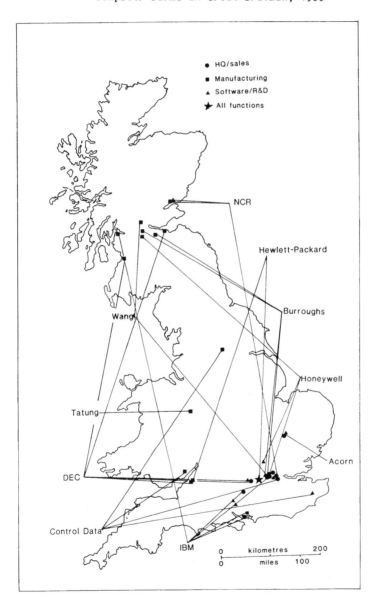

UK computer industry firms have manufacturing branch plants
which are potentially mobile. Other firms, such as Sinclair
Research (now part of Amstrad) and Acorn (now part of
Olivetti), do however subcontract much of their manufacturing
operations and some of this work is done in the assisted
regions.

3.5 Foreign-owned multinationals

Locational factors involved in the siting of
manufacturing facilities of inward investors appear to differ
in several respects from the indigenous sector discussed
above. Firstly, they are often geared towards a European
rather than a merely national market and therefore while
proximity to London may be important for their sales and
distribution functions other factors may determine the siting
of manufacturing facilities. These may include labour market
conditions, communications and attractive premises or
residential environment. Secondly, most of the inward
investors in the computer industry have started up during the
post-war period when regional policy has been active,
favouring manufacturing investment in the assisted areas.

For these reasons, many of the inward investors show a
hierarchical division of functions which is often mirrored by
a spatial division (Fig. 3.9). The average distance between the
UK HQ function and other manufacturing/sales functions is 245
miles for overseas firms compared with just 81 miles for UK
companies in the survey. The example of IBM, which has its HQ,
R&D and low volume manufacturing facilities in Hampshire but
high-volume manufacturing in Greenock, Scotland, is discussed
in more detail in section 3.3, and inward investment generally
in chapter four. While most of the major inward investors
maintain manufacturing facilities in the peripheral regions
only Burroughs and NCR have R&D facilities in assisted areas.
Where the inward investors do have R&D facilities in the UK,
they are mainly in the south of the country.

An important distinction may be drawn between inward
investors who have established branches in the UK, and others
who have acquired local firms. This latter category includes
several software and CAD firms such as CIS, Shape Data,
Compeda and ARC, all in Cambs/Herts and also some hardware
manufacturers such as Microdata (Hemel Hempstead, Herts) and
Systime (Leeds). In the early stages following acquisition the
locational characteristics of these firms more closely

The origins of the British computer industry

Figure 3.10: Distribution of computer establishments
              founded before 1975 (217)

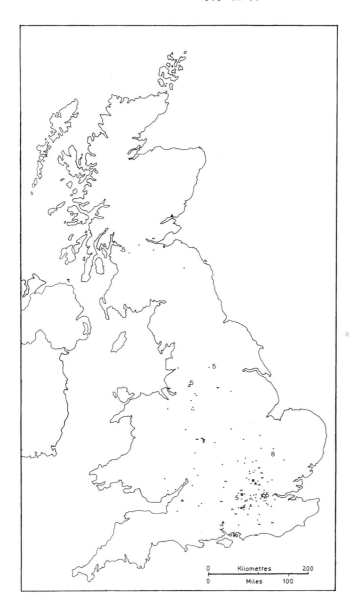

The origins of the British computer industry

Figure 3.11:   Distribution of computer establishments
founded post-1975 (471)

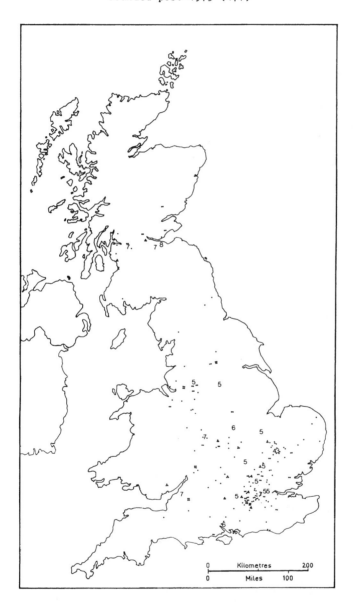

The origins of the British computer industry

Figure 3.12:   Distribution of sales offices of overseas
               computer firms (134)

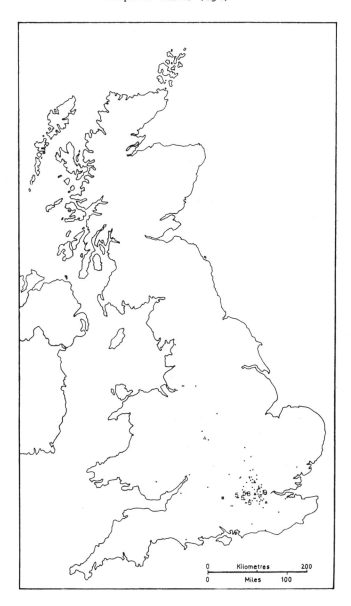

resemble those of the indigenous sector discussed earlier though they may later become more integrated through rationalisation into the corporate structure of the parent firm.

3.6 The geographical distribution of establishments

Figures 3.10 and 3.11 show dot-maps of the distribution of the 688 establishments included in the postal questionnaire survey. Where a number is shown, this indicates the presence of several establishments in one particular city, for instance inner London, Cambridge and Reading. The first two maps show firms founded before 1975 (217) and since 1975 (471). Both maps show roughly the same pattern with the main cluster of establishments around West London, particularly in the counties of Berkshire, Surrey and Hertfordshire. Lesser concentrations are found in Cambridgeshire, the West Midlands, in Manchester/Cheshire and the central lowlands of Scotland. However, important differences are discernible in detail between the two maps. In general, the later map shows a greater dispersal into small towns and rural areas of East Anglia, the South West and Eastern Scotland. The chief single difference is the remarkable growth of the computer industry in and around Cambridge since 1975. This so-called 'Cambridge Phenomenon' (Segal Quince & Partners, 1985) is discussed in more detail in chapters five and six.

Figure 3.12 shows the location of a further 131 establishments which are the UK sales and distribution offices of overseas firms. These establishments were excluded from the questionnaire survey, but are included here because of their distinctive locational pattern. The overseas distributorships are mainly located in the South East (87%). Greater London is well represented and also towns in the surrounding counties with good access to airports and motorway links such as Reading, Slough and Watford. These distributorships have become increasingly important over recent years, both in number and employment, as the UK trading deficit in Information Technology products has continued to increase. Furthermore, many overseas firms which begin as distributorships may later establish assembly or development facilities in the UK. For instance, Data General, the US minicomputer manufacturer, have had a sales operation at Hounslow in Greater London since 1971 and now employ over 500 people in the UK. In August 1985 they announced their intention to set up a development centre at Cambridge. It is likely that if current trends continue, it will be the location patterns chosen by these overseas multinationals and distributorships that will shape the geography of the British computer industry in the coming decades.

Chapter Four

THE GROWING CRISIS AND THE RESPONSE OF THE GOVERNMENT

In chapter two, the evolution and current structure of the
British computer industry was examined using macro-level
statistics for computer hardware and software. In chapter
three, the origins of the industry were studied by reference
to specific firms. This chapter explores the growing crisis in
the domestic computer industry since 1979 with an examination
of the financial collapse and ultimate takeover of ICL
(section 4.1), the increasing trade imbalance (4.2), and the
domination of the British industry by foreign-owned firms
through inward investment and acquisition activity (4.3). The
government's perception of, and response to, this growing
crisis is traced in section 4.4 in a critique of technology
policy since the mid-1960s. It is concluded that the
overcommitment to defence and the lack of a comprehensive
industrial policy has exacerbated rather than alleviated the
crisis.

4.1 The crisis at ICL

4.1.1 Financial collapse, 1979-81
     The Government's shareholding in ICL passed into the
hands of the National Enterprise Board (NEB) during the
period of the Wilson and Callaghan Labour Governments 1974-9.
The Government provided a further £40m to support the group's
Research and Development programme on the 2900 series over
the years 1972-6. The arrangements made for the repayment of
the loan between 1978 and 1984 were dependent upon pre-tax
profitability reaching the level of 7.5% of turnover - a
situation which did not prevail.
     When the Conservative Government took office in 1979, the
final 20% shareholding in the company was disposed of and the
principal   shareholders   became   the   city   institutional
investors. Early in 1980, ICL announced the closure of a
factory at Dukinfield near Manchester with the loss of 800
jobs. The annual results for the year end 30/9/80, however,

showed a 45% decline in profits to only £25m or just 3.5% of turnover, and in November 1980 a further 2,500 redundancies were announced, including the closure of a further factory at Winsford in Cheshire. By the beginning of 1981 it had become clear that ICL was in severe financial trouble and talks were opened with a series of foreign manufacturers concerning a possible takeover, including Burroughs, Sperry Univac, St. Gobain of France and at least one Japanese manufacturer. Reluctantly, the Government agreed to step in again to prevent the nation's computer flag carrier falling into foreign hands. In May 1981, a new senior management team was appointed and immediately broke off talks with foreign competitors. Sir Christophor Laidlaw, ex-deputy chairman of BP, was appointed as chairman and Mr. Robb Wilmot and Mr. Peter Bonfield were appointed Managing Director and Marketing Director respectively. Significantly, both had formerly been with the UK branch of Texas Instruments involved in managing the volume manufacture of pocket calculators. In addition, the Government extended loan guarantee facilities of £200m to the company in an agreement between ICL and four major banks. A further £70m in loan facilities were secured against the assets of ICL itself.

The Financial Times editorial of May 12th 1981 noted:

> The £200m of loan guarantees provided for ICL by the Government is the clearest sign to date of the strong and perhaps excessive strain of pragmatism with which the free-market doctrines of Mrs. Thatcher and Sir Keith Joseph have been tempered in practice ... Altogether the ICL saga ... is a disappointment to those who believe that a dynamic and successful economy is more likely to be created by efficiently functioning private capital markets, rather than Government officials allocating financial and managerial resources.

On June 5th 1981, the new ICL management announced 5,200 further redundancies of which 1,000 were to be from overseas operations and 4,200 to be from a general reduction in the staffing of UK operations including the closure of a further small factory at Bradwell Wood, in Cheshire. In addition, a freeze was announced on pay for the rest of the year. In September 1981, Dataskil, a wholly-owned computer software and services subsidiary of ICL was absorbed into the main organisation with its operations being transferred to two newly-formed ICL divisions of applications software and

consultancy and training. In September 1983, the Dataskil
branch at Dalkeith in Scotland was closed, and 91 jobs there
were relocated to Kidsgrove in Staffordshire. The Dalkeith
branch had been one of the few software houses in Scotland and
its closure was a blow to the Scottish Development Agency's
hopes of establishing a broadly based computer industry in
Scotland.

   In September 1981, the end of year results showed a pre-
tax loss of £49.8m in addition to the costs of redundancy
payment of £78.1m giving a total retained loss for the year of
£133.1m after tax. In November 1981, a further 1,500
redundancies were announced including the closure of a
factory at Plymouth Grove in Manchester employing 330 people.
The factory had been planned in 1977 when the company's
fortunes seemed buoyant following the acquisition of Singer
Business Machines in the previous year. Turnover was up by
45%, and orders by 53% in what the annual report termed "a
year of exceptional growth" disrupted only by labour disputes
(ICL Annual Report, 1977, p4). The new site was opened in 1979
to manufacture printed circuit boards for computers, and was
one of the most modern of its kind in Europe. However the
company had failed to appreciate the extent to which
technical change and electronics miniaturisation were
transforming manufacturing labour requirements. An indication
of this lack of foresight is shown by the fact that in the
period before the financial collapse in 1981, ICL was
investing heavily in an automated production control system
to handle thousands of parts while technical change was
eliminating the need for such capacity.

   Further job loss through natural wastage has reduced the
number employed in ICL's UK operations to 14,379 in 1985, more
than 11,000 less than the peak UK employment of 25,654 in 1980.
ICL employment overseas in 1985 was 6,149 (30% of total
employment in that year), reduced from a peak of 9,252 (27%) in
1978. ICL is highly unionised with 90% of the hourly paid
staff and a majority of the salaried staff belonging to trades
unions. However, throughout the period of restructuring and
pay freeze since 1980 there have been no serious labour
disputes. Financial restructuring has continued and two
rights issues of Ordinary Shares raised £136m. In addition,
three of the banks who had extended overdraft facilities
agreed to convert £50m into Redeemable Preference Shares.
ICL's borrowing was down to £86m in 1983 from a peak of £240m
in 1981, with interest payments similarly down to £15.9m from
£31.1m. Net assets of the company had risen from £73.1m in 1981

The growing crisis

to £234.1m in September 1983, and the company seemed in a much stronger position with a series of important product launches imminent. The company was therefore highly attractive to possible takeover.

Table 4.1: ICL employment by area, June 1981 and April 1985

Area	Employment June 1981	Employment April 1985	Change 1981-85	% Change
London	4,000	2,839	-1,161	-29.0%
Reading	1,200	1,088	-112	-9.3%
Bracknell	1,140	1,200	+60	+5.3%
Stevenage	1,400	1,039	-361	-25.8%
Letchworth	2,990	1,728	-1,262	-42.2%
Kidsgrove/Cheshire	3,600	2,438	-1,162	-32.3%
Manchester	3,750	2,259	-1,491	-39.8%
Other	3,034	2,529	-505	-16.6%
Total ICL	21,114	15,120	-5,994	-28.4%

Source: Financial Times, 6/6/81 p1
Unpublished ICL statistics, April 1985

Table 4.1 shows the extent of the recent redundancies (June 1981 - April 1985) by the main ICL locations. The plants which have suffered worst have been the manufacturing operations at Manchester, Kidsgrove and Letchworth which have each lost a third or more of their employees. Most of these sites have now lost their machine shop facilities and have moved towards 'assembly' rather than full manufacture. The HQ function in London has also lost 29% of its workforce during the enforced slimdown of operations. By contrast, company employment in Berkshire in the R&D, software and sales divisions in Bracknell and Reading has been relatively untouched. It is significant that the job losses have been sharply differentiated by skill composition with job shedding being most severe among unskilled and manual occupations. This is in line with general trends in in the industry towards

77

reskilling of the labour force illustrated in chapter two.

4.1.2 The acquisition of ICL by STC

In July 1984, the telecommunications multinational Standard Telephones & Cables (STC) acquired around 10% of ICL's Ordinary shares and made a cash-or-shares offer for the remaining 90%. Negotiations were opened with ICL management and on 16th August 1984 the two boards announced that agreement had been reached on a revised offer which valued ICL at around £411m. STC, which was founded in 1883, was formerly a subsidiary of the American electronics multinational ITT (Young, 1983). The US shareholding was reduced between 1979 and 1982 to 37% and since the acquisition of ICL, it has been further diluted to around 24%. This residual shareholding has now come under the control of the French company, CGE, with whom ITT has entered a joint venture for its European operations. There has been press speculation that the minority shareholding may be sold to Siemens of Germany but, at the time of writing, nothing had been resolved. Under the terms of the agreement, ICL is to be run as a management company within the corporate structure of STC, and has been renamed STC International Computers Ltd. STC still retains a joint agreement on research with ITT, but this is to be kept separate from ICL's collaboration with Fujitsu. This division between research orientation within the company is one of many anomalies which have still to be fully sorted out in the new corporate structure.

STC is a multinational company involved in research, development, manufacture and supply of telecommunications equipment and related services, the manufacture and distribution of electronics components and business systems, the wholesale distribution of electrical goods, and the supply of residential electronics. STC had a turnover of £920.6m in 1983 before the ICL takeover (9% higher than ICL in that year), 28,231 employees (25% more than ICL) and made a pre-tax profit of £92.2m (102% higher than ICL). Since gaining independence from ITT, STC has been a notable corporate predator acquiring International Aeradio Ltd. (IAL), the aviation electronics and medical services group, from British Airways; and Best & May Ltd., the electrical wholesalers. It also acquired ITT IDEC, a computer systems house founded in 1976 and now based in Stevenage, from its former parent. Following STC's recent financial difficulties, several parts of the operation have been demerged through management buy-outs or sold off. These include IAL (sold to British Telecom) and STC Exacta (printed circuit board manufacture).

The ICL management welcomed the takeover in that "the links between computer and telecommunications companies could give rise to benefits to both parties as their technologies converge" and because it would enable ICL "to compete more effectively in the worldwide computer market where ICL's major competitors can call on substantially greater resources than those available to ICL" (STC/ICL offer document, 1984, p3). In general, the merger reflects a convergence of complementary technologies, however there are also significant areas of overlap. In particular ICL was already moving towards becoming a telecommunications supplier in its collaborative agreement with Mitel. The 'One-per-desk' voice/data workstation is also similar to the STC 'Executel' product. For its part, STC is a volume manufacturer of IBM-compatible terminals at the rate of 20,000 p.a. and distributes ITT computer products such as the Xtra Personal Computer. There is also overlap between ICL and STC subsidiaries such as IDEC in systems/software and IAL in data communications. On the positive side, In July 1985, STC announced the setting up of a new division, STC Network Systems. This will initially have a staffing of around 1,000 and a turnover of £50m and will incorporate parts of both companies including STC IDEC and ICL's International Network Services.

It is likely to be several years before STC and ICL have fully integrated their businesses. However, the initial signs are not hopeful. During 1985, ICL shed a further 1,300 jobs including 470 at Letchworth and 300 from the manufacturing operation at Utica in the US which has been closed down. STC has also reduced its workforce in 1985 by 8,400 through management buy-outs of subsidiary units and redundancies. STC's operating profits fell by 46% during 1985. STC declared a post-tax loss of £54m due to the costs of reorganisation and a downturn in trading conditions since February 1985 that has affected the electronics sector as a whole (Collins & Williams, 1985, p61). Between December 1984 and July 1985, STC was second only to BSR International as the worst performing share on the UK stock exchange and its market capitalisation was reduced from £1.3 billion to just £535m, which was £80m less than three years previously before the takeover of ICL and IAL (Beresford, 1985, p63). This has prompted press speculation of a further takeover, possibly by GEC or British Telecom. If this was to occur then it would complete the process of rationalisation in the British electronics sector begun by the 1964 Labour Government. However, it would inevitably lead to a further loss of identity for ICL.

In the first six months of 1986, ICL has continued its recovery and increased its level of profitability to 7.6% of turnover, a level not reached for ten years. Sales of the Series 39 mainframe and the DRS 300 have done particularly well. By contrast, turnover in the rest of STC fell by 24% and more than 7,000 jobs have been shed since the start of the year. ICL now provides 63% of STC's turnover and 88% of its profits. It is not without irony that ICL's 'shining white knight' should turn out to be in much worse shape than ICL itself. For STC it was certainly a wise move to take over ICL, but for ICL the tarnished image of STC has undoubtedly hindered its recovery and made it difficult to attract outside investment.

Table 4.2: UK Trade statistics for computer hardware, 1984

Product	Exports Value (£m)	1984 %	Imports Value (£m)	1984 %	Balance Value (£m)
Computers	674.1	25.9%	939.3	26.3%	−265.2
Peripherals	683.6	26.3%	1,382.0	38.7%	−698.4
Subassemblies	1,240.5	47.7%	1,249.3	35.0%	−8.8
Total	2,598.3	100.0%	3,570.6	100.0%	−972.3

Source: Business Monitor PQ 3302 Fourth Quarter 1984
published Jan 1985 (HMSO)

4.2 Trade statistics

4.2.1 Computer hardware

Trade statistics for the computer electronics industry are presented in Business Monitor PQ 366 (now PQ 3302) by product headings. Table 4.2 shows the UK trading position in 1984. A trade deficit in that year was sustained in all parts of the industry. Sales of peripherals and computer subassemblies (excluding printed circuits) are more important in international trade than computer systems per se. This is partly due to the nature of tariff barriers and partly because basic hardware is more readily adaptable to international markets than fully operational systems which are often market-specific. The apparent anomaly that the volume of exports exceeds the volume of domestic production may be partially explained by the level of re-exports. This is especially true for computer subassemblies which may be re-exported after having value added to them in the form of software functions. One of the consequences of this is that most products of the UK computer industry contain some components made in the US, and are therefore subject to US government controls on their movement. The US government rules on export controls are chiefly intended to prevent export of high technology goods to communist nations but there is a widespread belief in the industry that they are used to enforce the de facto US hegemony of the information technology industry. There are many accounts of delays by the US government in issuing export licences, particularly to growing markets such as China, and this confers an unfair advantage on US firms. Some UK firms, including Systime, have been fined and other individuals jailed for contravention of the rules of COCOM, the co-ordinating committee amongst NATO members for the control of high technology exports.

The trade figures from the PQ Business Monitor series form the basis for calculation of import and export ratios which have been published in Business Monitor MQ 12 since 1977 (Table 4.3). These ratios show that both import penetration and exports sales ratios for the computer hardware industry are much higher than the average for manufacturing industry in the UK. Furthermore, these ratios have been growing at a faster rate in the computer sector than for manufacturing industry as a whole, illustrating the degree of 'openness' in the computer hardware market. Examination of the ratios suggests an increase in imports relative to exports since 1980, and this is confirmed by the trade statistics supplied by the Department of Trade (Business Monitor MQ 10) for product heading 75 – 'Office machinery and Automatic Data-Processing (ADP) equipment' (Fig. 4.1).

Between 1970 and 1980 the trade balance in office machinery and ADP equipment was only in surplus for two years, but the trade deficit never rose above £170m in historic cost prices. However, since 1980, while exports have increased more rapidly by almost 16% p.a., the rise in imports has been 30% p.a. leading to a trade deficit of over £1 thousand million in

The growing crisis

Figure 4.1: UK trade statistics for computers and office
machinery, 1970-83

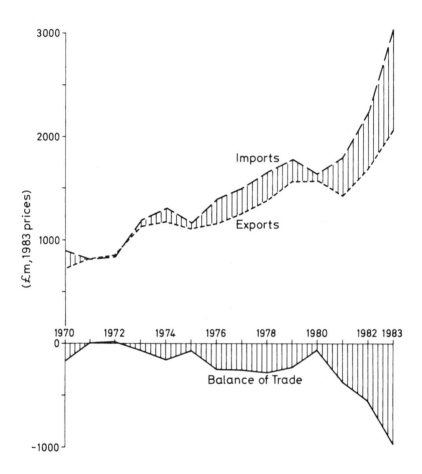

Source: Business Monitor MQ 10

Table 4.3:   Import and export ratios for computer hardware
             and all manufacturing industry in the UK,
             1977-83

	1977	1978	1979	1980	1981	1982	1983
Imports/Home demand							
MLH 366	77	82	90	91	91	98	106
All Mnfg. Ind.	25	24.5	24.5	26.1	24.5	28.8	29.7
Imports/Home demand plus exports							
MLH 366	50	52	52	51	53	59	62
All Mnfg. Ind.	20	19.5	20.5	20.8	19.4	22.8	23.5
Exports/Manufacturer's sales							
MLH 366	69	76	88	87	89	98	110
All Mnfg. Ind	25	25.3	24.6	25.2	25.9	27.2	27.0
Exports/Manufacturer's sales plus imports							
MLH 366	35	36	43	42	42	40	42
All Mnfg. Ind.	20	20.3	19.6	19.9	20.8	21.0	20.7

Source: Business Monitor MQ 12 - 'Import penetration and
          export sales ratios for manufacturing industry'

1984. Taking the electronics sector as a whole, electronic
consumer goods (MLH 365, 1968 SIC) has long been in trade
deficit and since 1970 electronic components (MLH 364, 1968
SIC) has also moved into the red. Only the electronic capital
goods category (MLH 367, 1968 SIC), made up chiefly of defence

electronics, has remained in surplus. Thus by 1983, the UK trade deficit in electronics had reached £1.7 bn. The deteriorating situation prompted the publication in 1984 of the 'crisis' report by the NEDO Information Technology Economic Development Committee chaired by Professor John Ashworth. The reasons for this severe deterioration are complex but probably include the following factors. Firstly, while the UK has experienced a 12% p.a. growth in output of information technology products (computers and telecommunications), this has not matched the growth of Britain's major international competitors, in particular West Germany (15% p.a. growth, 1970-82), the USA (18%), France (19%) and Japan (23%). Consequently, the UK share of the world market in information technology has slipped from 9% in 1970 to only 4% in 1982 (NEDO Information Technology SWP, 1983, p2-4).

Secondly, the major domestic manufacturer, ICL, nearly collapsed in 1981 following a £50m loss and three years of stagnation in turnover. During this period it lost a significant slice of its UK market share to IBM. Thirdly, and closely related to the above point, in 1980 the UK government, under pressure from the EEC and US multinationals with manufacturing facilities in the UK, ended the practice of preferential treatment to UK suppliers in favour of an 'open tender' policy. More recently, the liberalisation of public telecommunications and the privatisation of British Telecom in 1984 meant that formerly 'sheltered' markets were opened up to foreign competition. Fourthly, during the first two years of the 1979 Conservative Government both interest rates and the value of sterling were maintained at an artificially high level. This was partly because of the perceived value of UK oil reserves but also as a result of deliberate government policy directed against inflation. The outcome of this was to make imports cheaper and exports more expensive at precisely the time when acute and deepening recession was already taking a heavy toll of British manufacturing production and investment (Martin, 1986).

Finally, the Ministry of Defence has embarked upon a number of major rearmament projects including the 'Trident' programme using imported American technology and only a minimal component of local supply. While it is not possible to confirm from official trade statistics the relative contribution of civilian and military trade, it seems certain that the sophisticated electronic systems necessary for these programmes will have added to the balance of trade deficit.

One of the implications of the 'openness' of the computer industry in the UK is the large number of 'distributorships' - firms which act as importers for products manufactured overseas by parent, sister or unrelated companies. Distributorships generally do not possess manufacturing facilities of their own other than low-level assembly functions and are therefore probably not classified to MLH 366/3302 but rather to a service category. The same is true of overseas firms which have a HQ/sales site separate from manufacturing facilities in the UK, for instance IBM (UK). In these cases, the manufacturing site would probably be classified to MLH 366/3302 and the HQ/sales site to a service category. The service classification is likely to be either AH 6144 - 'Wholesale distribution of machinery, industrial equipment and transport equipment other than motor vehicles' (1981 employment, 93,400); AH 6530 - 'Retail distribution of books, stationery and office supplies' (1981 - 68,400) or AH 8430 - 'Hiring out of office machinery and furniture' (1981 - 900). The distributorships may add value to the imported product by means of service and maintenance contracts, and may also offer training and instruction to users. Value may also be added in the form of software - either 'package programs' of general applicability or 'custom software systems' written specifically for the user. More usually, a mixture of the two is offered so that the customer can be supplied with a 'turnkey system' - for which the user need only 'turn the key' to have a fully operational system. While 'turnkey' systems are usually classified to computer services (AH 8394), a large part of the value of the system will derive from the Original Equipment Manufacturer (OEM).

4.2.2 Computer services

Trade in computer services comes under the category of 'invisibles' for which information is much less readily available than for manufactured goods. Business Monitor SDQ 9 records 'billings' to clients abroad, but this is subject to the same caveats as for the value of sales and level of employment, namely that it probably records less than 10% of the firms, 60% of the employment and only 54% of the output of the sector. Nonetheless, the figures show a rapid increase in exports from £2.5m in 1971 (4.2% of total billings) to £78.9m in 1984 (6.8%) with a particular growth in 'turnkey' sales (British Business, 1985). However the value of this trade is less than 5% of the value of computer hardware exports. The computer services market is far less open therefore than the

The growing crisis

hardware market, reflecting the market-specific nature of
software.

No comparable figures for computer services imports are
available. However, the recent ACARD (1986) report on the
computer software industry in the UK estimates that the
current trade deficit in software billings is around £200
million and predicts that if current trends continue then the
trade imbalance will reach £2 billion by 1990. This
contradicts the popular idea that Brtain's software
capability be sufficient to offset any future trade imbalance
in hardware.

Table 4.4: Employment and number of establishments, 1984
by legal status

Legal status	Estabs in 1984	(%)	Employment in 1984	(%)	Average size
Independent UK firms	394	(57.3%)	15,240	(21.8%)	38.7
UK-owned branches	200	(29.1%)	30,521	(43.7%)	152.6
US direct branches	50	(7.3%)	17,409	(24.9%)	348.2
US acquired branches	22	(3.2%)	4,055	(5.8%)	184.3
Other overseas branches	12	(1.7%)	1,152	(1.6%)	96.0
Other acquired branches	10	(1.5%)	1,537	(2.2%)	153.7
All establishments	688	(100.0%)	69,914	(100.0%)	101.6

Source: Questionnaire survey data

4.3 The rise in foreign ownership

4.3.1 The legal status of computer industry establishments

Only limited information on corporate control in the
computer industry is available from published sources. The
Census of Production (1981) records that 36 establishments
(12%) in the office machinery and data processing equipment

86

sectors were foreign-owned and that they accounted for 14,700 employees (38.2%). This compares with 2.6% of establishments and 14.8% of employment under foreign ownership in UK manufacturing industry generally. An alternative source of information on overseas control in the computer industry is provided by the survey of computer firms carried out at Cambridge University between 1984 and 1985.

The legal status of establishments included in the questionnaire survey is shown in Table 4.4. A majority of establishments (394) are independent UK firms or the headquarters of multi-plant operations. However, because these firms are generally small (82% employ under 50 workers) they provide only 22% of total employment. Together with UK branch plants (both acquired and set-up directly), UK-owned firms comprise 86% of the total number of establishments in the survey but only 66% of the employment. The next largest category is US branches set up directly by the parent firm. These establishments are mainly involved in manufacturing and sales operations and their employment size is more than three times higher than the average for the survey. Branch plants owned by other overseas firms are fewer in number and generally smaller.

Around one third of all overseas-controlled firms in the UK computer industry were acquired rather than being set up directly by their current parents. As Table 4.5 shows, changes of status through acquisitions and management buy-outs have become more frequent over the last ten years. The increasing number of acquisitions can be seen as an inevitable part of the rationalisation process occurring within the industry following the high rates of new firm formation recorded in the later 1970s. The microcomputer sector in particular had become overcrowded and many of the acquisitions involved the buy-out of maintenance contracts and product rights of firms which had gone into liquidation. More than a quarter of the employees in the survey were in establishments which had been acquired by new parent firms. The average size of acquired establishments was twice the national average, though both these figures were inflated by the acquisition of ICL by STC in 1984. Table 4.6 shows that acquired firms grew in employment at a much slower rate than establishments which had not changed their status. However, if ICL is excluded then acquired establishments grew by almost 80%. Firms acquired by overseas concerns in particular grew by much faster rates than branches established directly, and faster even than independent firms. Thus the extra capital resources obtained

87

Table 4.5: Establishments involved in a change of legal
            status, 1975-85

Date of formation	Acquisitions	(%)	Buy-outs	(%)
1975-76	7	(7.1%)	2	(9.5%)
1977-78	9	(9.2%)	0	(0.0%)
1979-80	9	(9.2%)	0	(0.0%)
1981-82	25	(25.5%)	14	(66.7%)
Since 1983	48	(50.0%)	5	(23.8%)
Since 1975	98	(100.0%)	21	(100.0%)
Employment	19,931		1,675	
Average emp. size	203.4		79.7	

Source: Questionnaire survey data

from their new parents appears prima facie to have benefitted
these firms. However, it could also be argued that these firms
were acquired _because_ they were high-flyers. A thorough
assessment of the likely outcomes of acquisition by overseas
firms would require a comparison of pre- and post-acquisition
rates of growth and a larger sample size than is available
here.

Management buy-outs have become more frequent since 1981
following the involvement of several venture capital and
management consultancy companies in promoting the idea of
corporate decentralisation. Many of the early buy-outs were
achieved at very low cost and success stories were well
publicised so that the apparent decline in the number of buy-
outs since 1983 probably represents the end of this brief
phase of 'bargain buy-outs'. Nevertheless, it is likely that
buy-outs will continue to occur and the phenomenon should be
seen as part of the structural deconcentration occurring in
the computer industry associated with higher rates of new

The growing crisis

Table 4.6: Employment change 1980-84 in pre-1980 establishments
            by legal status

Legal status (No.[a])	Employment in 1980	Employment in 1984	Emp. Change 1980 - 84	% Change 1980 - 84
Ind. firms (140)	4,211	8,064	+3,853	+91.5%
Existing (132)	3,799	7,281	+3,482	+91.6%
Buy-outs (8)	412	783	+371	+90.0%
UK Branches (77)	22,504	20,239	-2,265	-10.1%
Existing (66)	19,043	17,479	-1,564	-8.2%
Acquired (11)	3,461	2,760	-701	-20.2%
US Branches (31)	12,325	14,551	+2,226	+18.1%
Existing (24)	12,075	14,065	+1,990	+16.5%
Acquired (7)	250	486	+236	+94.4%
Other Branches (9)	355	733	+378	+106.4%
Existing (6)	245	429	+184	+75.1%
Acquired (3)	110	304	+194	+176.4%
All Estabs (257)	39,395	43,587	+4,192	+10.6%
Existing (228)	35,162	39,254	+4,092	+11.6%
Acquired/BO (29)	4,233	4,333	+100	+2.3%

Notes

a - Data Coverage = 56.7% of relevant establishments

Source: Questionnaire survey data

firm formation. Employment growth in those management buy-outs for which pre-1980 employment figures are available was equal to that for independent firms generally (see Table 4.6). However, failure rates for these firms are not recorded in the survey data.

Table 4.7:   Employment and number of establishments founded since 1980 by legal status

Legal status	No. of estabs. founded since 1980	Employ. in 1984	(%)	Average size
Independent UK firms	143	2,018	(28.0%)	14.1
UK Branches	64	2,732	(37.9%)	42.7
US Branches	19	1,518	(21.1%)	79.9
Other overseas branches	8	937	(13.0%)	117.1
All new estabs.	234	7,205	(100.0%)	30.8

Source: Questionnaire survey data

Tables 4.6 and 4.7 show employment change 1980-84 by legal status for existing and new establishments respectively. New establishments created 63% of net new employment and within this category, new independent firms provided 28% of net new employment. Within existing firms, gains by independent firms and overseas branches offset losses by UK branches (principally ICL). Overseas firms provided 44% of the net new employment growth in the industry 1980-84 in new and existing establishments, compared with only a 32% percentage share of employment in 1980. In addition, 21 formerly UK-owned firms, employing 2,820 people in 1984, have been acquired by overseas concerns since 1980. By comparison, only two firms employing 180 people that were formerly foreign-controlled have undergone management buy-outs or been acquired by UK firms since 1980. Consequently, the level of overseas control in the UK computer industry has risen by a further 2% to just over a third of total employment in 1984. This compares with an average level of overseas control of only 14.8% in manufacturing industry as a whole for establishments included in the 1981 Census of Production (HMSO, 1984).

Foreign ownership is much more prevalent in the hardware sector (44% of employment) than the services sector (9%). This is because of the international nature of the hardware market compared with computer software which generally caters for a national market. However, the level of overseas control in the domestic computer services sector is increasing through acquisition activity. Software firms acquired since 1975 account for 51% of total foreign-controlled employment in the computer services sector. Software firms which have been acquired by US multinationals include Hoskyns (taken over by Martin Marietta Data Systems), Unilever Computer Services (Electronic Data Systems), Applied Research of Cambridge (McDonnell Douglas), Cambridge Interactive System (ComputerVision), Shape Data (Evans & Sutherland) and Metier (Lockheed). In most of these cases the motivation behind the acquisition appears to have been to gain local skills. Significantly, most of the acquiring firms have substantial defence interests. Consequently while most of the firms acquired have continued to grow under their new parents, their field of work has often changed towards defence systems, and UK sovereignty in this arena has diminished. Strategic Defence Initiative (SDI) work has come to Britain not so much by UK firms winning US government contracts as by UK firms being bought out by US defence contractors.

Independent firms and multi-plant HQs are numerically the most important form of establishment in the survey data. However, because of their small average size (39 employees), they provide little more than a fifth of total employment. UK-owned branch plants, though fewer in number, provide more than twice as many jobs as single plant and HQ establishments. Included in this category are STC ICL and Ferranti Computer Systems Limited who provide the bulk of employment in the UK-owned sector.

4.3.2 The geography of corporate control

The geographical breakdown of corporate control in the computer industry is presented in Figure 4.2. The category of 'local control' includes independent single plant firms, multi-plant HQs and branches of multi-plant firms in the same region as the parent, with the South East classified as one region. The core area has more than 60% of total employment under local control. In the intermediate areas, most employment is UK-owned but is mainly controlled from the

Figure 4.2: Computer industry employment by legal status
           in Great Britain, 1984

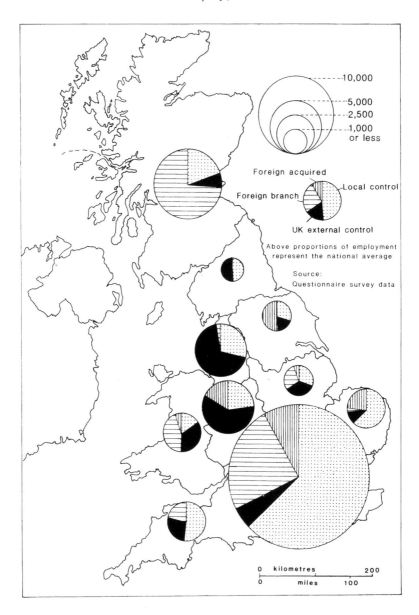

South East. In the periphery, overseas ownership is dominant particularly in direct branch plants. Clearly, therefore, there is an important regional dimension to variations in corporate control in the computer industry. East Anglia and Scotland form two extremes in this spectrum. The former has almost 60% of employment still under local control though this has declined recently due to overseas acquisition activity. The latter has almost three-quarters of total employment in US manufacturing branch plants.

Variation in corporate control by urban/rural status is less apparent than by region. However, some degree of filtering is evident in the fact that local control is of greatest relative importance in Greater London, UK external control in the conurbations, and foreign control in free-standing cities. The nature of corporate control in rural areas throws an interesting light on the phenomenon of 'rural industrialisation'. 'Rural industrialisation' has usually been viewed in terms of a 'branch plant economy', either as part of the filter-down hypothesis (Thompson, 1965) or the 'spatial division of labour' hypothesis (Massey, 1979). However, in the computer industry at least, the dominant form of control in rural areas is local rather than external or foreign. This is because of the high rate of new firm formation in rural areas which is discussed in chapter five.

4.3.3 Foreign control in the computer industry

Table 4.8 shows the breakdown of control by nationality of the 94 foreign-owned establishments included in the survey with manufacturing/software production facilities in the UK and for the 131 firms which have distribution facilities only (see figure 3.12). These firms were excluded from the survey data and the details have been compiled from secondary source material. The table reveals the extent to which North American firms are dominant, providing 89% of survey employment in the overseas sector. The other major industrial competitors in international electronics markets, Japan and Germany, currently have only distributorship facilities in the UK. However, Japanese firms primarily engaged in other sectors do manufacture magnetic media and VDUs in the UK, but these establishments were excluded from the questionnaire data. The database of distributorships is not comprehensive but the relative balance of ownership by nationality shown is probably representative.

Several of the overseas firms included in the survey data have a long history of investment in the UK. For instance,

Table 4.8: Distribution of foreign-owned computer firms in the UK
            by nationality, 1984

Nationality	Firms with production facilities				Firms with no production facilities	
	Estabs.	(%)	Emp.	(%)	No.	(%)
US	72	(76.6%)	21,464	(88.9%)	95	(72.5%)
Canada	6	(6.4%)	529	(2.2%)	5	(3.8%)
Netherlands	4	(4.3%)	43	(0.1%)	4	(3.1%)
Italy	2	(2.1%)	260	(1.1%)	3	(2.3%)
France	2	(2.1%)	125	(0.5%)	1	(0.8%)
Spain	2	(2.1%)	80	(0.3%)	0	(0.0%)
Norway	1	(1.1%)	750	(3.1%)	1	(0.8%)
Taiwan	1	(1.1%)	750	(3.1%)	0	(0.0%)
Sweden	1	(1.1%)	100	(0.4%)	2	(1.5%)
Eire	1	(1.1%)	13	(0.1%)	4	(3.1%)
Japan	0	(0.0%)	0	(0.0%)	9	(6.9%)
Germany	0	(0.0%)	0	(0.0%)	3	(2.3%)
Others	2	(2.1%)	39	(1.6%)	4	(3.1%)
Total overseas	94	(100.0%)	24,153	(100.0%)	131	(100.0%)

Sources: Questionnaire survey data
          Commercial directories, trade journals etc.

Burroughs and NCR started operations in the UK around the turn
of the century. Furthermore, the origins of both STC and ICL
lie originally in US multinational distributorships (Fig.
3.1). However, it was argued above that the level of foreign
control has increased recently. This is due to three factors.
Firstly, existing overseas branches and subsidiaries have
expanded employment at a faster rate (+20%, 1980-84) than UK
establishments (+6%, see Table 4.6). A large part of this
variation, however, is due to the expansion of IBM relative to

decline in ICL. If these firms are excluded, then overseas
firms grew by (only) +28% (1980-84) compared with +60% for
other UK firms. Thus it can be seen that the poor performance
of the UK domestic industry in fact equates solely with the
poor performance of ICL. Secondly, since 1980, 27 new overseas
branches have been opened in the UK with an average employment
size of 90 employees, which is more than twice that of new UK-
owned branches. Consequently, overseas firms have provided 34%
of employment in new openings compared with just 11% of new
plants (Table 4.7). Thirdly, acquisition activity by overseas
firms, particularly since 1980, has taken some of the fastest-
growing firms out of the domestic sector, including Systime,
Acorn, Microdata, CIS and ARC.

Just under a quarter of overseas-controlled employment
in the UK was in establishments which had been acquired rather
than being set up directly by the parent firm as branch
plants/subsidiaries. Acquisition activity by overseas firms
has increased in recent years, particularly since 1980 when 23
(72%) of the 32 acquisitions have taken place. In the regions
of East Anglia, the West Midlands and Yorkshire and
Humberside, acquired firms provide the bulk of employment in
the overseas sector, whereas in other areas, particularly
Scotland, all 13 overseas branches were established directly.
Acquired firms can be divided into two broad categories
according to the circumstances of their acquisition. Some
firms, such as Acorn and Systime were acquired because they
had encountered financial difficulties, or in the case of
Tatung, a loss-making branch plant was acquired from a UK
multi-plant firm. Generally, these acquisitions are followed
by job-shedding and rationalisation. Other firms, such as
Shape Data, CIS or ARC, have sought overseas corporate parents
as a means of financing their expansion plans, and in these
cases the acquisition is followed by growth of employment. In
relative terms, as Table 4.6 shows, the overseas acquired
sector has out-performed the direct branch plants in terms of
employment expansion, 1980-84.

Between 1980 and 1984, all but six (90%) of the overseas
establishments for which data is available increased their
employment. This growth of +5,059 jobs, accounted for 44% of
the total employment increase in the computer industry
recorded in the survey data, whereas overseas establishments
provide only 34% of survey employment. The net increase is
divided between 2,455 (48%) in new overseas establishments and
2,605 (52%) in in-situ change.

Table 4.9: Occupational composition among overseas branch plants,
            acquired establishments, and UK-owned establishments, 1984

Occupation	Overseas branches	Overseas acquired	All Overseas estabs.	All UK-owned estabs.
Management, sales and clerical	3,793 (30.3%)	785 (27.6%)	4,578 (29.8%)	12,151 (36.1%)
Research & Development	2,135 (17.0%)	529 (18.6%)	2,664 (17.3%)	7,968 (23.7%)
Technicians and skilled	3,032 (24.2%)	823 (29.0%)	3,855 (25.1%)	8,430 (25.0%)
Semi- and unskilled manual	3,563 (28.5%)	705 (24.8%)	4,268 (27.8%)	5,129 (15.7%)
Total	12,523	2,842	15,365	33,678
Establishments	39	20	59	361
Data coverage (employment)	67.5%	50.8%	63.6%	73.6%
(estabs)	62.9%	62.5%	62.8%	60.8%

Source: Questionnaire survey data

    The literature on job quality in branch plants reviewed
above suggests that they are likely to employ a lower
proportion of R&D and other white-collar employees than other
types of establishment. Table 4.9 shows that this is borne out
for the computer industry in the comparison between the
overseas and UK-controlled sectors. The level of
administrative, sales, clerical and R&D employment in the UK-
owned sector (60%) is higher than in the overseas sector
(47%), with a correspondingly lower level of manual

employment. There are also differences within the overseas sector between acquired firms and direct branch plants. On average, acquired firms have more R&D employment relative to management, sales and clerical; and more skilled, relative to unskilled employment. However, the differences which are shown to exist in Table 4.9 between the occupational composition of different organisational types are relatively marginal, when viewed at this broad national scale. Variations in corporate structure are much more apparent between regions within the national economy. In chapter six, two contrasting regional environments of computer industry concentration are examined in detail. These are Cambridgeshire/Hertfordshire in the 'core' area and Scotland in the 'periphery'.

4.4 The Government's response: Technology policy

4.4.1 The perception of crisis

In October 1964, when appointing Frank Cousins to the post of Minister for Technology, Harold Wilson, leader of the newly-elected Labour Government, told him that he had "one month to save the British computer industry" (Wilson, 1971 p9). Twenty years later, the NEDO Information Technology Committee, under the chairmanship of Prof. John Ashworth, published a report entitled 'Crisis facing the UK Information Technology Industry' (NEDO, IT SWP, 1984). Thus it could be argued that technology policy directed towards the UK computer industry has been formulated against the background of a perceived growing 'crisis'. The bare parameters of this 'crisis' outlined above are that in 1960 there were nine major UK computer manufacturers who cumulatively accounted for 90% of the computer installations in the UK (Moralee, 1981, p790) whereas twenty years later, ICL, the sole major UK-based manufacturer had been reduced to just 25% of the domestic market (Cane, 1982). Even more serious is the UK balance of payments deficit in computers and office machinery which had slipped from £21m in 1973 to £1 billion in 1984 (Annual Abstract of Statistics).

Since 1979, the crisis in the computer sector has been worsened by the onset of a national industrial recession unparalled since the 1930s. Many commentators have argued that this represents the downswing of a Kondratiev long-wave. Freeman (1974, 2nd ed. 1982) has argued that the structural depression of the Kondratiev downswing marks the period when the allocative efficiency of the market is at its weakest and he therefore stresses the importance of public policy directed towards the "...promotion of major new technology systems and of productivity based on technical change". (Freeman, 1982, p220). Thus 'technology management' policies could be used in a Keynesian counter-cyclical manner to overcome market inertia in periods of depression. The components of such a technology policy are spelt out by Freeman et al (1982, p192-5) as being:

"i/ Policies which aim directly at encouraging firms to take up radical inventions/innovations ...

ii/ Policies aimed at improving the diffusion of existing, but still relatively new and radical innovations throughout the various sectors ...

iii/ Policies aimed at improving the import and internal diffusion of foreign technology ..."

Significantly, in this policy prescription, the authors acknowledge their debt to observation of the post-war economic miracle of Japanese technology-led growth.

Such an interventionist stance is not, however, in tune with current government thinking on the role of the state. The perceived objectives of the Department of Trade and Industry (DTI) are: "...to encourage, assist and ensure the proper regulation of British trade, industry and commerce; to increase the growth of world trade and the national production of wealth" (Cabinet Office, 1984, p106). This is to be done by promoting a climate for British industry conducive to enterprise and competition; by enhancing the international competitiveness of British firms through increased efficiency and adaptability; and by innovation to improve the products and services on offer. The evolution of government policy towards technology since the early 1960s described below illustrates this swing away from 'intervention' towards 'regulation'.

4.4.2 1964-70 'Mintech'

The general tone of the 1964-70 Labour Government towards technology was set in the oft-quoted Wilson speech to the Labour Party Conference in Scarborough 1/10/63 which alluded to "the Britain that is going to be forged in the white heat of the technological revolution". The speech outlined a four-fold programme to produce more scientists, to reverse the 'brain drain', to improve the planning of Science and to "organise British industry so that it applies the results of scientific research more purposively to our national production effort" (quoted in Clarke, 1973, p26). These proposals were enshrined in the new Ministry of Technology ('Mintech') which was established in October 1964.

Mintech acquired responsibility for the computer industry and was generally active in promoting its interests through the setting up of the National Computer Centre (NCC) in 1967, the Computer-Aided Design Centre in Cambridge in 1969, the Advanced Computer Technology Project and the Computer Advisory Service. Computers also received special treatment in investment grants and in lease finance. However, as Sir Richard Clarke, the Permanent Secretary of the Department 1966-70, recounts:

> The ministry's aim was "to bring advanced technology and new processes into British industry", but it soon appeared that the essential ability to create competitiveness and profitability depended more upon the structure of industry than upon technological considerations as such. (Clarke, 1973b, p153)

In terms of the computer industry, this involved the formation of International Computers Ltd. (ICL) by a merger of International Computers and Tabulators (ICT) and English Electric Computers through the midwifery of the 1968 Industrial Expansion Act. The explicit aim of the merger was "...to establish one strong British-owned computer company able to compete with IBM, Honeywell etc" (Clarke, 1973b, p156). This intervention in the computer industry paralleled that of the Industrial Reorganisation Corporation (IRC) in other sectors of the economy between 1966-71 (Hague & Wilkinson, 1985: Massey & Meegan, 1978). Mintech took a 10.5% share of equity in the new company associated with R&D grants of £13.5m over four years, and thus established the principle of government support for the domestic computer industry. ICL also benefited from the British government's stated policy of buying from British firms "wherever reasonably possible" (House of Commons, 1970, vol. 137 p358) and in the first year of its existence it received 94% of central government orders for computers, two-thirds of which were by single tender (Moonman, 1971 p216).

The growing crisis

4.4.3 1970-79 Rothschild and after

In October 1970, the incoming Conservative administration disbanded Mintech and absorbed most of its functions into the new Department of Trade and Industry. The abolition of Mintech necessitated a review of the administrative arrangements for government-funded R&D and following the publication of the Rothschild Report (Rothschild, 1971) the government published a White Paper on 'The framework for government R&D' (HM Govt., 1972). The Government adopted the Rothschild 'customer-contractor' principle which involves particular Government sectoral interests commissioning research from intra- or extra-mural contractors rather than centralised allocation of resources. Thus while the Department of Education and Science (DES) funds 'basic' research through the Research Councils, 'applied' research is funded through 'mission oriented' departments acting as customers (Williams, 1984). In 1976, in a series of amendments to the Rothschild system, the Advisory Council for Applied Research and Development (ACARD) was set up to oversee applied research, and there has subsequently been further fine-tuning of the system including the publication in 1983 for the first time, of an 'Annual Review of Government Funded R&D' (Cabinet Office, 1983).

Despite the change in Government in 1970, support for ICL continued under the Conservatives with a further grant for R&D of £40m over four years in 1972. In 1974, the incoming Labour Government, in its controversial White Paper on the regeneration of British Industry (Dept of Industry, 1974), proposed the creation of the National Enterprise Board (NEB) as a state-holding company. In its most idealistic form, it was seen as an agent of social change and employment creation, but ultimately it was run on commercial lines with a brief "...to combine the advantages of public sector financial resources and the private sector's entrepreneurial approach to decision-making". (House of Commons, PAC, 1978, p150). Its history was dominated by the inheritance from the Department of Industry of the 'lame ducks', principally British Leyland and Rolls-Royce Ltd., which collectively accounted for almost 90% of expenditure to March 1979 (Grant, 1982, p108). However, it also acquired the government's stake in ICL which was increased to a 24.4% shareholding, plus majority shareholdings in Ferranti and Data Recording Instruments.

The major break with previous policy came in the establishment of 'green field' ventures in areas of technology not perceived as being covered by existing British companies

100

(Willott, 1981, p206). The most publicised venture was the
setting up of INMOS to establish a UK manufacturing base in
Very Large-Scale Integration (VLSI) microchips. Inmos
received £115m in grants and guaranteed loans from successive
Governments and £8m in Regional Assistance for its Welsh
manufacturing plant before its takeover by Thorn-EMI in 1984.
Less successful ventures undertaken by the NEB were the
setting up of INSAC (later split into Aregon and IPL) in
computer software/viewdata and NEXOS in Office Machinery. The
latter was severely criticised by the Public Accounts
Committee (House of Commons, 1984, vol. 144, pages xi-xiii) for
the loss of all but £0.5m of the £31.5m which the NEB had
invested, before it was split up between Logica, ICL and
Muirhead.

In the later years of the 1974-79 Labour Government a
series of initiatives were launched by the Department of
Industry to promote the microelectronics industry and the
application of new technology. In July 1977 the Product and
Process Development Scheme (PPDS) was introduced guaranteeing
up to 50% government funding from the design stage to the
point of commercial production for an innovative product or
process. In 1978, the Microprocessor Application Project (MAP)
was set up to increase awareness in industry of the benefits
of new technology (initial funding £55m) and the
Microelectronics Industry Support Programme (MISP) with
initial funding of £70m over five years. In addition, the
Software Products Scheme (SPS) which was initiated in 1973
and administered by the NCC was expanded during this period.
The scheme provides up to a third of the development costs for
new software products.

4.4.4 The neo-market strategy of the Conservative Government

Since its election in 1979, the present Conservative
administration has shown an ambivalent attitude towards
technology policy. Figure 4.3 shows that the Department of
Trade and Industry (DTI) expenditure specifically earmarked
for 'Scientific and Technology Assistance' has risen from
£170m in 1980-1 to £369m in 1984-5 but in the context of an
overall cut in DTI spending of almost half in real terms.
Indeed, if Exchequer gains through the sale of public assets
are taken into account, then in 1984-5 industry was a net
sponsor rather than recipient of government industrial
policy. Thus technology policy is in the paradoxical position
of being an 'interventionist' enclave within a 'laissez-faire'
policy. This paradoxical position reflects Conservative

Figure 4.3: Department of Trade & Industry expenditure
and 'income', 1981-85

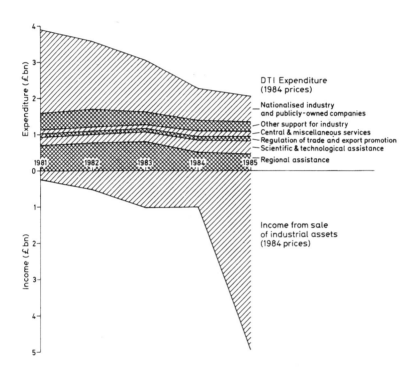

unease with interference in the operation of free market forces but fear of falling behind the heavily-subsidised industries of international competitors. Thus Conservative policy has fluctuated more between individual ministers, being most energetic under Patrick Jenkin and Kenneth Baker, than according to any overall plan. For example, the cash limits for the MISP package were cut from £70m to £55m in 1980, but later increased to £120m in 1984 (Johnstone, 1984). Similarly, when the PPDS scheme had been repackaged into the Support for Innovation programme in 1983, the high level of demand prompted a five-month embargo on new claims, Nov. 1984 - March 1985, following a ministerial changeover.

The change of government also witnessed a change in the locus of government intervention: Labour strategy had been geared towards the restructuring of industry through mergers and public ownership to create an internationally competitive UK presence in key sectors. But the Conservative approach has been to encourage the operation of free market forces through the sale of public shareholdings (ICL, British Telecom, Ferranti, INMOS etc) and through the abandonment of preferential procurement policies for British-made computers. Instead government assistance has been targeted towards the small firms and new firms sector. For instance, the DTI policy statement on new telecommunications equipment specifically states that it will "...encourage development ...particularly by small and medium-sized firms" (Cabinet Office, 1984, p107). In 1982 the Government introduced the Small Engineering Firms Investment Scheme (SEFIS) to assist small firms in the engineering industry in undertaking investment in certain types of advanced capital equipment including Computer Numerically Controlled (CNC) machine tools, through selective capital grants of up to one-third or project costs (Mason & Harrison, 1985a).

Nevertheless, on occasion the Government has intervened when the consequences of the free operation of the market would have proved unacceptable. In March 1981, the Government provided £220m in secured loans to bail out ICL from financial collapse or foreign takeover in what Grant (1982, p98) at the time called "the most significant policy modification in relation to the private sector by the Government in its first two years in office". In addition, in October 1984, the Government intervened to prevent the joint venture between IBM and British Telecom, codenamed JOVE, to set up a Value-Added Network (VAN) which would have had a near-monopoly status and would have made IBM's System Network Architecture

(SNA) the de facto interface protocol in opposition to the European-preferred Open Systems Interconnection (OSI) (Computer News, 18/10/84; 8/11/84).

Administrative changes in government technology policy include the merger of the NEB and the National Research and Development Corporation (NRDC) to form the British Technology Group (BTG) in 1981 with greatly reduced scope. Following a period of rundown, when the BTG was instructed to sell off its inherited NEB shareholdings, and lost its statutory rights to first refusal of the results of publicly-funded research, a new role for the group was outlined in 1985. Its activities are to be carried out "on commercial terms", and it is expected to be "both profit-making and self-financing" (BTG 1985, p1). Its annual budget, to be funded by patent revenue but not from the sale of NEB assets which are to go towards the reduction of the Public Sector Borrowing Requirement, is to be £15m p.a. (cf NEB borrowing limits of £4.5bn in 1979). Its new role is to concentrate on 'technology transfer' between University and Industry and 'Finance for Innovation' providing up to 50% of development costs under a joint venture finance scheme based on risk- and revenue-sharing rather than on taking equity shareholdings as the NEB had done.

4.4.5 Evaluation: International Comparisons

The structure of government-funded R&D in five leading OECD nations is shown in Table 4.10. The most striking feature of the table is the dominance of defence in the UK which constituted almost 60% of government-funded R&D in 1980. As a percentage of the R&D budget this is the highest of all 24 OECD nations; it is higher even than the US (47.3% 1980) and much higher than Germany (15.3%) or Japan (4.9%). Despite the fact that two-thirds of defence R&D is spent in industry, there has been relatively little commercial spin-off. This concern has prompted the publication of the Maddock Report (Maddock, 1983) on the civil exploitation of defence technology. In other areas of the R&D budget too, the structure of allocation restricts the potential for commercial benefit. In energy spending, for instance, the UK R&D programme is more heavily biased towards Nuclear Power (82:18) than any of the other OECD nations except France. In Higher Education spending on Science Research (through the Science & Engineering Research Council, SERC) there is a bias towards the 'big science' of Astronomy and Nuclear Physics (43.7% of 1983/4 budget) as opposed to engineering (26.5% of 1983/4 budget, Cabinet Office, 1984, p86-7)

Table 4.10: Allocation of government-funded R&D (excluding
general university funds) for five major OECD
nations, 1980

	Percentage of R&D funds				
	US	JAPAN	GERMANY	FRANCE	UK
Defence	47.3	4.9	15.3	40.1	59.4
Space	14.5	12.0	6.6	6.8	2.3
Civil Aeronautics	1.9	-	2.4	2.4	3.1
Agriculture	2.7	25.4	2.9	4.3	3.1
Industrial growth	0.3	12.2	12.4	7.9	3.8
Energy & Infrastructure	14.2	34.4	30.9	16.0	10.1
Health & Welfare	15.2	11.2	15.3	7.5	3.9
Advancement of Knowledge	3.0	4.1	14.2	15.0	12.9
TOTAL	100.0	100.0	100.0	100.0	100.0
Govt. support for R&D as a % of GDP	1.2%	0.5%	1.2%	1.3%	1.3%

Source: OECD, 1984; (Table 2.9, p87)

    In short, therefore the post-Rothschild abdication of
responsibility for taking a central overview of R&D
allocation has, in effect, ossified the current R&D budget as
an anachronistic hangover from former times with its roots in
"Britain's former perception of itself as a leading world
power with, in particular, major interests in aviation and a

determination not to lose out in the new nuclear industries" (Williams, 1984, p40). The pattern of R&D spending has been sustained more through "habit" (Freeman, 1982, p189) than a realistic assessment of changing circumstances, and indeed, the proportion of the R&D budget devoted to defence, which declined during the 1964-70 Wilson Government, actually rose from 46.2% in 1971 to 59.4% in 1980 (Freeman, 1982, p193).

Recently attention has been drawn to the shortage of 'seedcorn' or 'strategic' research (Irvine & Martin, 1984: Freeman et al, 1982), defined as "having some application in view (ie it is not undertaken purely in order to gain knowledge) [but] is not expected to find application for some years, typically of the order of a decade" (Cabinet Office, 1984, p39). A notable exception to this is the Alvey Programme (1982) which has committed £200m of public money and £150m from industry over five years to the development of key technologies. The programme is being conducted through 'pre-competitive collaborative research into advanced Information Technology' with the specific objectives of building up a UK expertise in Very Large-Scale Integration (VLSI) microchips, software tools, Intelligent Knowledge-Based Systems (IKBS) and Man-Machine Interface (Alvey Committee Report, 1982). However, this is small in comparison with state support for Information Technology in Japan where the Ministry for International Trade and Industry (MITI) in 1980 committed $623m to the much-publicised 'super-computer' and 'fifth generation computer' projects (OECD, 1984, p135). In France too, where the Government in 1981 made a commitment to an 11% p.a. increase in real terms in R&D 1980-85, growth is to be concentrated in six priority areas, including biotechnology, electronics and robotics, to which the French Government committed £750m in 1983. In the US, government support for R&D is less important because the major multinationals have sufficient resources to compete in a near-monopoly fashion (for instance the number of researchers employed in the Computers and Office Equipment sector in the US (41,100 1978) is more than twice that of Japan, Germany, France and the UK combined). However, government support exercised through the space programme and the defence budget, including recent SDI contracts, has been important in the growth of many of these leading companies (Malecki, 1984b).

In conclusion therefore, even though government-funded R&D in the UK is as high as a percentage of GDP as its major international competitors, there is relatively little support for applied industrial technology. The same is true in the computer industry: of £33.2m government support in 1981/2 £20m was for defence applications (Bowles, 1984). However, despite slipping down the OECD league table of R&D spenders from second in the 1960s to fifth currently (OECD, 1984, p141), Britain continues to maintain a surplus in overseas technology royalty transactions as an exporter rather than an importer of technology (£131.6m 1982, Bowles, 1984). This is in contrast to Japan and West Germany who have consistently imported technology throughout the period of their so-called 'economic miracles' (Williams, 1984, p39). Thus the sins of inertia discussed earlier have been compounded with insularity. As Williams concludes:

> The overall balance of Britain's technological effort is ... almost certainly wrong, and the culture, institutions and procedures of the state are at best neutral, and probably antipathetic, to market-dominated technological change. (Williams, 1984, p51)

Chapter Five

NEW LAMPS FOR OLD: NEW FIRM FORMATION

In recent years, small firms and in particular new technology-based firms have been championed by Government and media alike as harbingers of industrial revival. After the Conservative Government's first year in office, 1979-80, an opinion poll commissioned by the McCann Erickson Advertising Group, and quoted in the Financial Times 9/9/80, found that 'assistance for new firms' was the issue most people identified as being central to the government's economic strategy. Indeed, since 1979, the government has set up a number of schemes aimed at encouraging the formation and expansion of small businesses through financial aid, advisory services and reduction of the financial burden placed upon entrepreneurs. Some of these were discussed in chapter four. In this chapter recent trends in new firm formation and industrial deconcentration are reviewed (section 5.1). Evidence for temporal and spatial variations in the pattern of new firm formation in the computer industry and throughout the economy is assessed in sections 5.2 and 5.3. Attention is turned to the origins and characteristics of entrepreneurs in 5.4 with particular attention to the new firm formation process in the contrasting environments of Cambs/Herts and Scotland. In section 5.5 the role of new firms in technological change is examined and finally, in 5.6 the contribution of new firms to the local economy is assessed.

5.1 Recent trends in new firm formation

5.1.1 Definitions

The definition of a 'new firm' implies both a recent date of formation and no prior existence. Both of these components of the definition are open to several interpretations as Mason (1983) has illustrated. For the purposes of this study, 'date of formation' is regarded as the year in which the firm was registered or 'incorporated' as a limited company. While it is true that some firms may be deterred initially by the costs and bureaucracy involved in incorporation, nevertheless those which survive the start-up phase will eventually take up limited liability status for the legal protection which it offers. The choice of date of incorporation thus affords a standardised definition of foundation while avoiding the arbitrariness and problems of obtaining accurate data for alternative definitions such as the date on which trading commenced or the date of recruitment of the first full-time paid employee.

The second requirement of the definition 'new firm' is that it should be a net addition to the economy. Again alternative definitions are available from the literature according to the degree of independence of the company at its foundation. Independence can be interpreted to mean either 'legal' independence or 'independence of action' but the rule of thumb adopted here will be that put forward by Johnson & Cathcart (1979, p270) namely that new firms should have "no obvious parent in any existing business or organisation".

For the purposes of this chapter, those firms which were founded as new independent enterprises since 1975 plus branches set up directly by them have been included in analysis of the questionnaire data. In all, 325 new, independent and currently surviving computer firms are recognised in the survey data employing 7,992 people on their main site plus a further 1,027 in 34 branch plants set up directly. New firms and their branches constitute 13% of the total employment in the survey data. A further 393 people are employed in regional sales offices in the UK and at least 144 in overseas branches, neither of which are covered by this survey. Altogether therefore, the 325 firms have created a total of 9,556 new jobs at an average size of 29.4 employees each. Since formation and before August 1985, some 30 (9.2%) of the new firms have been acquired, of which 9 have been acquired by overseas firms. However, it seems certain that this figure will increase as rationalisation proceeds apace, particularly in the microcomputer sector.

5.1.2 Industrial Concentration

When the Bolton Committee of inquiry on small firms reported in 1971, it was clear that the small firms manufacturing sector had undergone a period of decline in terms of share of UK output and employment. Indeed, Bolton stated that:

...there are many powerful forces, some of them

New firm formation in the computer industry

apparently irreversible, making for a greater
industrial concentration and a reduction in the
number of small firms. It is indeed possible that
the danger point has already been reached. (Bolton
Committee, 1971, p86)

The decline in importance of the small firms sector has been
coincident with what Hannah (1976) has termed the "rise of the
corporate economy" and in particular the rise to dominance of
the multi-plant, multinational corporation. Thus the share of
UK output of the top 100 UK manufacturing firms rose from
approximately 16% in 1909 to 41% in 1970 (Prais, 1976, p4).
Over the period 1930–68, Prais calculates that the number of
establishments with 10 employees or less fell by 63% from
93,400 to 34,800.

Table 5.1: Percentage of manufacturing employment in small
            establishments in the UK and selected other
            countries

Country	Total mnfg. employment (millions)	Year	% of emp. in estabs 20–200	Year	% of emp. in estabs 20–200
United Kingdom	6.58	(1978)	24%	(1978)	30%
West Germany	7.39	(1979)	30%	-	n.a.
South Africa	1.30	(1976)	32%	(1976)	35%
Austria	0.59	(1980)	33%	(1980)	35%
United States	18.35	(1972)	34%	(1977)	39%
Sweden	0.80	(1979)	37%	-	n.a.
Canada	1.54	(1976)	43%	(1976)	48%
Italy	3.61	(1971)	48%	(1971)	65%
Spain	1.74	(1978)	52%	(1978)	64%
Switzerland	0.72	(1975)	52%	(1975)	64%
Norway	0.31	(1979)	54%	(1979)	62%
Japan	7.56	(1978)	54%	(1978)	68%

Sources: Ganguly & Povey, (1982, p486)
         Business Monitor PA 1002, 1979

New firm formation in the computer industry

The process of industrial concentration appears to have gone further in the UK than in other advanced industrial economies, yet this does not seem to have made UK industry more competitive. One measure of industrial concentration is the percentage of employment in small firms. In Table 5.1, the Bolton Committee definition of small firms as having less than 200 employees is adopted. The table shows that the UK has the lowest percentage of employment in small establishments of 12 industrialised nations for which comparable data is available. While establishment-level data does not provide a wholly adequate surrogate for industrial concentration (enterprise-level data would be preferable) nevertheless it does allow for a standardisation of industrial statistics between nations. It might be expected that the level of industrial concentration would be greater in economies with a larger base of manufacturing employment, for reasons of economy of scale, but these figures lend little support to this hypothesis. Particularly instructive is the comparison between the UK and Japan which has a manufacturing employment base of similar size, but has a percentage employed in small establishments which is more than twice that of the UK. The importance of the small firm in the Japanese economy has been advanced as one source of its industrial dynamism over the post-war period (Rothwell & Zegveld, 1982; Anthony, 1983).

The Bolton Committee were indeed concerned that the contraction of the small firms sector might affect adversely the ability of small firms to fulfil what they regarded as "the most important function, namely to act as a breeding ground for new industries" and "the seedbed from which new large companies will grow to challenge and to stimulate the established leaders of industry" (Bolton, 1971, p84). Since the publication of the Bolton Committee report, the rate of increase of industrial concentration seems to have slowed as the number of mergers and acquisitions of manufacturing firms in the UK has fallen from a peak of 700 in 1964 to 202 in 1982 (Annual Abstract of Statistics). Since 1968, the small manufacturing firms sector also seems to have regained some of the share of output and employment lost to larger enterprises. Figure 5.1 shows that the number of small manufacturing enterprises in the UK (ten employees or less) reached a nadir in the mid-1960s but has subsequently risen substantially (Keeble, 1986a; Census of Production, 1981). Some of this apparent increase is undoubtedly due to changes in the scope of the Census of Production from which these figures are derived, for instance the new register of businesses adopted

New firm formation in the computer industry

Figure 5.1:   Small manufacturing establishments*in the
              United Kingdom, 1930-1980

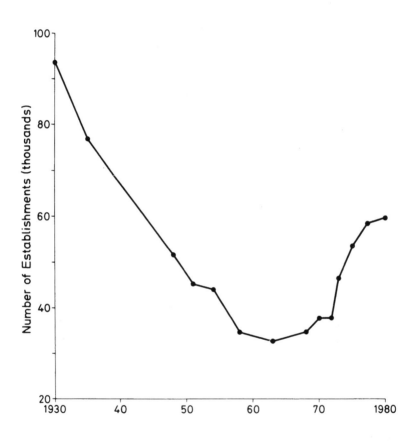

*Ten employees or less

following the 1968 revision of the standard industrial classification. However, changes in statistical definitions can not fully account for the reversal of the trend which has been observed since 1970.

An alternative measure of industrial concentration is to consider the market share of the largest firms. The Business Monitor Series PO 1006 - 'Statistics of Product Concentration of UK Manufacturers' - shows the percentage of total sales by industry accounted for by the top five enterprises for selected years since 1963. For computer hardware, the index initially rose from 73.3% in 1963 to 87.2% in 1968, the year of the formation of ICL. Since then however, it has declined progressively to 81% in 1979. Between 1970 and 1979, the number of enterprises recorded as being engaged in computer manufacture rose from 75 to 153, and the number of establishments from 84 to 162. Since 1979 the 1980 SIC has been used in the Census of Production and it has not been possible to differentiate between computers and office machinery, but the degree of concentration in the combined group (AHH 330) has continued to decrease from 71% in 1980 to 69% in 1982. This has been associated with a rise in the number of enterprises from 244 to 282 (+15%). Thus it can be inferred that 1968 marked something of a watershed in the process of concentration in the computer sector.

Three major reasons may be advanced to explain this turnround in industrial concentration observed in both the computer manufacturing sector and all manufacturing since the late 1960s. Firstly, it may be a result of improvements in productivity and increasing capital:labour substitution which has allowed substantial manufacturing operations to be established with a smaller labour force. This would imply that the process of industrial concentration has not necessarily ceased, but rather that the arbitrary 200 employee cut-off point used for defining small manufacturing firms is an inadequate scale for identifying its operation. Strong support for this comes from the data on declining average establishment size examined in chapter six. Both EITB figures for computer manufacturing 1978-84 and questionnaire survey data for all computer industry employment 1980-84 indicate a reduction of between a quarter and a third in the average size of establishments. However this does not explain the decrease in market share by the largest enterprises in the computer industry noted above. Secondly, it may be explained in terms of the effects of recession on the operations of large manufacturing units which has enforced the rationalisation, or even the hiving off of whole departments. Evidence presented in chapter six on employment change by size band shows that the 12 largest establishments in the computer industry collectively lost 15% of their employment between 1980 and 1984. Deliberate firm fragmentation policies (Shutt & Whittington, 1984) are less evident in the computer industry. However the increase in the number of management buy-outs in the survey data since 1981 (see table 4.5) may give some support to this hypothesis.

Thirdly, the rising importance of the small business sector may be explained by higher rates of new firm formation (Gudgin, 1984). Examination of the ratio of manufacturing establishments to enterprises in the computer industry in the Census of Production shows that the ratio actually fell from 1.12:1 in 1970 to 1.09:1 in 1982. This suggests that in the computer industry at least, the process of industrial deconcentration has taken place through the formation of new firms rather than through the opening of new manufacturing branch plants by existing enterprises. This has more than counter-balanced the high level of acquisition activity in the microcomputer sector. The remainder of this chapter examines in more detail the phenomenon of increased new firm formation.

5.2 Temporal Variations

5.2.1 Time-series trends

Despite growing interest, the small firms and particularly the new firms sector in the UK remains underdocumented at the national level. The use of business registrations is subject to the problem of overestimation because many companies are registered purely for legal purposes and never trade. Furthermore, business registration data does not differentiate between industrial and commercial sectors, and so cannot be used to provide information on new manufacturing firms. Nevertheless, the rise in new registrations from just 20,654 in 1968 (4.3% of the total stock of businesses registered on 1/1/68) to 87,166 in 1982 (10.0% of the total stock of businesses registered on 1/1/82) is an impressive indication of higher rates of new firm formation during recent years.

An alternative data source which has only recently become available to the industrial economist is registration of businesses and other organisations for the purpose of VAT

Table 5.2:   Registrations and deregistrations of businesses
             for VAT in the production industries sector,
             1980-84

Year	Births	Deaths	Surplus	Stock at year end	% Change
1980	14,555	13,134	+1,421	122,385	+1.2%
1981	14,796	11,514	+3,282	125,667	+2.7%
1982	16,557	14,028	+2,529	128,196	+2.0%
1983	18,794	14,275	+4,519	132,715	+3.5%
1984	19,229	13,787	+5,442	138,157	+4.1%
1980-1984	83,931	66,738	+17,193	138,157	+14.2% +2.8% p.a.

Source: VAT registration data from Ganguly (1985c)

which has been carried out since UK membership of the EEC in
1973. VAT registrations for the years 1980 to 1984 have been
analysed in a series of articles by Ganguly (1983, 1984, 1985a,
1985c). In 1981 the number of firms registered for VAT (1.33m)
was 61% higher than the number of firms incorporated with
limited liability status (0.82m). This reflects the number of
sole-proprietorships, partnerships, clubs and associations
which register for VAT purposes but do not seek limited
liability status. This limits the value of VAT registration
data for study of new firms in the economy as a whole. However
for the industrial production sector, the data is reasonably
reliable. Taking new registrations and deregistrations to
represent 'births' and 'deaths', Table 5.2 shows that in 1984
births of production firms (19,229) added almost 15% to the
existing stock of production businesses. The annual volume of
new births rose by almost a third between 1980 and 1984 but
there was no appreciable rise in the number of firm deaths.
Consequently, the surplus of births over deaths rose from
1,421 in 1980 to 5,442 in 1984 (Figure 5.2). Thus it can be
inferred that the rise in the stock of manufacturing firms has

Figure 5.2:   New firms in production industries in the
              United Kingdom, 1980-1984

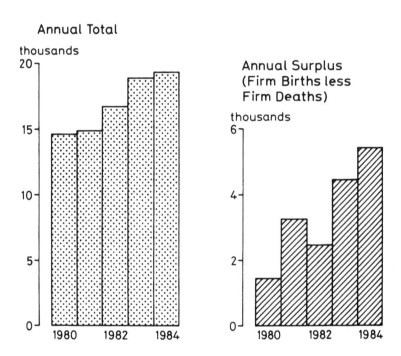

been of the same order of magnitude as that for all firms shown in the company registration data, with a particularly significant increase since 1980. Higher rates of new firm formation are common to most of the economies of Western Europe (Keeble & Wever, 1986) and three major hypotheses have been put forward in the literature to explain them. These are discussed below.

5.2.2 Recession-push hypothesis

In view of the timing of the rise in new firm formation, it has been argued by some researchers that there is a causal relationship between higher levels of unemployment and increased entrepreneurship. Fothergill & Gudgin (1982) recognise such a relationship in the East Midlands over the period 1947-75, and argue that recession forces people into self-employment. However Gould & Keeble (1984) doubt the existence of such a relationship in East Anglia after 1973. Moreover, while there is an upwards trend in the time series for both company registrations and unemployment, Binks and Jennings' (1983) work on monthly data for company registrations and the adult unemployment rate between 1971 and 1981 suggests that the true regression relationship between the two is actually inverse. That is, once serial autocorrelation has been taken out of both time series, higher levels of unemployment are associated with lower levels of company registrations, even after allowing for likely time lags.

In the survey data for the computer industry, there were few entrepreneurs who had previously been unemployed. However, there are local instances where entrepreneurs left a unit which was later closed down. Notably in Edinburgh, several small software firms were founded by ex-employees of the ICL software development unit at Dalkeith which was closed in 1983. On the whole though, the theory of recession-induced entrepreneurship does not seem to explain adequately higher rates of new firm formation.

5.2.3 Income growth hypothesis

A second possible reason behind the rise in new firm formation is the growth in real incomes. Data from Social Trends (CSO, annual) shows that real household disposable income per capita in the UK has risen by 27% between 1970 and 1983 in constant prices. Interestingly, the biggest growth area in consumer expenditure has been on electronic forms of home entertainment such as TV, video, Hi-fi, and home computers. Consumer spending on these products increased 40% in real terms between 1980 and 1983 compared with only a 5% increase in total spending. The market for home computers in particular has been made feasible by increased spending power. Bolton (1971) considered that increased income would lead to a higher demand for 'one-off' goods and services which the small firm sector was most suited to supplying. Brusco (1982, p171-3) argues that the increase in demand for more varied and customised goods, produced in short series, is one of the two main reasons (the other being increased trade union militancy) underlying the decentralisation of the production structure in the Emilia region of Italy. This has been associated with a rising number of new firms, increased self-employment and the growth of the 'black' economy generally.

5.2.4 Technological change hypothesis

A third explanatory approach to rising new firm formation which has been advanced in the literature (Keeble & Kelly, 1985a; Soete & Dosi, 1983; Markusen, 1985) is technological change theory. Though perhaps more industry-specific than recession-push or income growth hypotheses, technological change provides a useful framework for understanding the changing rate of firm formation in the computer industry. In chapter two, it was argued that the computer industry has experienced a 'technological paradigm shift' since the advent of microelectronics in the mid-1970s. The thesis is predicated upon a link between technological change and market structure. In the particular case of the computer industry, the following factors have favoured new firm formation. Firstly, electronic component miniaturisation has greatly reduced the unit costs of computing power and has therefore lowered the 'barriers to entry' for new firms. Secondly, the pace of technological change has been extremely rapid and small firms are arguably more flexible and responsive to change than larger units with hierarchical decision-making structures. Thirdly, the introduction of the microcomputer has undercut profit margins and shortened projected life-cycles for existing product ranges such that R&D and capital investment can not be fully redeemed. In this context, longer-established firms are less likely to adopt the 'subversive' technology of microelectronics than new firms which have no past investments to protect. Finally, the lack of standardisation in operating systems, interface protocols and programming languages has created a diversity of market niches where economies of scale do not operate and which can

118

Figure 5.3:   Formation rate of computer new firms in
relation to technological change, 1965-1983

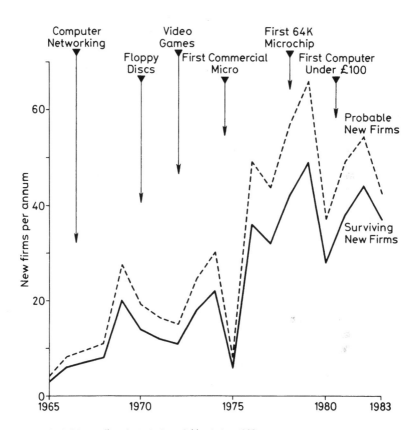

Probable new firms include those failing before 1985

best be exploited by small firms with low overheads and a close contact with changing market requirements.

Figure 5.3 shows the date of formation of the 438 firms in the survey founded as new independent units between 1965 and 1983. 1984 has been excluded from this graph because data is available for only half the year. Within this time series, there appears to be a definite 'business cycle' effect leading to recession-induced decline in firm formation rates in the years 1971/2, 1975 and 1980. However, the most striking feature is the increasing rate of firm formation, particularly after 1975, which peaked in 1979 when almost 50 new and currently surviving firms were formed in the industry. It might be expected that the low rates of firm formation before 1975 signal a higher rate of failure amongst older firms. In fact the rising trend after 1975 is still apparent even when the time series is corrected to allow for the probable rate of firm failure (the dotted line in Fig. 5.3) which is calculated using firm failure rate probability tables derived from Ganguly's (1983) study of VAT registration data. Looking in more detail at the composition of the new firms, it can be seen in Figure 5.4 that an earlier smaller 'cycle' of increased firm formation in the computer industry is apparent in the late 1960s and early 1970s. This may be associated with the widespread diffusion of minicomputers, but this cycle was in decline after 1972 in the hardware sector and after 1974 in software. The major 'cycle' of firm formation apparent after 1975 associated with the introduction of microelectronics, again shows an earlier peak among hardware firms (1978 - 24 new firms) than among software (1982 - 27). Figure 5.4 also shows the number of acquisitions in each sector. The process of rationalisation is apparent from an earlier date in the hardware sector and has proceeded further than in the software sector. Thus it is possible to infer that the effect of the microelectronics revolution filtered down first to the hardware sector and later to software, but that the 'mushroom' of growth in the stock of businesses is now subsiding in each.

5.3 Spatial variations in new firm formation

5.3.1 Theoretical issues

Spatial variations in the pattern of new manufacturing firm formation have been interpreted by Fothergill & Gudgin (1982, p113-133) as reflecting variations in the local size structure of the existing stock of establishments. They argue

New firm formation in the computer industry

Figure 5.4: Formation rate of computer hardware and
             software new firms, 1965-83 and cumulative
             number of acquisitions

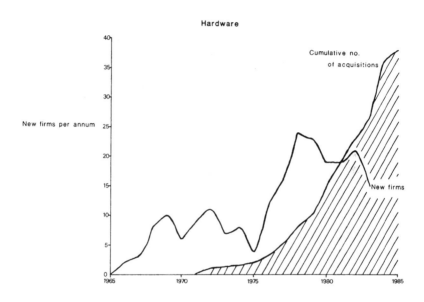

Hardware

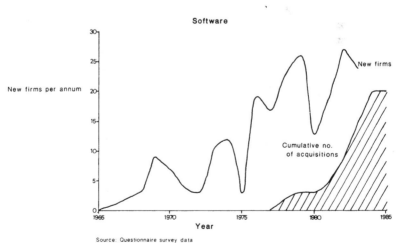

Software

Source: Questionnaire survey data

that small firms, because they offer a better training ground for potential entrepreneurs, produce more entrepreneurs per employee than larger establishments. It must also be added that in areas dominated by small plants, the 'turnover' of the stock of businesses is likely to be higher than in areas with a larger average size of establishments. Thus small plant areas may not necessarily produce a greater number of surviving new firms. Nevertheless, Fothergill & Gudgin's work in the East Midlands does show that entrepreneurs come preferentially from backgrounds in small firms. Support for this hypothesis comes from Keeble & Gould's (1985) work on small manufacturing firms in East Anglia which shows that 51% of founders came from firms which employed less than 50 workers. In the more specific environment of Glasgow, Checkland (1981) has argued that the historical paucity of new firms is due to the 'Upas tree' effect of large dominant firms, especially in the shipbuilding and iron and steel industries. The legendary Upas tree was reputed to kill off all smaller plants in the surrounding area by the shade of its branches.

Beaumont's (1982a) study of new high technology electronics companies in the South East of England differs from other work in showing that a majority (60%) of founders come from larger multi-plant companies. He emphasises the difference between companies in their attitudes to internal entrepreneurship. Some firms have binding agreements with their employees preventing the independent development of discarded technologies. Other firms operate incentive schemes to encourage innovation within the firm. But an increasing number of companies are participating in 'sponsored spin-outs' of innovations which can not be profitably developed in-house, and several venture capital companies have publicly stated their interest in initiating such schemes.

Most other explanations of variations in the rate of new firm formation relate to the socio-economic characteristics of the resident population. Whittington (1984) using regional data for VAT registrations for 1980 and 1981 found some correspondence between size structure and birth rate but this was not statistically significant (at the 95% level). The variables which were significantly correlated with higher levels of firm formation were low level of manual employees and a high level of owner-occupation in the local housing market. In regional case-studies, Gould & Keeble (1984) found a positive relationship in East Anglia between rate of new firm formation and the percentage of the resident population

New firm formation in the computer industry

Figure 5.5:   New firm formation rate in production
               industries, 1980-83

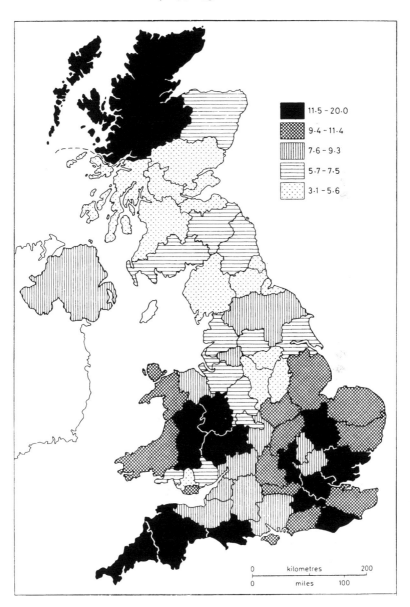

in non-manual occupations. This often implied that areas which had not previously experienced industrial growth on any substantial scale recorded relatively high levels of new firm formation. A similar phenomenon of non-metropolitan industrialisation was found by Cross (1981, p246-281) in Scotland. Storey (1982, p196) has taken several of these variables relating to size structure, occupational composition, socio-economic class and housing market characteristics (though not urban structure) to devise an index of regional entrepreneurship. According to this index, the most favoured region is the southern 'core' of the country, and the least favoured are the 'peripheral' regions of Wales, Northern Ireland and the North of England.

5.3.2 Spatial variations in new manufacturing firm formation

The recent publication of county data (Ganguly, 1985a) on business formation as measured by new VAT registrations permits for the first time analysis of the detailed spatial pattern of new firm creation in the United Kingdom. The figures recorded in Table 5.3 and Figures 5.5 and 5.6 refer to all new VAT registrations during the four years 1980 to 1983 inclusive in production industries. In rate terms, expressed per one thousand employees in production industries in 1981, Table 5.3 reveals that in the 1980s, the geography of new production firm formation in the UK has been dominated by the South East, together with adjacent East Anglia and South West England. The lowest regional rates have been recorded by Northern England, Scotland and Yorkshire/Humberside. The county-level data (Figure 5.5) highlights very high rates in Greater London and surrounding counties, including those in East Anglia, together with three perhaps surprising rural/peripheral zones of high formation rates, in the far south-west, rural West Midlands and Wales, and the Scottish Highlands. In these latter cases, the high rate chiefly reflects the low base of production employment in 1981. The volume map (Figure 5.6) is dominated by Greater London (over 12,000 new firms, or 20% of the UK total), with much smaller clusters in other English conurbations.

5.3.3 Spatial variations in new computer firm formation

Table 5.4 shows the geographical distribution of new firms formed since 1975 in the computer electronics industry. The 'new firm formation rate' is obtained by dividing the number of new computer firms by the number of information technology employees (defined in Table 5.5) in each county and

124

Table 5.3:   New firm formation rate in the production
             industries by region, 1980-1983

Region	No. of new businesses 1980 - 1983	Business formation rate[a]
South East	24,473	13.8
East Anglia	2,132	11.0
South West	4,412	10.3
West Midlands	6,733	8.0
Northern Ireland	1,026	8.0
East Midlands	4,717	7.7
North West	6,039	7.1
Wales	2,052	7.0
Yorks & Humberside	4,387	6.4
Scotland	2,869	5.1
North	1,803	4.5
United Kingdom	60,643 [b]	9.0 [b]

Notes

a - New businesses per 1,000 production industry employees,
    1981
b - Excluding 4,207 new businesses unallocated by region
    Full UK rate = 9.6

Source: Ganguly (1985a)
          Dept. of Employment Gazette, Occasional Supp. No 2
          (Dec. 1983)

multiplying by 1,000. The information technology sector was
chosen as a suitable base because survey data on the origins
of computer industry founders (see Table 5.11)
     Perhaps the most striking feature of the table is the
high rate of new firm formation in East Anglia (6.32). This is

Figure 5.6: Volume of employment in new firms in the
production industries, 1980–1983

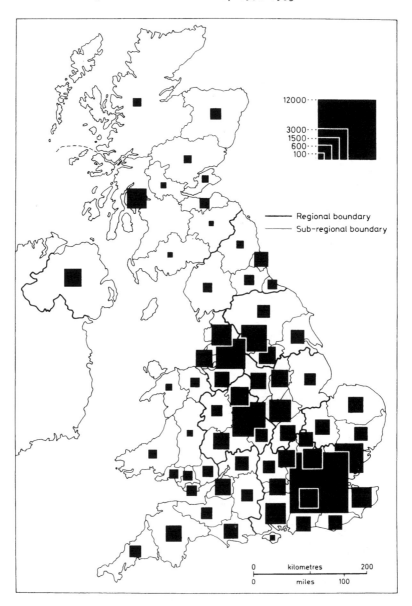

Table 5.4: The geographical distribution of new firms in
            the computer industry by region, 1984

Region	No. of new firms	Employment 1984	(%)	Firm formation rate[a]
Greater London	57	1,398	(15.5%)	0.61
Rest of South East	100	2,488	(27.6%)	0.68
All South East	157	3,886	(43.1%)	0.66
East Anglia	68	1,624	(18.0%)	6.32
South West	15	583	(6.5%)	0.67
West Midlands	16	418	(4.6%)	0.51
East Midlands	10	420	(4.7%)	0.44
North West	15	348	(3.9%)	0.43
Yorks & Humberside	9	388	(4.3%)	0.80
North	2	36	(0.4%)	0.12
Wales	7	354	(3.9%)	0.47
Scotland	26	962	(10.7%)	0.81
Great Britain	325	9,019	(100.0%)	0.74

Note
 a - New firms 1975-84 per 1,000 information technology
     employees, 1981

Source: Questionnaire survey data
         Dept. of Employment Gazette, Occasional Supp. No. 2
         (Dec. 1983)

partly explained by the low level of existing information technology employment in the region (10,756 - 2.6% of the GB total in 1981). But it is mainly the result of the extraordinarily high rate of new firm formation in Cambridgeshire (60 firms - NFF Rate = 14.8: see Table 5.5 and Figures 5.7 and 5.8). This represents more than a sixth of all new firms founded in the computer industry over the last ten years. It might be argued that this reflects a 'study base' effect such that more smaller firms have been identified in the researcher's home area. However, the average size of new firms in East Anglia (23.9) is not significantly smaller than the UK average (27.8), while the survey results are entirely in line with the independent work on the Cambridge high technology complex by Gould and Keeble (1984) and Segal Quince and partners (1985). Interestingly, the next highest county new firm formation rate is Oxfordshire (7 firms - NFF Rate = 5.1) which is similarly a predominantly rural county with a premier university.

Figures 5.7 and 5.8 show the rate and employment volume respectively of new computer firm formation 1975-84 by county. In general terms, Figure 5.7 shows a band of higher firm formation rates running approximately East-West along a Bristol-Norwich axis (Hall, 1981). This is consistent with arguments advanced in chapter six concerning the growth of new computer industry employment at the growing 'fringe' of the economic 'core' area of the country. This area arguably affords a pleasant living environment for mobile entrepreneurs and highly-qualified workers, together in several cases with a research environment generated by a major university or other existing R&D establishments.

After East Anglia, the next ˙highest regional new firm formation rate is Scotland (26 firms - NFF rate = 0.81) This is of course in some contrast to Scotland's overall very low new production firm formation rate (Table 5.3), and reflects a concentration of new computer firms in the central lowlands. Furthermore, the Scottish new firms are bigger in size than the national average (37.0 employees per firm; GB = 27.8). Given that the growth of the electronics sector in Scotland has been largely induced by the influx of branch plants of foreign-owned multinationals partially attracted by regional policy incentives, it might be reasonable to assume that these firms had grown up because of the subcontracting opportunities offered by the multinationals.

Figure 5.8 shows the volume of new employment created by new computer firms and their branch plants by county. The arc

Table 5.5: New computer firm formation rate 1975-84 by
county: The top ten counties

County	No. of new firms[a]	Employment in new firms	Information Technology Employment[b]	Firm formation rate[c]
Cambridgeshire	60	1,349	4,056	14.8
Oxfordshire	7	164	1,373	5.1
Cheshire	10	126	3,986	2.5
Avon	9	234	3,747	2.4
South Yorks	3	108	1,528	2.0
Warwickshire	3	130	1,628	1.8
Surrey	19	562	12,991	1.5
Buckinghamshire	7	357	4,855	1.4
Hertfordshire	28	471	20,100	1.4
Suffolk	5	100	3,694	1.3
Great Britain	325	9,019	483,390	0.7

Notes

a - Counties with less than 3 new firms excluded

b - Information Technology employment includes:

   AH 3302 'Computer hardware'

   AH 3440 'Telecommunications equipment and
         electronic components'

   AH 3450 'Other electronics equipment'

   AH 8394 'Computer services employment'

c - New firms 1975-84 per 1,000 information technology
   employees, 1981

Sources: Questionnaire survey data
         Census of Employment, Sept. 1981, Unpublished
         county estimates

New firm formation in the computer industry

Figure 5.7: Firm formation rates by county for new
computer firms, 1975–1984

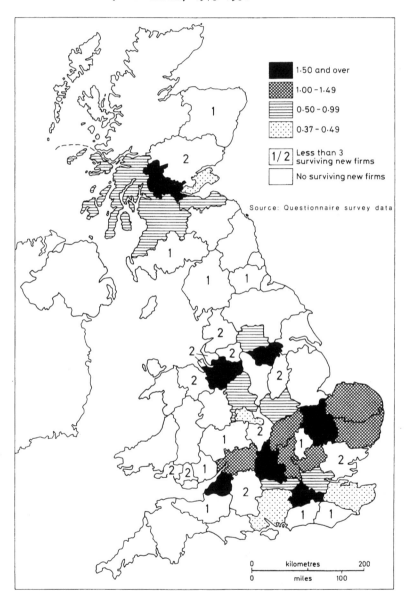

of counties to the north and west of London plus the metropolis itself all show high levels of employment creation. In comparison to the location of all computer industry employment by county (1981 Census of Employment), two counties in particular show higher levels of employment than would be expected. In the case of Fife, the employment total is inflated by the presence of one particular firm, Rodime, a manufacturer of disc drives, which has expanded since its formation in 1979 to employ more than 500 people worldwide. In the case of Cambridgeshire however, the survey records 1,349 employees in 1984 in new firms and their branches compared with the census of employment estimate for 1981 of just 725 employees in all establishments, both hardware and software. As explained earlier, the reasons behind this discrepancy lie in the so-called 'Cambridge phenomenon' of new high technology growth. This is discussed in section 5.4.

The new firm formation rate index does show something of a bias towards rural and small town areas. For instance, of the 13 counties with a firm formation rate greater than 1, only two (Avon and South Yorks) contain urban areas of any significant size (greater than 200,000 population 1981 Census). Conversely, Table 5.6 shows that, with the notable exception of Greater London, the conurbations and other free-standing cities (greater than 250,000 population) are relatively under-represented by new firm formation and employment. More than 52% of the new employment is in small towns and rural areas, and if Cambridge, with a non-student population of less than 100,000, were included in this category, it would exceed 57%. The main exception to this trend of high technology growth in lesser urban settlements is Greater London. The Greater London case is interesting in having both a higher share of new firms (17.5%) and a higher share of new firm employment (15.4%) than that which would be predicted by the 1981 share of manufacturing employment (11.0%). This is consistent both with the high rates of new production firm formation in Greater London noted earlier (Figures 5.4 and 5.5) and with the turnround in the relative employment performance of Greater London since 1977. In the specific case of the computer electronics industry it would seem to be accounted for by the growth of software firms in the City and other small office automation firms which have their HQ in London but manufacturing facilities outside the metropolis, either in branch plants or through subcontract (GLC, 1985, p311-29). The unique role of London as the dominant UK market for high technology products may thus play a part in

New firm formation in the computer industry

Figure 5.8:   Distribution of computer employment by county
              in new computer firms, 1984

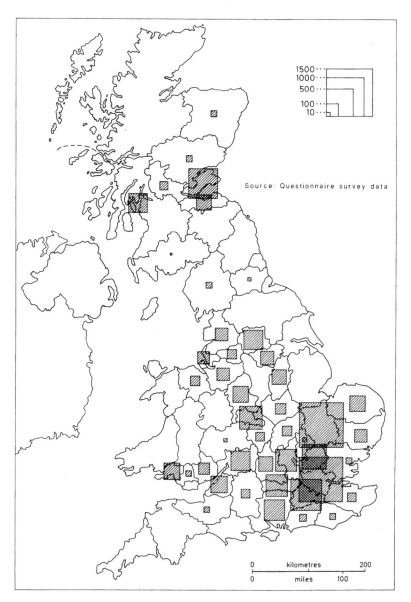

New firm formation in the computer industry

its above average firm formation rate, along with firm size, occupational characteristics, and volume of existing scientific research activity.

Table 5.6: Urban-rural distribution of computer industry new firms and employment, 1984 and all manufacturing employment, 1981

Urban/rural status	Firms	(%)	Employment	(%)	Total Mnfg. Emp. 1981 ('000s)	(%)
Greater London	57	(17.5%)	1,398	(15.5%)	650	(11.0%)
Conurbations	26	(8.0%)	735	(8.1%)	1,295	(21.9%)
Free-standing cities	34	(10.5%)	955	(10.6%)	950	(16.1%)
Large towns	55	(16.9%)	1,177	(13.1%)	756	(12.8%)
Small towns	100	(30.8%)	2,809	(31.1%)	1,609	(27.2%)
Rural areas	53	(16.3%)	1,945	(21.6%)	655	(11.1%)
Great Britain	325	(100.0%)	9,019	(100.0%)	5,916	(100.0%)

Sources: Questionnaire survey data
          Fothergill et al (1984)

On the whole, new firm formation would appear to be further intensifying existing patterns of concentration of the electronics industry in the expanded South Eastern core at the expense of intermediate and peripheral areas. For instance, some 73.8% of all surviving new firms and 67.6% of new firms employment in the computer industry is in the regions of the South East, East Anglia, the South West. This compares with 47.7% of GB firms (1982) and 44.4% of GB employment in these regions (Regional Trends, 1984 Tables 7.1 & 10.6). This finding is in accordance with other work on the location of new high technology-based firms (Mason, 1985; Rowlinson, 1985) and with other high technology employment, Research and Development establishments and product innovation.

5.4 The firm formation process

5.4.1 Industry/Academic structure

In the previous section it has been shown that there are significant spatial variations in the rate of new firm formation. In this section the focus of the study shifts to examine the relationship between the existing industrial and academic base in an area. From the 325 new independent firms founded since 1975 identified above, the questionnaire survey yielded information on entrepreneurship for 198 firms (60.9%). Altogether 443 founders were involved in these firms at an average of 2.2 per firm. From this total, more detailed information is available for 177 founders in Cambs/Herts and Scotland from the interview survey. In these case study areas a few firms founded before 1975 for which entrepreneurial data is available have been included to increase the sample size.

In chapter six, the composition of the computer industry in the two study areas of Cambs/Herts and Scotland is contrasted in terms of legal status, size and age of establishments, product range and skills composition. It is argued here that these differences are likely to affect both the potential rate and, more importantly, the nature of entrepreneurship in the two areas. One assumption of this methodology is that entrepreneurs tend to stay in the same market sector and geographical area in which they were previously employed. This assumption is supported by other studies of new firm founders (Beaumont, 1982; Fothergill & Gudgin, 1982; Keeble & Gould, 1985). In Cambridgeshire and Scotland the assumption is corroborated by the low percentage of in-migrant founders (19% in Cambs, 18% in Scotland) and high percentage of founders who came from backgrounds in academic research, computer firms or the electronics industry (92% in Cambs, 85% in Scotland). In order to study the industrial composition effects, it is necessary to look at the personal characteristics of the founders themselves. Here it becomes pertinent to distinguish between new firms in Cambridgeshire and Hertfordshire because it is clear from the survey data that the new firm formation process in Cambridgeshire is a distinctive phenomenon. Hertfordshire is included as a separate entity only when data availability does not allow for comparison with the rest of Great Britain.

Table 5.7: Average age of founders of new firms in Cambridgeshire, Scotland and the rest of GB

Age of founders	New firms in Cambs		New firms in Scotland		Other new firms		All new firms	
Under 25	11	(16.9%)	3	(4.7%)	11	(4.1%)	25	(6.3%)
25 - 34	37	(56.9%)	29	(45.3%)	137	(51.5%)	203	(51.4%)
35 - 44	15	(23.1%)	21	(32.8%)	102	(38.3%)	138	(34.9%)
45 plus	2	(3.1%)	11	(17.2%)	16	(6.0%)	40	(10.1%)
Total	65	(100.0%)	64	(100.0%)	266	(100.0%)	395	(100.0%)

Source: Questionnaire survey data

5.4.2 Age and education of founders

Tables 5.7 to 5.9 show a selected range of characteristics relating to the age, education and previous employment of new computer firm founders in Cambridgeshire, Scotland and the rest of the UK. One feature immediately apparent in these tables is the 'university effect' in Cambridgeshire and to a lesser extent in Scotland. This is shown by the number of founders coming directly from academic research (Cambs: 24 founders, 13 firms); or possessing Ph.Ds or other post-graduate qualifications (Cambs: 39 founders, 24 firms); many of these are also relatively young (Cambs: 73.8% of founders under 35; 16.9% under 25). Examples of firms which have been started up from ex-university connections in Cambridge include Applied Research of Cambridge (Architecture Dept.), Shape Data (Computer Science Lab) and Laserscan Laboratories (High Energy Physics). These statistics fully corroborate the argument over the crucial role of major science-based universities in the initiation and development of technology-oriented complexes. Moreover, in addition to the direct role of the university in generating entrepreneurs there is an equally important secondary effect as a provider of skilled graduates. Acorn Computers, for example, calculate that at least 50% of their 100 plus graduates come from Cambridge University.

In Scotland, university/industry relationships are not quite as evident as around Cambridge (12 founders; 8 firms). Nevertheless, several firms, particularly in the Edinburgh area, owe their origins directly to ex-university personnel; for instance Raannd and CAS (Heriot-Watt); Intelligent Terminals and Memex (Edinburgh University). The Scottish Development Agency (1982) also quotes the high number of technically oriented research and teaching establishments (8 universities and 55 technical colleges) as one of the selling points of the area to potential investors. Thus while other researchers have found few formal or direct links between university and industry in terms of research collaboration or information flows (Oakey, 1981 p39-46: the scientific instruments industry), or have been unable to show any locational pull exerted by universities (Howells, 1984 p24-5: the pharmaceuticals industry), nevertheless in the computer industry there is a clear university influence as a source of entrepreneurs and skilled personnel. Interestingly, Hertfordshire, which has few direct university links except through the spillover of founders from Cambridge and London, has the lowest percentage of founders coming directly from university (7.7%) and the highest percentage of in-migrant founders (42.9%; see tables 5.10 and 5.11).

In the rest of the UK, the average age of founders is much older than in Cambridgeshire and more than a third had sub-degree level or no technical qualifications. Thus it is reasonable to take the area around Cambridge, and to a lesser extent the area around Edinburgh as distinctive forms of high technology entrepreneurship.

Table 5.8: Technical qualifications of founders of new firms in
            Cambridgeshire, Scotland and the rest of GB

Qualification	New firms in Cambs		New firms in Scotland		Other new firms		All new firms	
Ph.D or other post-graduate								
qualification	39	(52.0%)	16	(27.1%)	44	(17.5%)	99	(25.6%)
Computing/electronics								
degree	16	(21.3%)	17	(28.8%)	77	(30.6%)	110	(28.5%)
Other type of								
degree	9	(12.0%)	11	(18.6%)	40	(15.9%)	60	(15.5%)
Other technical								
qualifications	8	(10.7%)	7	(11.9%)	49	(19.4%)	64	(16.6%)
No technical								
qualifications	3	(4.0%)	8	(13.6%)	42	(16.7%)	53	(13.7%)
Total	75	(100.0%)	59	(100.0%)	252	(100.0%)	336	(100.0%)

Source: Questionnaire survey data

5.4.3 Previous employment of founders

Tables 5.9 to 5.11 deal with the previous employment of
founders by type, size and ownership/location of the
'incubator firms'. Table 5.9 shows that over the country as a
whole, around one sixth of all computer industry founders have
come directly from academia. In addition to Cambridge and
Edinburgh, there are other clusters of ex-academic founders in
Avon (5), Greater Manchester (4), and Greater London (4).
Almost half of the founders came from other computer firms.

New firm formation in the computer industry

Table 5.9: Former employment of founders of new firms in
            Cambridgeshire, Scotland and the rest of GB

Former employment	New firms in Cambs		New firms in Scotland		Other new firms		All new firms	
Academic research	24	(30.8%)	12	(19.4%)	35	(13.2%)	71	(17.5%)
Computer firm	41	(52.6%)	37	(59.7%)	123	(46.4%)	201	(49.6%)
Electronics firm	7	(9.0%)	4	(6.5%)	47	(17.7%)	58	(14.3%)
Other firm	6	(7.7%)	9	(14.5%)	60	(22.6%)	75	(18.5%)
Total	78	(100.0%)	62	(100.0%)	265	(100.0%)	405	(100.0%)

Source: Questionnaire survey data

Thus it can be seen that the growth of new computer firms in
an area is self-reinforcing when established. A further 14%
came from other electronics firms. Less than a fifth of
founders came from other backgrounds. This particular subset
of founders are generally people with a background in
accountancy or financial services who have joined a 'team' of
entrepreneurs, or who formerly worked in the data processing
department of a non-electronics firm. Thus it seems improbable
that new computer firms would emerge spontaneously in an area
which had no previous links with the industry or local
computer industry research bodies. In such areas,

New firm formation in the computer industry

entrepreneurs, established firms or mobile branch plants could only be attracted from outside.

Table 5.10: Former employment of founders of new firms in
Cambridgeshire, Hertfordshire and Scotland by size of firm

Size of firm (employees)	New firms in Cambs		New firms in Herts		New firms in Scotland		Case study areas	
Under 25	6	(9.4%)	1	(3.8%)	2	(4.0%)	9	(6.4%)
25 - 99	11	(17.2%)	2	(7.7%)	5	(10.0%)	18	(12.9%)
100 - 499	17	(26.6%)	4	(15.4%)	2	(4.0%)	23	(16.4%)
500 plus	6	(9.4%)	17	(65.4%)	29	(58.0%)	52	(37.4%)
University	24	(37.5%)	2	(7.7%)	12	(24.0%)	38	(27.1%)
Total	64	(100.0%)	26	(100.0%)	50	(100.0%)	140	(100.0%)

Source: Questionnaire survey data

Again from these tables the distinctive nature of the firm formation process in Cambridgeshire is apparent. Table 5.10 shows that it has acted through 'splitting' and spin-off of entrepreneurs from small and medium-sized firms (Dale, 1979) rather than from larger establishments as in Herts and Scotland. This correlates with the findings of Table 5.11 which shows that founders in Cambs have come principally from local firms and the university, whereas in Herts and Scotland the externally-owned sector is more important. These figures undoubtedly reflect differences in the size distribution of firms in the two regions. Fothergill and Gudgin (1982, p 125-6), in their study of new firm formation in the East Midlands 1968-78, show that firms employing less than 25 people provide over a quarter of all founders. It is likely therefore that the smaller average size of firms in the industry in Cambridge (25.5) in comparison to Herts (143.4) or Scotland (123.0) contributes to the higher rate of firm formation observed there. Segal Quince and partners (1985, p65) mention the importance of local 'role models' of successful entrepreneurs such as Sir Clive Sinclair of Sinclair Research; Christopher Curry and Hermann Hauser of Acorn; and the so-called 'USM millionaires club'. While their image has recently been tarnished by the much publicised financial difficulties of their firms, they still engender a feeling of competitive emulation amongst would-be entrepreneurs. Work in other countries has emphasised the importance of a psycho-sociological entrepreneurial culture (Illeris, 1985; Larsen & Rogers, 1984) and certainly in Cambridge there is a strong 'mythology of entrepreneurship' (Levi, 1982; Marsh, 1985a). This is encouraged by local organisations such as the 'Cambridge Computer Club', (now the 'Cambridge Technology Association') set up in 1979, which is an informal grouping of local computer executives.

The role of the foreign-owned sector, often attracted by regional policy, in stimulating or alternatively suppressing an indigenous industry, has been much debated in the literature. McDermott (1979) in his study of the electronics industry in Scotland in 1975 showed that only one indigenous firm at that time owed its origin to a major externally-controlled establishment. By contrast, table 5.11 shows that 11 founders (8 firms) in Scotland came from backgrounds in the foreign-owned sector and 16 founders (9 firms) from firms owned in the rest of the UK. It appears therefore that almost 40 years after the first foreign-owned electronics company came to Scotland, and ten years after McDermott's study, a spin-off effect from the foreign-owned sector is becoming apparent, in what the Scottish Development Agency (1982a p3-4) has termed a 'third generation' of indigenous enterprise. By contrast the decision by the Ministry of Technology in the Labour Government of 1969 to locate the Computer Aided Design Centre (now the privatised CADCentre) in Cambridge has had a rapid effect and it has been instrumental in the formation of at least 14 software/consultancy firms in the Cambridge area. This would appear to have clear implications for a

Table 5.11: Former employment of founders of new firms in
Cambridgeshire, Hertfordshire and Scotland by ownership/
location of firm

Ownership/ Location	New firms in Cambs		New firms in Herts		New firms in Scotland		Case study areas	
In-migrant founders	13	(19.1%)	12	(42.9%)	10	(18.5%e	35	(23.3%)
Locally-owned firms/ University	52	(76.5%)	3	(10.7%)	17	(31.1%)	72	(48.0%)
Other UK-owned firms	2	(2.9%)	11	(39.3%)	16	(29.6%)	29	(19.3%)
Foreign-owned firms	1	(1.5%)	2	(7.1%)	11	(20.4%)	14	(9.3%)
Total	68	(100.0%)	28	(100.0%)	54	(100.0%)	150	(100.0%)

Source: Questionnaire survey data

technology-oriented regional policy (Ewers & Wettman, 1980).

5.5 New firms and technological change

5.5.1 Innovation

In chapter two and section 5.2 of this chapter, the
thesis was put forward that new firms and small firms have
been particularly well placed to take advantage of recent
technological opportunities in the computer electronics
industry associated with the introduction of
microelectronics. It may therefore be thought that new firms
are more likely to be at the 'leading edge' of advanced
research. Limited support for this hypothesis comes from the

'innovation data bank' held at the Science Policy Research Unit (SPRU) at the University of Sussex. The data bank, which includes 54 innovations in the computer industry, shows that up to 1969 innovation was wholly the preserve of the largest companies, but since then small firms (less than 500 employees) have provided 40% of the innovations in the industry (Rothwell & Zegveld, 1982). It is possible from the questionnaire survey data to identify several new firms which are involved in advanced research, such as Sinclair Metalab, working on wafer-scale VLSI technology; Intelligent Terminals Ltd., on artificial intelligence/expert systems; and Meiko, a spin-off from Inmos, which has incorporated the latters' 'transputer' microchip into a low-cost 'supercomputer'. On the whole though, few new firms have the resources of capital or personnel to engage in basic research with only long-term promise of financial gain. Furthermore such assessments of 'leading edge' technology are highly subjective and it is only really possible to recognise successful innovation in retrospect.

5.5.2 Technological sophistication

An alternative formulation of the problem is to consider the 'technological sophistication' of a particular firm and its product range. This is difficult to measure directly and therefore three surrogates have been used in the questionnaire survey data: These are patenting activity; the modernity of the product range; and the percentage of products originally developed 'in-house' or by parent/sister firms, rather than being bought-in or merely distributed. Table 5.12 shows the evidence for patenting activity amongst new firms and other establishments. Relatively few hardware firms had applied for patents over the previous five years and the question was irrelevant for computer services firms because currently software can only be copyrighted and not patented. It was clear from the interview survey that the patenting system was widely viewed as inadequate because of the slowness and the bureaucracy involved, and because of the lack of protection it affords. Nevertheless, there was a marginal tendency for new firms to be less active in patenting their products than older establishments.

Table 5.13 shows the approximate age of the product range of new firms and other establishments as a percentage of turnover weighted by the employment size of the firm in 1984. New firms are shown to have a younger average age of product than older establishments. This conclusion is hardly

Table 5.12:   Evidence of patenting activity 1980-84 among
new firms and other establishments

	New firms[a]	(%)	Other estabs[b]	(%)
Patents applied for/ granted	28	(7.8%)	33	(10.0%)
No patents applied for	177	(49.3%)	153	(46.5%)
Not known/missing data	154	(42.9%)	143	(43.5%)
Total	359	(100.0%)	329	(100.0%)

Notes:

a - Firms founded as independent units since 1975
    and their branches
b - Firms founded before 1975, overseas firms and
    their branches

Source: Questionnaire survey data

unexpected, but nevertheless the table shows that Scottish new
firms, and to a lesser extent Cambridgeshire new firms, have a
younger average age of product than new firms in other areas.
There are problems however in simply equating 'newness' with
'technological sophistication'. Most products, particularly
program software, go through many successive updates before
being finally discarded from the product line. Furthermore, in
defence contracts in particular, 'reliability' is afforded as
high a priority as other criteria such as efficiency or cost,
and this may preclude purchasing the very latest product
releases. Overall therefore 'age of product' is of dubious
merit as a measure of technological sophistication.

New firm formation in the computer industry

Table 5.13: Percentage of product range (by value) originally
introduced at different times for new firms and other
establishments (weighted by employment size in 1984)

Product age	New firms in		Other new	Other estabs.
	Cambs	Scotland	firms	
% of products				
introduced since 1981	87.7%	99.1%	87.1%	64.6%
% of products				
introduced 1974-1980	12.3%	0.9%	12.7%	33.9%
% of products				
introduced before 1974	0.0%	0.0%	0.3%	1.5%
All products	100.0%	100.0%	100.0%	100.0%
Data Coverage (employ.)	70.7%	89.6%	47.1%	52.5%

Source: Questionnaire survey data

The least problematic of the three technological
sophistication indices is the location of original
development of products. Table 5.14 shows that on average new
firms gain around one sixth of their revenue from
distributing products originally designed by unrelated firms,
whereas other UK—owned establishments included in the survey
gain only one ninth from such arrangements. Distributorships,
along with subcontract and consultancy work, provide a steady
income flow during the early and most vulnerable years of a
firms existence. This can be used to finance R&D work or to
establish funds for investment. Some firms use 'low tech' work
such as this as a 'soft start' (Bullock, 1983) before moving
into production of their own products, for example Apricot and
Irvine Business Systems. However new firms in Cambridgeshire
and Scotland can be shown to be considerably less dependent

Table 5.14: Percentage of product range (by value) originally
developed in different locations for new firms and other
establishments (weighted by employment size in 1984)

| Product development | New firms in | | Other new | Other UK-owned |
	Cambs	Scotland	firms	estabs.
% of products				
developed in-house	80.4%	86.0%	70.6%	60.9%
% of products developed in the UK				
by a parent/sister firm	11.7%	4.7%	8.6%	24.1%
% of products developed in the UK				
by an unrelated firm	3.0%	4.8%	6.7%	5.0%
% of products developed overseas				
by a subsid./sister firm	0.0%	0.0%	2.3%	3.9%
% of products developed overseas				
by an unrelated firm	4.9%	4.4%	11.9%	6.0%
All products	100.0%	100.0%	100.0%	100.0%
Data Coverage (employ.)	71.2%	89.6%	50.7%	58.2%

Source: Questionnaire survey data

than other new firms on distributed products. Indeed more than
90% of the product range of new firms and their branches in
these areas were originally designed in-situ or by a
parent/sister firm in the UK, rather than being bought-in.
This suggests a high level of independence and, in the terms
adopted here, technological sophistication.

5.5.3 Percentage of the workforce involved in R&D
Indices of 'innovation' and 'technological
sophistication' discussed above are both subject to problems
and neither can be used with unqualified applicability. It is
necessary therefore to go back to the original definition of

'high technology' advanced in chapter one and to examine the skills composition of new firms. This is discussed in more detail in section 5.6 but here attention is focussed on the percentage of the workforce involved in research and development. The orthodox position on R&D in small firms is that put forward by Freeman (1971) and reiterated by Rothwell & Zegveld (1982, p43-77), namely that while small firms produce slightly less innovations per unit of output or per employee than larger firms, they appear to produce more innovations per unit of R&D expenditure. The rationale for this is that most small firms do not have a formal R&D department but rather employees divide their time between a variety of tasks and because most innovations in new firms tend to come from the founder. In the survey data however, new firms were found to employ a marginally higher percentage of their workforce in R&D (22.3%) than for all establishments included in the survey (21.8%). Furthermore, only 42 (13%) of all new firms for which data was available employed no R&D staff. This compares with Rothwell & Zegveld's estimate (1982, p55) that 95% of small manufacturing enterprises (employing under 200 people) perform no formal R&D.

On the balance of evidence presented in this section there seems to be little difference in the level of technological intensity between new firms and other establishments in the UK computer industry. On the one hand, new firms may be less inclined to engage in basic 'patentable' research and may, in the early stages of growth, depend on products developed elsewhere for part of their income. But on the other hand, new firms are equally committed to R&D and often have a more contemporary product range. In certain areas, notably around Cambridge, new firms can be shown to be more research intensive, and many maintain close links with university research departments, for instance Acorn, Topexpress and GEMS in Cambs; Intelligent Terminals and Memex in Scotland.

5.6 The contribution of new firms to the local economy

5.6.1 New firms and employment growth

Studies of new firm growth have characteristically shown that while new firms may contribute a large percentage of net new jobs in an area or in an industry, they have little short term effect on overall employment patterns. The same could be said to be true of the computer industry, where the UK jobs lost by a single company, ICL, over the period 1979-84 (-9,775) exceed the number of jobs created in all the computer new firms in the survey over the period 1975-84 (+9,556). This initially pessimistic conclusion must, however, be tempered by the fact that many small firms subcontract much of the manufacture and distribution of their products and thus create additional indirect employment. As an extreme example, one leading new firm in Cambridgeshire, which had a 1984 turnover in excess of £75m, claims to have created indirect to direct employment in the ratio of more than 20:1 through its subcontracting arrangements. Furthermore, new technology-based firms do exhibit a much faster rate of growth in both employment and turnover than other new firms in more stable technologies. For instance, of the 325 new firms identified by this study, 19 (5.8%) exceeded 100 employees and 46 (14.1%) exceeded 50 by 1984. This compares with Storey's (1982 p22-3) estimate of only a 0.5-0.75% probability that new manufacturing firms in Cleveland would employ more than 100 workers by the end of a decade (based on a total sample of 159 firms, 1965-76).

Table 5.15 shows that the average 1984 employment size of new computer firms in this survey is just under 30 workers. This is higher than that recorded in similar studies. For instance, Fothergill & Gudgin (1982, p117) find an average size of 15 for new manufacturing firms in Leicestershire at the end of an eight year period (728 firms, 1968-75); while Gould and Keeble (1984, p191) record an average size of only 12.1 in East Anglia at the end of a ten year period (703 firms, 1971-81). Only in Scotland does Cross (1981, p134; 504 firms 1968-77) find a comparable average firm size of 24.2 for new manufacturing firms over ten years, and this is consistent with the higher average size of firms in Scotland of 37.0 recorded in this survey. While a straight comparison between these studies is invalidated by the variation in the industrial sector, region and period, nevertheless it does serve to illustrate the relatively high rates of growth within surviving new firms in the computer industry.

It may be argued, however, that the real potential contribution of new firms to employment creation lies in the long rather than short-term. One approach to assessing the possible longer-term contribution of the new firms in this study is to look at their recruitment intentions. The questionnaire survey asked two questions: 'Do you expect to recruit any new workers over the next six months?' and 'If so, approximately how many?'. Such an approach is clearly subject

Table 5.15: Number of firms and growth of employment by age
             cohort for new firms in the computer industry,
             1975-84

Date of formation	Firms	Employment	Average size
1983-84	41	415	10.1
1981-82	85	1,543	18.2
1979-80	81	2,613	32.3
1977-78	80	2,941	36.8
1975-76	38	2,044	53.8
1975-1984	325	9,556[a]	29.4

Notes

a – Employment figures used here includes employment in
    sales offices and overseas branches not included in the
    questionnaire survey

Source: Questionnaire survey data

to the fluctuations of the business cycle and is also
vulnerable to the inflated expectations of entrepreneurs and
executives. Nevertheless the answers to the question are
broadly comparable between firms. Table 5.16 shows that the
new firms and their branches who responded to the question
expected to add a total of 1,116 new jobs over the next six
months or approximately an extra 20%! This was more than a
quarter of all new jobs anticipated by respondents to the
questionnaire whereas new firms only currently contribute 13%

Table 5.16: Future recruitment expectations over next six
             months among new firms and other establishments

Recruitment expectations	New firms		Other estabs.	
	No.	(%)	No.	(%)
Establishments expecting to recruit	174	(48.5%)	155	(47.1%)
Establishments not expecting to recruit	30	(8.4%)	39	(11.9%)
Not known/ missing data	155	(43.2%)	135	(41.0%)
Total	359	(100.0%)	329	(100.0%)
Current employment size[a]	5,722		37,159	
Anticipated growth	+1,116		+3,170	
Percentage change	+19.5%		+8.5%	

Notes
 a - excluding 'don't knows' and missing data

Source: Questionnaire survey data

of survey employment.
     It is likely however that a large minority of these new
firms will fail over the next five years which will reduce
their potential job creation. Ganguly (1983a) for instance in

his survey of new VAT registrations shows that 35% of new production firms fail in the first five years. Nevertheless, the presence amongst the new firms of just one future IBM, Apple or Racal would clearly make a major contribution to a local economy. This suggests that an effective policy of identifying and backing 'high flyers' could have a significant impact on local employment in particular areas. However, diagnostic procedures for identifying such 'winners' are poorly developed and anyway successful firms are likely to attract sufficient venture capital for expansion from private sources. Therefore the government policy for small firms assistance should continue to be targeted at a wide number of new firms in the hope that future 'winners' will be helped through the early vulnerable years.

5.6.2 Skill divisions in new firms

The contribution of new firms to the local economy must be evaluated not only in terms of the absolute quantity but also the quality of jobs they provide. The economic multiplier effects of highly-paid professional jobs are obviously greater to the local economy than low-paid, part-time unskilled jobs. Furthermore, the evidence of the origins of entrepreneurs presented above suggests that successful entrepreneurs are generally graduates from non-manual professions. Thus the creation of white-collar jobs in new firms provides a pool of potential entrepreneurs in an area. However, it could also be argued that unless the skills required by the new high technology firms match those of the local population, then they will do little to reduce local unemployment. The Science Park in Cambridge, for instance, has been criticised for creating few long-term opportunities for local residents but rather for recruiting nationally mobile graduates. Moore and Spires (1983) show that around 60% of the jobs created by firms on the Cambridge Science Park were for managerial/professional and scientific/technical occupations, and that around three-quarters of these personnel were recruited from outside the Cambridge subregion.

Table 5.17 shows the full occupational breakdown for new firms in Cambridgeshire, Scotland and the rest of GB compared with the computer industry average for the questionnaire survey data. The percentage of the workforce involved in R&D in the Cambridgeshire new firms (41.1%) is abnormally high by the standards of the industry. It is clear also that the high level of management, sales and clerical jobs (38.2%) is also above average for new firms and for the computer industry as a

Table 5.17: Occupational division of the workforce in new firms in
             Cambridgeshire, Scotland, the rest of GB and all
             establishments

Occupation	New firms in Cambs	New firms in Scotland	Other new firms	All computer firms
Management, sales and clerical	371 (38.2%)	163 (18.9%)	1,300 (31.3%)	16,729 (34.1%)
Research and Development	399 (41.1%)	100 (11.6%)	837 (20.1%)	10,632 (21.7%)
Other skilled employees	154 (15.9%)	138 (16.0%)	1,518 (36.5%)	12,285 (25.1%)
Semi-skilled and unskilled employees	46 (4.7%)	461 (53.5%)	499 (12.0%)	9,397 (19.2%)
Total	970 (100.0%)	862 (100.0%)	4,154 (100.0%)	49,043 (100.0%)
Data Coverage (employment)	71.9%	89.6%	61.9%	70.1%

Source: Questionnaire survey data

whole. Perhaps the key to this is indicated by the low level
(less than 5%) of semi-skilled and unskilled manual jobs in
the Cambs new firms. Insofar as Cambs new firms are involved
in the hardware market it is through subcontract of product
manufacture to firms elsewhere in the country. Acorn for
instance subcontracts manufacture to A.B. Electronics of South
Wales, and to Singapore. Sinclair/Amstrad has manufacturing
links with Timex in Dundee, Thorn-EMI Datatech in Feltham,
West London, A.B. Electronics, and with Samsung in Korea.
Another option is to set up a branch plant to manufacture away
from the main site: Torch Computers, for instance, has a branch

plant at Caernarfon in North Wales.

By contrast, more than 50% of employment in the Scottish new firms is in semi-skilled and unskilled manual occupations. The Scottish example is biased by the presence of a few new firms, notably Rodime and Future Technology Systems, which have grown very rapidly and have in-house manufacturing facilities, rather than using subcontractors. With the exception of Scotland and Cambridgeshire, new firms differ little from other computer industry establishments. Perhaps the main difference is the higher percentage of the workforce in the 'other skilled employees' category which covers technicians, programmers, analysts and skilled manual workers. Employees in small firms rarely have official job titles and this perhaps explains the higher than expected number in this category.

5.6.3 Conclusions

This chapter has traced the importance of new firms in the computer industry in terms of their growing numbers, increasing employment, and their contribution to technical change and the local economy. It has been asserted that the opportunities presented by the microelectronics revolution have been particularly favourable to market entry by new and small firms. The 'technological paradigm shift' which beset the computer industry in the mid-1970s has created a far more mobile and volatile market structure than that which had prevailed in the decade up to 1975. The slowness with which the established multinationals moved into the burgeoning microcomputer sector allowed several new firms to grow rapidly to a considerable size and to challenge the existing market leaders.

The evidence presented above suggests that the boom in new firm formation has slowed since its peak in 1979, particularly in the hardware sector. Furthermore, the number of competing firms in the market is being reduced through firm failure and market rationalisation. Other evidence suggests that start-up costs have risen recently in the electronics industry (Beaumont 1982b, p7; Barron & Curnow, 1979). Nevertheless, in certain areas computer firms have had a considerable impact on the local economy, in particular in the area around Cambridge. The area has long-established university research links with computing and there are a number of older firms in related industries such as Pye, Cambridge Electronic Instruments and Cambridge Consultants. Thus it would not be true to say that the computer industry in the Cambridge area has grown 'out of nothing'. Nevertheless, the survey shows that computer industry employment in firms founded since 1975 considerably exceeds that in firms created before that date. Furthermore, the stock of young, small high technology firms in the area employ a large number of graduates and other highly-qualified personnel which has created a pool of potential entrepreneurs. Thus the recent Segal Quince study of new firms in the Cambridge subregion argued that the 'Cambridge Phenomenon' is still 'very young' (Segal Quince, 1985, p83) and they estimate that new firms are still being formed at the rate of about two per month (p24).

The second area studied here where new firms have had a considerable local impact is in Scotland particularly in the eastern counties of Lothian and Fife. Here the emergence of an indigenous computer industry can be partially seen as a long-term 'success' of regional policy in attracting internationally-mobile branch plants of the US electronics industry to Scotland. The externally-controlled sector has both created markets for the independent Scottish firms and, indirectly, provided entrepreneurs for two of the most successful 'start-up' firms, Rodime and Fortronic. However the hypothesis put forward by other workers that the indigenous sector is 'dependent' upon the externally-controlled branch plants seems now to be far less valid than in the past. In the area around Edinburgh at least the growth of new firms through 'organic' splitting and spin-off of entrepreneurs from existing small firms, and through technology transfer from university departments is akin to the 'Cambridge Phenomenon' though, as yet, on a much smaller scale.

Overall new firms have made a considerable contribution to restoring the employment and competitive edge lost by the established domestic UK computer industry since the mid-1970s and they may well offer significant potential for future growth. However, new firm formation rates have been markedly higher in the regions of the economic core, particularly on the growing semi-urban fringe of the core area rather than in the conurbation areas where job loss has been greatest. This spatial concentration of new firms has, if anything, been intensified rather than reduced by entrepreneurial and industrial mobility. Thus measures taken at the national level to foster new firm growth should not be seen as a substitute for regional policy. There is therefore a strong case for a regionally-selective new firms policy which might focus on the provision of venture capital finance for young firms and on encouraging academia/industry technology transfer. The importance of both of these is evident in the area around Edinburgh. Taking lessons from the Cambridge experience, it is apparent too that the location of Government-funded research establishments, as the CADCentre once was, can also have considerable local impact. However, on balance the government's role in stimulating local enterprise is directive and protective rather than initiatory and ultimately it must be concluded, along with Marsh's (1985a) verdict on Cambridge that "the most important ingredient in the area's success is people".

Chapter Six

THE GEOGRAPHY OF THE BRITISH COMPUTER INDUSTRY

6.1 Introduction

The discussion in chapter two of the relationships between technological change and market structure highlighted the uneven nature of adoption of technology between firms and between industrial sectors. From this it is reasonable to infer that technological change will also vary over geographical space, if only because of spatial variations in industrial structure and the mix of enterprise types. In section 6.2 of this chapter some of the possible causes of geographical variation in the location of high technology industry are examined and a typology of 'technology-oriented complexes' (TOCs) is developed. The later parts of the chapter apply this theoretical understanding to the practical example of the computer industry in Britain. In section 6.3, the current pattern of employment and recent employment change is examined. These aggregate patterns are analysed in further detail in section 6.4 using questionnaire survey data. Attention is focussed on spatial variations in the occupational composition of the workforce and the age and size of establishments. It is shown that the employment displacement effects of technological change, most evident in larger, older hardware manufacturing plants, are often spatially removed from the employment creating effects of technological change which have acted through new firm formation and the rising demand for software and R&D jobs. Finally, in sections 6.5 and 6.6, two contrasting examples of technology-oriented complexes in Scotland and Cambridgeshire/Hertfordshire are examined as case-studies of the evolution of the computer industry in different areas.

Three major sources of data are used in the description and analysis of employment data in this chapter. The first in the Annual Census of Employment (ACE), carried out by the Department of Employment, for which the most recently available data in September 1981. Unpublished county-level records are used for analysis of the spatial pattern of hardware and software employment in 1981, and employment change for hardware between 1976 and 1981. The second source is the statutory returns to the Engineering Industry Training Board (EITB) which provides employment data by occupational composition for the computer hardware sector up to April 1984. Finally original survey data collected at Cambridge University between March 1984 and April 1985 by postal and face-to-face questionnaires is used for more detailed analysis. In total, some 822 establishments were included in the three phases of data gathering by postal questionnaire, interview questionnaire or company case-study. During the course of the survey, 82 (10.0%) units were found to have closed down, or gone out of business, and a further 52 (6.3%) were later rejected because they were found to have no UK manufacturing or software development facilities, or were not primarily involved in the computer industry. The remaining 688 units represent 543 separate firms of which 484 (89.1%) are UK-owned. Positive responses to the survey were received from 447 establishments, or 65% of those in the database. There is no reason to believe that non-respondents have introduced any bias into the survey data either by region or type of establishment. For the remaining 241 establishments, a range of basic data covering location, date of formation, legal status, product range and employment, was collated from company annual reports, trade directories and telephone interviews.

6.2 High technology industry and location theory

6.2.1 Technology-Oriented Complexes

The conventional view of the geography of high technology industry is that it is free from the usual locational constraints such as raw materials, energy, or proximity to markets and can therefore be regarded as 'footloose' or 'randomly-located' (Bale, 1976). However, in practice, most studies of the spatial location of high technology industry have tended to highlight the fact that it is generally clustered in specific regions or more localised 'Technology-Oriented Complexes' (TOCs) defined by Keeble and Kelly (1985, p80) as:

> ...highly localised clusters of new high technology
> firms which exhibit dynamic growth through a

process of 'synergy', or intense interaction, between new firms and entrepreneurs, research institutions, local banks and finance agencies, and business service organisations... underpinning if not initiating this dynamism in most documented cases is the impact of existing major scientific research institutions, such as large science-based universities or government research facilities, together with a high-quality local residential environment which attracts and retains the crucially important but intrinsically highly mobile research scientists and entrepreneurs whose activities create the complex.

A slightly broader view is taken by Steed and deGenova (1983, p264-5) who define a typology of TOCs as follows:

I. TOCs which are principally the product of locally initiated firms and spinoffs, and arising from a well-developed science and technology infrastructure. This is the form of TOC described by Keeble and Kelly above and is most closely identified with areas such as Palo Alto, California, or 'Silicon Valley' (Larsen & Rogers, 1984; Saxenian, 1983a); Route 128 around Boston, Massachusetts (Dorfman, 1983), West Berlin (Allesch, 1985) or Cambridge (Segal Quince and Partners, 1985).

II. Research-oriented TOCs restricted to a park site, such as the Research Triangle Park of North Carolina or the Sheridan Park in Toronto. To this category could be added other 'planned' research communities such as Sophia Antipolis in France, or Tsukuba in Japan.

III. TOCs which are initiated by attracting manufacturing facilities of high technology companies, often through the operation of regional policy incentives. Examples of these include Phoenix, Arizona, or the Central Lowlands of Scotland (Hood & Young, 1983; Scottish Development Agency, 1985). However, other 'offshore' manufacturing bases of the US and Japanese electronics industry such as Eire (Fox, 1982; Murray & Wickham, 1982; Matthews, 1984), Malaysia (SEAD, 1985) or elsewhere in South East Asia (Froebel et al, 1980) have, arguably, more to do with cheap labour and tax incentives than technological sophistication.

IV. TOCs which have resulted from very large expenditures of government funds at a research or military establishment.

The geography of the British computer industry

The role of US defence spending in regional development is documented by Malecki (1984b) and deGrasse (1983). In the UK too the role of defence spending, military research establishments and Ministry of Defence sales contact points has been stressed in the evolution of the 'M4 corridor' area to the west of London (Breheny & McQuaid, 1985; Breheny 1986; McQuaid, 1985; Lovering, 1985).

The typology of 'Technology-Oriented Complexes' outlined above is not intended to be a set of mutually exclusive categories, and many examples of TOCs, as Steed and deGenova show for Ottawa, contain elements of each. Furthermore, in an evolutionary model of TOC formation it should be possible for a regional economy to develop from the 'induced' growth of TOCs II, III and IV to the 'indigenous' growth of TOC I. For instance, in the UK over recent years there have been several local initiatives by local government, regional development agencies and university/commerce alliances to establish 'science parks', including Cambridge, Salford and Aston (Cross, 1982; Taylor, 1985). While these have met with mixed success, the aim has generally been to establish a 'growth pole' which would attract investment and capitalise on local potential for academic/commercial spin-offs. The example of the Cambridge Science Park,which was opened in 1975 at the start of the 'Cambridge Phenomenon', might be seen as a role model for successful evolution from TOC II to TOC I.

A similar case could be made for the long term aims of technology-based regional development plans which often underlie TOC IIIs. The Scottish Development Agency (SDA) (1982a, p3-4) for instance claims that in the evolution of the electronics industry in Scotland, after almost 40 years of the operation of regional policy, a transition from TOC III to TOC I has been successfully made and that indigenous potential for economic growth and innovation is now being mobilised (Goddard, 1980).

Examples of TOC IV, where government spending and procurement policies have had a significant local multiplier effect on regional economic development, have usually been unintentional side-effects of government policies rather than their chief objective. However, in France a specifically spatial innovation policy has been in operation since 1954 when a movement to decentralise government R&D laboratories from Paris to the regions was initiated. Since 1958 it has been deliberate policy to focus electronics research and spending in the Brittany region (Cooke, 1985), and in 1981 the region employed 13,670 people in electronics industries. However, it has recently been overtaken by newer concentrations of electronics growth industries in Grenoble and the Cote d'Azur (Aydalot, 1984, 1985).

6.2.2 Academia/industry relations

In discussing the location of high technology industry, the textbook example usually given is the Palo Alto area of California, universally known as 'Silicon Valley'. The phenomenal growth of high technology electronics companies over the post-war period in this former agricultural area has been widely documented (Thompson, 1978; Hanson, 1982; Saxenian, 1983a; Larsen & Rogers, 1984). Recent work on the origins of Silicon Valley has stressed the importance of Stanford University, particularly during the early years of growth. The university attracted war-time investment for the development of electronic components for use by the military. In the immediate post-war years, an ambitious programme to establish a centre of excellence in Stanford in the emerging electronics technology attracted further military and commercial investment. The university had close connections with the Shockley Transistor Company and Fairchild Semiconductor, two of the important 'ancestor' firms in the Silicon Valley family tree of entrepreneurial spin-offs. In Boston too, MIT played a seminal role in the route 128 complex (Dorfman, 1983), and the Research Triangle Park in North Carolina contains no less than three universities.

In the UK, the links between academia and high technology-based new firms are perhaps best developed around Cambridge, where recent unpublished work by Segal Quince Wicksteed has shown the existence of more than 400 such firms within 30 miles of the city. While a relatively small proportion of these firms (17%) have founders who came directly from the university, a much larger number (52%) owe their origins, directly or indirectly, to these firms and other research organisations in the area (Segal Quince, 1985, p30-2). The 'Cambridge phenomenon' is explored in more detail later in this chapter.

In theoretical terms, university links with high technology industry are important for four reasons. Firstly, information linkages between industry and academia may be formed either through formal research collaboration or through less formal social contacts. In North America, private funding of university research is more widespread than in the UK. Furthermore, institutional and financial arrangements for promoting academic spin-off are better developed in the US (Bullock, 1983). In the UK, there is a greater emphasis on 'big science' - theoretical rather than applied science, and defence-related rather than commercial projects (Irvine & Martin, 1984; Freeman, 1974, 2nd ed. 1982). However, University Grants Committee cuts have forced many technically-biased universities such as Aston and Salford to seek closer links with industry as a source of finance (Eglin et al, 1983). Perhaps, therefore, what Wiener (1981) has described as a fundamental cultural distaste for industrial and entrepreneurial enterprise in British life, embedded in the academic system, may be eroded by financial stringency. As yet however, there is little evidence that information linkages and research collaborations have had any significant locational pull on industry in the UK (Oakey, 1981, p39-46; Howells, 1984, p24-5).

Secondly, academic institutions are important sources of high technology firm founders. In the US, some companies with university roots have grown into major corporations, such as Digital Equipment Corporation (DEC), Xerox and Wang. Beaumont's (1982a) study of new firms in the electronics industry in the South East of England showed that 22% of founders had come directly from research and that 85% were graduates. Fothergill and Gudgin (1982, p128-131) show from their study of new firms in the East Midlands that firms founded by graduates are generally more successful and expansion-oriented than firms founded by 'craftsmen'. Thirdly, universities can provide a significant local market for high technology goods, particularly for prototypes and low volume production runs rather than mass-produced products (Beaumont, 1982a; Oakey, 1979). Finally, university towns provide an important source of highly-skilled recruits. While graduates are theoretically one of the most highly mobile segments of the population, in practice they show considerable inertia when it comes to leaving the university environment. This applies particularly to post-graduate students or research assistants with a higher degree who have settled in a particular university town.

In many areas, non-university research establishments have also had an attraction and spin-off effect which has promoted new firm growth. In the Ottawa case discussed by Steed and deGenova (1983), a third of entrepreneurs had come from federal government funded research and administration organisations. A further third came from the Northern Telecom group including Bell Northern Research laboratories. In

Norway, some 50 new technology-based firms have been initiated around a marine research establishment at Horton, close to Oslo. In Britain, Breheny et al (1985) point to the important role of Government Research Establishments in the genesis of the 'M4 Corridor' in the Thames Valley area. Thus it must be emphasised that the interface between commercial and scientific research discussed above that has proved so productive in initiating 'Technology-Oriented Complexes' is not restricted to university towns, but any community which has a high concentration of scientists and technologists. Clearly, therefore, the key factor is not the institutional structure but the availability of highly-skilled labour in these areas, which is discussed below.

6.2.3 Labour

Most studies of spatial patterns of high technology industry are in agreement on the major importance of labour as a locational factor. However, there is considerable debate over the exact nature of changing skill requirements. Oakey (1981, p125-7) argues that for the scientific instruments industry at least, it is the relative immobility of skilled shop floor workers that is the critical locational factor. However, other studies have shown that demand for skilled manual work has fallen in manufacturing industry as a whole (Frost & Spence, 1981; Johnstone, 1982; Martin, 1985). Massey (1984) (see also Braverman, 1974; Conference of Socialist Economists, Microelectronics group, 1981) has argued that the effect of technological change on the labour process is predominantly one of 'deskilling':

> ...the dual process of separating the functions of conceptualisation from those of execution, and of the increasing fragmentation of the tasks of execution. (Massey, 1984, p33)

Co-incident with this increasing technical division of labour, Massey argues, has been a spatial division and a sexual division of functions in the production process. In this latter case, Massey argues that a secular trend towards increasing female participation rates has been associated with a 'feminisation' of the semi-skilled and unskilled routine production occupations, and that availability of unskilled, semi-skilled, and non-unionised labour in peripheral areas is becoming of greater importance as a locational factor (Massey, 1984 p139-45).

Corporate restructuring, in response to perceived labour market characteristics, is at the root of the 'spatial division of labour' hypothesis (Massey, 1984). The argument is summarised by Martin & Hodge:

> A new form of regional specialisation based on an intra-sectoral spatial division of labour is being overlaid on the historical pattern of inter-sectoral spatial specialisation of production, with more peripheral and depressed regions increasing their share of low-skilled, part-time and often female employment as a result of the attraction of these types of labour within spatially specialised multi-plant production structures. (Martin & Hodge, 1983, p142)

Drawing on the work of Westaway (1974) and Lipietz (1977), Massey (1979) describes how the 'bottom' end of the hierarchy of mass-production and assembly stages are characteristically located in areas of the periphery and seaside resorts with surplus unskilled labour and little tradition of trade union militancy. Increasingly volume production functions are being transferred internationally to the low pay 'sweatshops' of the third world or, in the case of the US, across the border to Mexico. The 'second stage' of production, which is less automated and requires input of skilled manual labour, would still be found in older industrial cities and conurbations. The 'top' of the hierarchy, including HQ and R&D functions, is located in the 'central metropoli' of the core region and in surrounding residentially-pleasant semi-rural environments.

One format for resolving the 'deskilling/reskilling' debate may be to consider how the balance of skill requirements changes over the course of a product life-cycle. Hirsch (1967, p16-24) shows that the critical labour inputs in the production process change during the transition from early to mature phases. During the labour-intensive 'early' phase, scientific and engineering skills are the major requirement. During the competitive 'growth' phase, successful companies will be those with the right blend of management and marketing abilities. Finally in the mature phase of capital-intensive mass production, semi-skilled and unskilled labour in branch plants often in third world locations, will be the dominant labour input.

Markusen (1985, p38–42), using a slightly different concept of a five stage 'profit cycle' shows, in theoretical terms, that the ratio of production to non-production workers will initially fall, but then rise towards the end of the 'growth' phase. She demonstrates this characteristic in practice in the steel, aluminium and brewing industries. High technology sectors such as computers, semiconductors and pharmaceuticals currently show the first stage of the cycle of a declining percentage of the workforce involved in production, whilst other 'low technology' sectors, such as textiles or automobile construction show the later stage of relative increase in the proportion of blue-collar workers. Markusen (1985, p43-50) describes the 'spatial manifestations of the profit cycle' in terms of a 'spatial succession' whereby the level of geographical concentration will initially increase until profits begin to decline but will then decrease as multiplant firms open regional and international sales offices and branch plants. Dispersion may also be encouraged if unionisation and inflexible working practices have become entrenched amongst skilled workers in the initial area of concentration. This point is, however, disputed by Pasinetti (1981), who argues that workers in high technology industries form a 'labour aristocracy' whose skills and goodwill are maintained by high salaries and therefore exhibit low unionisation. In the final stages of what Markusen terms 'negative profit', the closure of excess capacity may have the effect of increasing the aggregate level of spatial concentration, though this will be dependent on the restructuring policy adopted. Furthermore, this final stage of 'abandonment' may well overlap with a new start to the profit cycle through technical change and the creation of new product markets.

Given that the ratio of production to non-production workers is used as one of the defining characteristics of high technology industry in chapter one, it is likely that 'high technology industry' as such will be restricted to the first two stages of what Markusen terms 'zero profit' and 'super profit'. In the early stages, location may reflect merely the 'historical accident' of invention or innovation, but during the 'super profit' stage:

> ... the strategy of the rapidly growing firms will be on product design, professional expertise in research, development and marketing, and flexibility. These needs emphasise the creation of a skilled labour pool, skewed heavily toward the professional-technical categories. Infant firms will tend to draw subcontracting firms and

suppliers around them. The need to be near the centre of ongoing innovative activity and to have ready access to new information results in the continued gravitation of new firms to the original location. Indeed, new firms frequently are formed from employees spinning off from older companies to found competitors. This spatial pattern I call agglomeration. (Markusen, 1985, p45).

It is likely therefore that high technology industry will be more sensitive to spatial variations in the socio-economic composition of the resident population, and that in turn, the concentration of high technology industry will act to shape those spatial variations in a positive feedback cycle. Only at a later stage of the cycle do 'agglomeration diseconomies' (Keeble, 1976, p74-8) become apparent.

6.2.4 The role of Government

Government policies, both spatial and sectoral, may be shown to have a major impact on locational patterns of high technology industry. Recent work by Lovering (1985) and Boddy & Lovering (1985) has emphasised the importance of the 'indirect' spatial effects of government policies, for instance in defence procurement. Most geographical work on the role of government has concentrated on regional policy. Thwaites (1978) has criticised regional policy for attracting capital-intensive industry, dependent upon 'imported' technology, with an inferior growth record. It has also been suggested that the provision of Regional Development Grants for rationalisation, and new investment in process technologies aimed at enhancing long-term competitiveness, may lead to labour displacement in certain industries in the short-term (Martin & Hodge, 1983; Moore, Rhodes & Tyler, 1983). It is evident that the conventional focus of regional policy on mobile firms is weakened in the context of nationally high unemployment (Chisholm, 1976), and a lack of firms seeking to expand (Oakey, 1983b). Furthermore, it has been argued that high technology industry, which has been the source of the few new jobs to be created in manufacturing industry, is inherently spatially immobile owing to its dependence on a highly qualified manpower (Oakey, 1981b).

There have been a number of recent 'scandals' which have lessened the credibility of regional policy. While the De Lorean saga in Northern Ireland received much media attention, there have also been other less-publicised cases in the electronics industry. Some firms have made extravagant claims over the number of jobs to be created, or have transferred money given for local investment to parent firms overseas. There have been investigations into the regional development grants made to the Parrott Corporation in South Wales and National Semiconductor in Scotland, amongst others. Nevertheless, it is still recognised by most economists that there is a need for a regionally-based technology policy in order to encourage regional economic development and to alleviate skill shortages in the core regions (Ewers & Wettmann, 1980; Rothwell, 1982).

6.2.5 Other factors in the location of high technology industry

Three major factors explaining the location of high technology industry have been put forward so far; namely, university/industry links, the availability of labour skills and government policy. A number of other factors have been suggested in the literature as being relevant to high technology industry.

An important influence on a region's innovative and entrepreneurial environment is inherited industrial structure. Beaumont's (1982a) study revealed that 78% of founders in the high-technology electronics firms surveyed had previously worked in an electronics company, and the remainder came from research work, consultancies or allied trades. Moreover, 92% of initial locations were within 40 miles of the founder's former employer. Oakey et al (1980) use a form of shift-share analysis to show that industrial structure accounts for part of the South East's advantage in innovation potential, but fails to predict the poor performance of the development areas. Taking industrial structure as a whole, Fothergill & Gudgin (1982, p48-67) find that while it was an important determinant in shift-share analyses of variance of overall regional manufacturing performance during periods of growth (1952-66), it has had little explanatory power during the more recent period of job loss associated with recession and de-industrialisation (1966-1979). Martin (1982) argues that it is necessary to take into account industrial 'character' as well as 'composition'. In particular, he finds that size structure of manufacturing plants, labour intensity and level of foreign ownership are important in regional economic performance, but because of multicollinearity it is difficult to isolate their separate effects.

Secondly, the availability of suitable premises may be a limiting factor on local industrial growth. Fothergill & Gudgin (1982, p104-112) argue that it is the 'constrained location' of large urban areas which underlies the operation of the urban-rural shift in manufacturing industry as a whole. High technology firms often require premises of exacting technical specifications, for instance 'clinically' clean, air-conditioned, with good lighting, a high proportion of office space, and a good customer image (Coopers & Lybrand, 1982). Furthermore, rapid growth firms may typically need to change premises several times in their early years. Beaumont (1982a) found that two-thirds of founders surveyed had experienced difficulty in finding suitable initial premises. Only 6% started in completely new industrial premises because the high rents proved prohibitive. However, with rapid expansion their highly specific demands often called for purpose-built premises.

An alternative explanation for the observed 'urban-rural' shift in manufacturing employment put forward by Tyler et al (1984) is the impact of geographical variation in industrial costs, particularly the level of wages/salaries, and the cost of rents, rates and bought-in services. It is argued that the high costs associated with urban locations will encourage firms to seek alternative locations in small town and rural areas in which to expand their operations or to relocate important functions.

A fourth factor explaining shifts in high technology industry, argued persuasively by Keeble (1980, 1986a), is the quality of the physical social and residential environments of different areas. As incomes and car-based personal mobility have risen, highly skilled workers have been able to 'vote with their feet' by moving out of congested urban areas to more spacious, tranquil and attractive semi-rural environments. 'Residential space preference' is difficult to quantify as desired lifestyles cannot be assumed to be universally similar, but nevertheless environmental image-making has become a familiar feature of national recruitment campaigns for skilled personnel. Marked and consistent spatial variations in perceived residential amenity amongst industrialists and managers have been documented by Gleave, 1967 (quoted in Keeble, 1980).

Fifthly, market accessibility may be regarded as less important for high technology industries than more traditional sectors, because they serve international markets and high technology products characteristically have a high value to volume ratio. Nevertheless, in certain instances, accessibility may still be regarded as a locational factor. Proximity to airports for instance is important, particularly for overseas firms, and the concentration of UK HQs of US electronics firms in North West London, Berkshire and Surrey, close to Heathrow and Gatwick, has been commented on by Hoare (1974), and Breheny & McQuaid (1985) amongst others. For high technology services sectors, such as computer software, consultancy or contract R&D, access to clients is often important because of the need for personal contact and because work may be carried out on clients' premises.

Finally, spatial variations in the availability of venture capital for high technology firms has been shown to be a locational determinant in the US (Norton & Rees, 1979). While the spatial dimension of capital availability is generally of less importance in the UK, several studies have shown regional variations in the uptake of external finance, for instance USM-listed firms are dominantly located in London and the rest of the South East (Mason, 1985; Rowlinson, 1985). This would indicate the better provision of financial advice in the core region.

6.3 The spatial distribution of employment

6.3.1 Computer hardware

Figure 6.1 shows the distribution of computer hardware employment by county and Table 6.1 shows the distribution by region at the September 1981 census of employment. Three main areas of concentration are apparent – the South East and North West of England and Scotland – which together account for 87% of national computer hardware jobs. The North West however has declined in employment recently due to ICL's redundancies. In terms of relative concentration, only the South East and Scotland have location quotients greater than unity. Within these two areas, particular absolute concentrations are found in the counties of Greater London (8,812 jobs), Hertfordshire (7,722), Berkshire (6,544), Hampshire (5,880) and Strathclyde (4,274). Elsewhere in the country there are more localised clusters of employment in Greater Manchester (4,737) and Staffordshire (2,554).

The relative share of computer manufacturing employment in each county is shown by means of location quotients in Figure 6.2. Again the concentration of the industry in the South East and Scotland is apparent and five counties,

167

The geography of the British computer industry

Figure 6.1: The distribution of computer manufacturing
employment by county, Sept. 1981

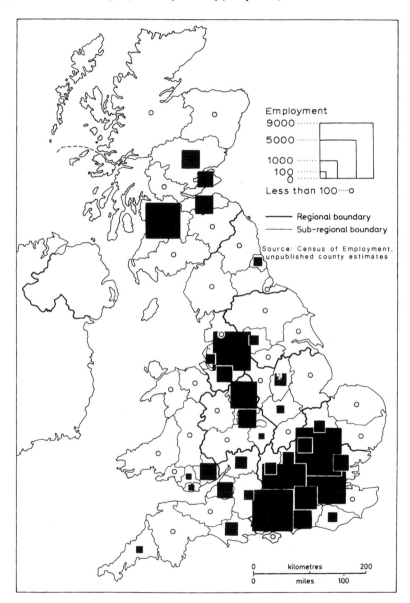

The geography of the British computer industry

Figure 6.2: Location quotients for computer manufacturing employment by county, 1981

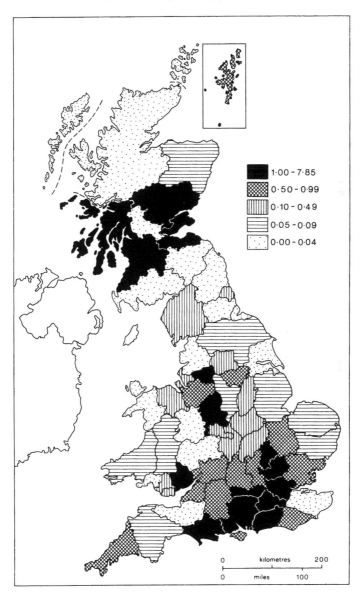

Table 6.1: Regional distribution of computer hardware employment
            in Great Britain, Sept. 1981

Region	Computer H/W AH 3302	(%)	All manufacturing industry ('000s)	(%)	Location Quotient[a]
Greater London	8,812	(15.8%)	686.0	(11.3%)	1.40
Rest of South East	25,303	(45.5%)	997.5	(16.5%)	2.76
All South East	34,114	(61.3%)	1,683.5	(27.8%)	2.20
East Anglia	461	(0.8%)	186.0	(3.1%)	0.26
South West	2,138	(4.0%)	395.7	(6.5%)	0.61
West Midlands	3,675	(6.5%)	800.7	(13.2%)	0.49
East Midlands	816	(1.5%)	533.4	(8.8%)	0.16
North West	5,853	(10.8%)	799.8	(13.2%)	0.80
Yorks & Humberside	413	(0.7%)	578.9	(9.6%)	0.07
North	348	(0.6%)	339.4	(5.6%)	0.11
Wales	1,175	(2.1%)	238.2	(3.9%)	0.53
Scotland	7,070	(13.1%)	502.0	(8.3%)	1.58
Great Britain	56,064	(100.0%)	6,057.5	(100.0%)	1.00

Note

a - The location quotient is calculated using the following formula:

$$\frac{AH\ 3302_i / AH\ 3302_n}{SIC\ 2\text{-}4_i / SIC\ 2\text{-}4_n} \qquad \text{Where } i = \text{reference region}$$
$$n = \text{national}$$

Source: Unpublished county estimates for the Census of
         Employment, Sept. 1981

Berkshire, Hertfordshire, Hampshire, Surrey and Tayside have location quotients greater than two. In other words, these counties have more than twice the level of computer manufacturing employment that would be predicted by their share of total manufacturing employment. Ten other counties have location quotients greater than unity: three of these are in the South East - Greater London, West Sussex and Bedfordshire; three in Scotland - Fife, Lothian and Strathclyde; and the rest are divided among the regions - Gwent, Dorset, Greater Manchester and Staffordshire. In short therefore the computer hardware industry is concentrated in a western arc of counties around London and in the Central Lowlands of Scotland with other small clusters in Greater Manchester, the North Midlands and Avon/South Wales areas.

A second major source of employment data by region for computer hardware is the unpublished EITB statutory returns (Table 6.2). This source is more up-to-date (April 1984) than the Annual Census of Employment (ACE) data but is subject to certain limitations, in particular a poor coverage of small firms (less than 50 employees). This may partly explain the smaller percentage of EITB employment recorded as being in the 'core' of the country (56.7%) compared with ACE (67.9%). However the major difference between the employment distribution displayed by the ACE and the EITB appears to be the inclusion in the latter of more overseas firms, especially in Greater London, Wales and Scotland which might have been classed as 'distributorships' in ACE. Thus the EITB data shows a much higher volume of employment in the 'peripheral' regions (15,898) than does ACE (8,593). Scotland and Wales also have much larger average plant sizes than the rest of the country which is consistent with a concentration there of branch plants. Establishments which are new to the EITB since 1978 formed just over a quarter of all establishments in 1984. However, in East Anglia, the South West and Wales new establishments accounted for almost half of the total stock.

Table 6.3 shows the distribution of computer hardware employment in 1984 by urban-rural classification. This table uses the questionnaire data rather than the ACE data and therefore the absolute total (50,645) is around 10% less than the ACE estimate. However it is unlikely that there is any substantial spatial bias in the establishments which have been missed by the questionnaire. The relative percentage, if not the absolute volume, of employment in each urban-rural class may therefore be taken as broadly accurate. In comparison to manufacturing industry as a whole, the

The geography of the British computer industry

Table 6.2: Establishment size structure by region for the computer
hardware sector, 1984

Region	Emp. 1984	(%)	No. of Estabs 1984	Average size	Estab. change 1978-84
Greater London	13,216	(18.3%)	95	139.1	+16
Rest of SE	24,050	(33.3%)	159	151.2	+48
All South East	37,266	(51.6%)	254	146.7	+64
East Anglia	264	(0.3%)	9	29.3	+4
South West	3,361	(4.7%)	37	90.8	+18
West Midlands	4,125	(5.7%)	30	137.5	+6
East Midlands	1,308	(1.8%)	16	81.7	+6
North West	7,977	(11.1%)	42	189.9	+4
Yorks & Humb	1,961	(2.7%)	21	93.4	+6
North	317	(0.4%)	9	35.2	+2
Wales	4,746	(6.6%)	23	206.3	+10
Scotland	10,835	(15.0%)	47	230.5	+15
Great Britain	72,160	(100.0%)	488	147.9	+135

Source: Unpublished EITB statutory returns

conurbations and large free-standing cities are markedly
under-represented in their share of employment while small
towns are heavily over-represented. The main exception to this
pattern is Greater London which has a slightly higher
percentage of computer hardware employment (14.1%) than all
manufacturing employment (11.0%). However, more than 60% of
London's computer hardware employment recorded in the survey
is in establishments which have no manufacturing or R&D
facilities on site. These establishments are mainly HQ

Table 6.3: Computer hardware employment, 1984, and all manufacturing
employment, 1981, by urban-rural status

| Urban/rural status | Computer hardware | | | All Manufacturing | |
	Employment	(%)	Estabs.	Employment (thousands)	(%)
London	7,139	(14.1%)	48	650	(11.0%)
Conurbations	4,590	(9.1%)	27	1,295	(21.9%)
Free-standing cities	3,892	(7.7%)	40	950	(16.1%)
Large towns	5,729	(11.3%)	59	756	(12.8%)
Small towns	24,452	(48.3%)	143	1,609	(27.2%)
Rural areas	4,843	(9.6%)	61	655	(11.1%)
Total	50,645	(100.0%)	378	5,916	(100.0%)

Sources: Questionnaire survey data
Fothergill et al (1984, p53)

functions and sale offices of multiplant firms and they give
the occupational profile of London a distinctive character
biased towards non-manual occupations.

Almost 60% of computer hardware employment in the
questionnaire survey was located in rural areas and small
towns of less than 100,000 population. This compares with only
38% of manufacturing employment as a whole. This is not to say
that all small towns and rural areas have benefitted equally.
There is for instance little computer industry employment in
Devon and Cornwall, rural Wales, Lincolnshire or the north of
England. Indeed, more than 70% of establishments in small
towns and rural areas are in the area of southern England
defined as the 'economic core' of the country, particularly the

173

counties of Cambridgeshire, Hertfordshire, Berkshire and Surrey. Thus there is a strong sense in which this apparent 'dispersal' of industry represents merely the growing fringe of the metropolis. These areas have many of the advantages of London such as access to clients, qualified personnel and financial and business services of all kinds, without the associated disadvantages of congestion and high rents and rates. Given the importance of purpose-built, prestige premises in the computer industry, it is more cost-effective for property developers to develop greenfield sites in these areas than to redevelop industrial areas of the inner cities and suburbs of the conurbations and large towns. In view of the high rates of unemployment prevalent even in the South East during the early 1980s, local authorities in semi-urban areas are also more inclined to grant planning permission for light industrial or R&D use than was perhaps the case ten years ago. Furthermore, given the politicisation of local government which has occurred over recent years, many local authorities are keen to identify themselves with the high-tech high-growth successful companies which the computer industry has produced. Consequently, they are often willing to put together attractive packages of premises, lower rents and rates to keep start-up firms in these areas.

6.3.2 Computer software

Figure 6.3 shows the volume of computer services employment by county in 1981, while table 6.4 shows the distribution by region using a location quotient derived from the regional share of software employment divided by its share of private service employment. The main area of concentration in software employment is in Greater London (17,491 = 32% of national employment) which is more than five times greater than the next highest county, Hampshire (3,901 jobs). As a service industry, the software sector is more concentrated in the conurbations than the hardware industry with both Greater Manchester (3,737) and the West Midlands (3,278) being well represented. This is due to the market orientation of computer services, particularly computer bureaux, recruitment agencies and software distribution companies all of which are excluded from the survey data. Most multisite computer services firms are organised on a regional basis and logically the conurbations offer the largest potential market. Thus the highly urbanised regions of the South East, the West Midlands and the North West all have location quotients greater than unity. The firms covered by

The geography of the British computer industry

Figure 6.3:   The distribution of computer software
              employment by county, Sept. 1981

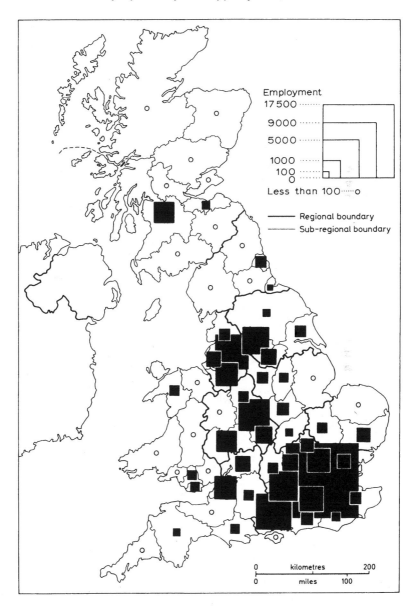

175

The geography of the British computer industry

Table 6.4: Regional distribution of computer services employment
in Great Britain, Sept. 1981

Region	Computer S/W (%) AH 8394		Private services[b] (%) ('000s)		Location Quotient[a]
Greater London	17,491	(31.9%)	2,539.5	(20.4%)	1.58
Rest of South East	13,108	(23.9%)	2,213.2	(17.7%)	1.37
All South East	30,599	(55.9%)	4,752.7	(38.2%)	1.48
East Anglia	950	(1.7%)	389.2	(3.1%)	0.58
South West	3,101	(5.7%)	911.7	(7.3%)	0.77
West Midlands	5,931	(10.8%)	1,018.0	(8.2%)	1.33
East Midlands	1,257	(2.3%)	715.1	(5.7%)	0.41
North West	6,322	(11.5%)	1,388.7	(11.2%)	1.01
Yorks & Humberside	3,519	(6.4%)	986.0	(7.9%)	0.74
North	595	(1.1%)	590.8	(4.7%)	0.27
Wales	805	(1.5%)	524.5	(4.2%)	0.35
Scotland	1,660	(3.0%)	1,163.3	(9.3%)	0.33
Great Britain	54,739	(100.0%)	12,440.0	(100.0%)	1.00

Notes:

a - The Location Quotient is calculated using the following formula:

$$\frac{AH\ 8394_i / AH\ 8394_n}{Private\ Services_i / Private\ Services_n}$$

Where i = reference region
      n = national

b - Private Services = SIC (1968) 6-9 minus Civil Servants in Post

Sources: Dept. of Employment Gazette, Occasional Supplement no. 2
Dec 1983 'Report on Sept 1981 Census of Employment'
Regional Trends 1983 Table 7.7
Civil Servants in Post: at 1/1/1982

the questionnaire survey data mainly develop software packages, or offer turnkey systems or consultancy services. A centre-of-town location is less important for these types of 'producer services' firms and while they still serve a primarily urban market, many choose to locate in small towns in counties fringing the conurbations (table 6.5). These areas are generally more residentially attractive and afford better quality and cheaper premises. Semi-urban locations may also be more convenient for staff and often for the founders themselves.

Table 6.5: Computer software employment, 1984, and all manufacturing employment, 1981, by urban-rural status

| Urban/rural status | Computer software | | | All Mnfg. | |
	Employ.	(%)	Estabs.	Employ. (thousands)	(%)
London	4,410	(22.9%)	77	650	(11.0%)
Conurbations	1,710	(8.9%)	38	1,295	(21.9%)
Free-standing cities	1,080	(5.6%)	22	950	(16.1%)
Large towns	2,436	(12.6%)	38	756	(12.8%)
Small towns	8,785	(45.6%)	103	1,609	(27.2%)
Rural areas	848	(4.4%)	32	655	(11.1%)
Total	19,269	(100.0%)	310	5,916	(100.0%)

Sources: Questionnaire survey data
Fothergill et al (1984, p53)

6.3.3 Inter-regional employment change (Computer hardware)

Because the computer services sector (AH 8394) was only defined as a distinctive entity following the 1980 standard industrial classification, it is not possible to study employment change by area from official statistics. For computer hardware however, this is possible and table 6.6 shows the pattern of employment change in the computer manufacturing sector derived from the censuses of employment in 1971, 1976 and 1981. The South East recorded an increase in absolute numbers employed in the industry 1971-81 of over 4,000 (+13%). However, this overall change masks a decrease of 9,000 jobs to 1976 followed by an increase of 13,000 to 1981. Interestingly, in terms of volume of employment change, this parallels almost exactly the national position during these years. From study of ACE data for the intervening years it is clear that the striking reversal in the relative performance of the South East occurred only after 1978. Because censuses of employment were not carried out in 1979 and 1980 it is not possible to date the change with any more precision than this. Several possible reasons may be put forward to explain this pattern of employment change. Firstly, the 1981 figures for the census of employment may be suspect. The provisional figures from the Department of Employment released in December 1982 showed an estimated rise of 40% to a total of 61,000 employees in the industry including around 13,000 in London. This was later downgraded to just 56,064 with less than 9,000 in London. This suggests that some double-counting or misclassification did originally occur but was later corrected. There was also improved collection of data on small firms (less than 20 employees) in the 1981 census which served to inflate the employment estimate relative to earlier counts (Dept. of Employment Gazette, Dec. 1983, p504-13).

A second possibility remains that since 1978 there <u>has</u> been a substantial reversal of trading conditions in the South East relative to the rest of the country. Support for this hypothesis comes from Keeble's (1986a) discussion of the regional reversal apparent in manufacturing industry as a whole since 1977. Figure 6.4, which is taken from Keeble's paper, shows the dramatic nature of this turnaround in terms of the South East's share of national manufacturing employment. Keeble explains this partly in terms of a cessation of factors which, up to 1977, had been causing a dispersal of manufacturing employment from the South East including regional policy and the urban-rural manufacturing shift. However, he argues that it also reflects a growth of high-technology industry in the South East particularly new firms. Evidence presented in chapter five on the rate of new firm formation in the computer industry suggests that it is considerably higher in the South East than in the rest of the country.

Within the South East there was a trend in employment change away from Greater London particularly between 1971 and

The geography of the British computer industry

Table 6.6: Employment in the computer hardware industry in the UK
by region, 1971, 1976 and 1981

Region	1971	(%)	1976	(%)	1981	(%)
Greater London	13,177	(25.8%)	5,699	(13.3%)	8,812	(15.8%)
Rest of SE	16,877	(33.1%)	15,257	(35.5%)	25,303	(45.5%)
All South East	30,054	(58.9%)	20,956	(48.8%)	34,115	(61.3%)
East Anglia	217	(0.4%)	334	(0.8%)	461	(0.8%)
South West	489	(1.0%)	2,037	(4.7%)	2,138	(3.8%)
West Midlands	4,135	(8.1%)	3,695	(8.6%)	3,675	(6.6%)
East Midlands	247	(0.5%)	117	(0.3%)	816	(1.5%)
North West	6,500	(12.7%)	8,295	(19.3%)	5,853	(10.5%)
Yorks & Humb.	309	(0.6%)	172	(0.4%)	413	(0.7%)
North	718	(1.4%)	604	(1.4%)	348	(0.6%)
Wales	100	(0.2%)	406	(0.9%)	1,175	(2.1%)
Scotland	8,214	(16.1%)	6,328	(14.7%)	7,070	(12.6%)
Great Britain	50,983	(100.0%)	42,944	(100.0%)	56,064	(100.0%)

Source: Annual Census of Employment
         Unpublished County Employment estimates

1976 and such growth that has occurred subsequently has
tended to be concentrated in the Rest of the South East
(+10,046 = +66%, 1976-81). Figure 6.5 shows the spatial pattern
of employment change by county 1976-81. The most dramatic
employment gains by county have been made in Berkshire
(+5,912) and Greater London (+3,113) though in both cases this
may have been exaggerated due to reclassification of
establishments. The improved performance of Greater London
after 1976 is in contrast to the other conurbations.

179

The geography of the British computer industry

Figure 6.4: Regional percentage shares of UK
            manufacturing employment, 1965-83

The geography of the British computer industry

Figure 6.5: Employment change in the computer
manufacturing industry, 1976-81

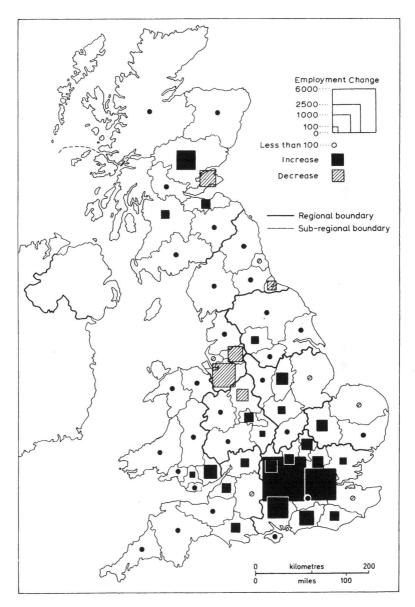

The highly urbanised areas of the West Midlands and North West both lost jobs between 1976 and 1981 mainly due to ICL job-shedding which has continued since 1981. With few exceptions, the whole of southern England records employment gains, and only the counties of Staffordshire, Cheshire, Greater Manchester, Cleveland and Fife have experienced significant employment declines.

6.4 Employment change analysis

6.4.1 Employment change by occupational composition

Two data sources on occupational composition for establishments in the computer industry are available for geographical analysis. One is the unpublished EITB statutory returns which cover only hardware but allow comparison of employment change between 1978 and 1984. The other is the questionnaire data which includes both hardware and software but only permits a cross-sectional examination for 1984. Generally speaking, they can be treated as compatible, though a higher percentage of employees is recorded as being involved in management, sales and clerical work and a lower percentage employed in semi-skilled and unskilled manual occupations in the EITB data. This probably reflects the inclusion of regional sales offices of multi-plant firms which were excluded from the questionnaire survey. The major difference lies in the survey data between the hardware and software sectors with the latter employing a much higher percentage in research and development work, principally as consultants, analysts and software engineers. A relatively small proportion of software employees are in semi-skilled or unskilled occupations, mainly keyboard/VDU operators.

Figure 6.6 shows that there are considerable regional differences in skill composition within the computer industry. To take two extreme examples, Greater London, with its concentration of firm HQs and sales offices, has 80% of its computer hardware employment (1984) in non-manual occupations compared with just 45% in Wales. In general terms, the assisted areas of Wales, Scotland and the North of England all have a lower percentage of non-manual employment and a higher percentage of unskilled manual employment than the national average. This would seem to conform to the hypotheses of the product life-cycle (Vernon, 1966; Hirsch, 1967), or spatial hierarchies of functions (Westaway, 1974; Massey, 1979). However, as Morgan & Sayer (1983, p6-7) warn, caution

The geography of the British computer industry

Figure 6.6: Computer industry employment by skill
division, April 1984

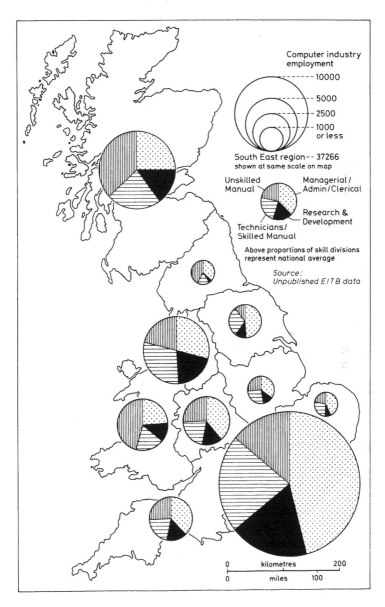

Figure 6.7: Computer manufacturing employment change
1978-84, for R&D and all employment

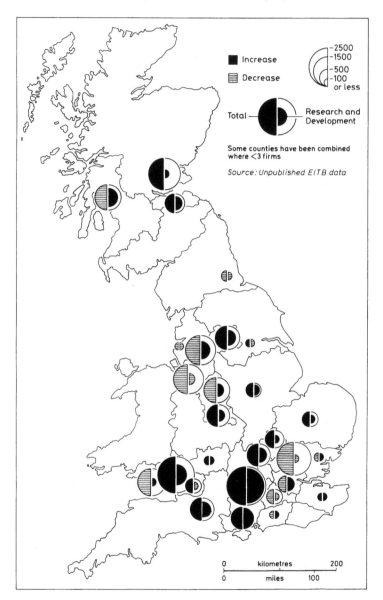

The geography of the British computer industry

Figure 6.8: Computer manufacturing employment change
1978-84, for manual occupations and all
employment

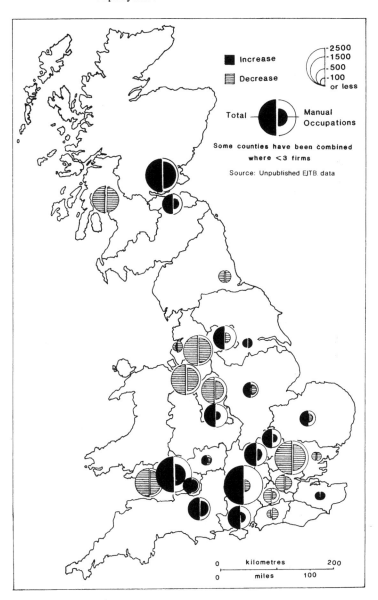

should be exercised over the use of percentage figures to define regional stereotypes. The dominance of the South East in the electronics industry means that it has, for instance, a greater absolute number of unskilled manual employees (5,408) than any other region and more than a third of the national total.

In general the hardware sector has experienced an upgrading of skill requirements with a national gain of more than 90% in R&D employment but a decline of one fifth in semi- and unskilled manual jobs between 1978 and 1984. Figures 6.7 and 6.8 show the extent to which overall employment change in each county has been determined by occupational composition. The EITB data on employment change (see also table 6.2) shows that the fastest growing counties are clustered in a western arc around Greater London, particularly Berkshire (+2,498 = +47.5%), Buckinghamshire (+818 = +244.2%) and Hampshire (+806 = +15.3%). In each of these counties, most of the employment gain is in R&D with only slow growth or decline in manual occupations. By contrast, those counties with a loss of more than 1,000 employees, Strathclyde, Greater Manchester, Cheshire, Staffs, Mid Glamorgan have all recorded substantial declines in manual employment.

The only areas in which manual employment grew by more than 500 were, significantly, counties in the peripheral regions of Wales (Gwent) and Scotland (Fife). In both areas there are a number of newly-established branch plants engaged in routinised volume manufacture of computer peripherals. Both areas also have high levels of female participation in the labour force of around 50%. In the South East there was a net loss of 1,700 (-24%) manual jobs over the period 1978-84. However, this was more than offset by the gain in R&D jobs (+3,420 = +102%) which exceeded the total employment increase (+2,352 = +6.7%). Thus the existing regional bias in occupational composition of R&D and managerial jobs in the South East and semi-skilled and unskilled manual jobs in the periphery, has been accentuated by recent employment change. This gives strong support to the hypothesis that there is an emerging functional division of labour within multi-plant corporate organisations (Massey & Meegan, 1979; Frost & Spence, 1981).

6.4.2 Employment change by age of establishment

Figure 6.9 shows the date of formation of establishments and their employment included in the questionnaire survey data 1945-1984 as a cumulative percentage graph. Eight

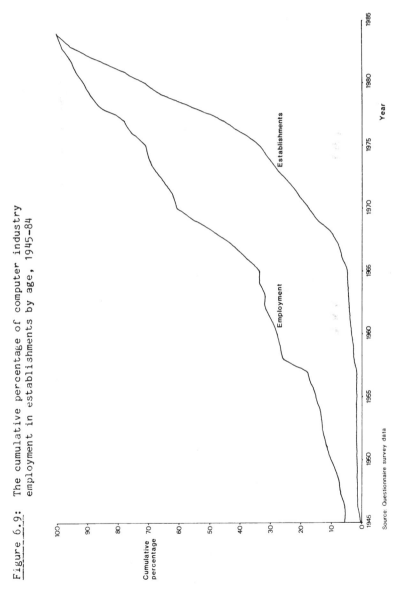

Figure 6.9: The cumulative percentage of computer industry employment in establishments by age, 1945–84

Source: Questionnaire survey data

The geography of the British computer industry

Table 6.7: Employment and average size of establishments, 1984
            by age band of establishments

Age band	Estabs. 1984	(%)	Emp. 1984	(%)	Average size
Less than 5 years	234	(34.0%)	7,205	(10.3%)	30.8
6 - 10 years	232	(33.7%)	13,251	(18.9%)	57.1
11-20 years	185	(26.9%)	26,004	(37.3%)	140.6
21 plus years	37	(5.4%)	23,454	(33.5%)	633.9
All establishments	688	(100.0%)	69,914	(100.0%)	101.6

Source: Questionnaire survey data

establishments were opened before 1945. The peak year for new
establishments opening was 1979, which was also the peak year
for new independent firms in the computer industry (see
figure 5.3). In a macro-economic context, 1979 marked the
downturn in the business cycle and preceded a major
industrial recession. The lower formation rate for
establishments after 1979 probably reflects this period of
economic instability and lower investment. The rate of
formation of establishments shows an upward trend over most
of the period up to 1979. Some 60% of establishments are less
than ten years old with 90% being less than 20 years old.
Despite being few in number however, the older establishments
are of major importance in employment terms by virtue of their

much larger average size. The 'employment by age' profile of
computer industry establishments is also demonstrated in
tables 6.7 and 6.8 which show employment in 1984 and
employment change 1980-84 by age band. Almost one-third of
employment in 1984 was in plants more than twenty years old.
However these plants shed 1,195 jobs between 1980 and 1984. In
general the pattern of employment change by age of
establishment favours newer concerns which showed the
greatest absolute and percentage increase.

Table 6.8:   Employment 1980, and employment change 1980-84,
by age band of establishments

Age band	Estabs.	Employment in 1980	Employment in 1984	% Change 1980-84
Founded since 1980	234	0	+7,205	–
6-10 years	129	6,052	+1,922	+31.8%
11-20 years	106	13,755	+3,465	+25.1%
21 plus years	22	19,588	-1,195	-6.1%
All establishments[a]	491	39,395	+11,397	+28.9%
Pre-1980 estabs.[b]	256	39,395	+4,192	+10.6%

Notes

a - Data coverage = 71.3% of establishments

b - Data coverage = 56.6% of establishments

Source: Questionnaire survey data

6.4.3 Employment change by size of establishments

It would be expected that the size of an establishment is
partly a function of its age, and there is indeed a strong
positive correlation between the two (from the questionnaire
data, Pearson's $r = 0.45$, which is statistically significant at
the 99% level). However, the size of the establishment is also
affected by other factors. For instance the average employment
size of hardware plants in the survey is 134.0 compared with

The geography of the British computer industry

62.2 for software. As table 4.4 shows, the average size of establishment also varies according to its legal status with branch plants generally being larger than independent firms. For independent firms, the rate of employment growth (size/age) is dependent on the competitive success of the firm. Thus, employment size, while clearly a dependent variable, cannot be presumed to be solely determined by any of the variables discussed.

Table 6.9: Establishments and employment size 1984 by size band of establishments

Size band	Estabs. 1984	(%)	Employment 1984	(%)
0-50	483	(70.2%)	8,851	(12.7%)
51-100	87	(12.6%)	6,322	(9.0%)
101-250	66	(9.6%)	10,994	(15.7%)
251-500	23	(3.3%)	8,884	(12.7%)
501-1000	17	(2.5%)	12,664	(18.1%)
1000 plus	12	(1.7%)	22,226	(31.8%)
All estabs.	688	(100.0%)	69,914	(100.0%)

Source: Questionnaire survey data

Table 6.9 shows the number and employment of establishments by size code in 1984. While four-fifths of the establishments in the survey employ 100 or less workers, they account for only one-fifth of total employment. Conversely, the twelve largest establishments (ICL - 6; IBM - 4; Ferranti Computer Systems Ltd. - 2) employ almost one third of the total. Comparison with table 6.10, which shows employment by size of establishment in 1980 and the pattern of employment change 1980-84, shows that the employment size distribution has undergone a considerable shift in favour of smaller plant sizes. Indeed the average size of establishments has fallen from 152.5 in 1980 to 101.2 in 1984. The quality of data is impaired by the lack of information on plant closures between

190

Table 6.10:   Employment size 1980 and employment change
1980-1984

Size band	Employment in 1980[a]	(%)	Change 1980-4 A	Change 1980-4 B
0-50	3,467	(8.8%)	+3,814	+11,268
51-100	1,644	(4.2%)	+2,525	+1,193
101-250	2,697	(6.8%)	+4,371	+982
251-500	2,786	(7.1%)	+1,833	+915
501-1000	2,036	(5.2%)	+1,403	+1,083
1000 plus	26,765	(67.9%)	-2,549	-4,044
All estabs.	39,395	(100.0%)	+11,397	+11,397

Notes

a - Data coverage = 71.3%

A - Classified by employment size 1984

B - Classified by employment size 1980

Source: Questionnaire survey data

1980 and 1984 and there may be a higher turnover of stock of establishments among smaller size bands. Nevertheless, the scale and direction of the shift is impressive. This is also confirmed by the EITB data for hardware establishments for which the average employment size fell from 194 in 1978 to 148 in 1984. Some 99% of the net gain and 68% of the gross gain in employment 1980-84 occurred in establishments which either did not exist, or employed less than 50 people in 1980. This employment gain was offset by a net decline of 15% among the largest establishments. Thus the relationship between size of establishment (1980), and employment increase (1980-84) even excluding new establishments, showed a strong negative correlation (Pearson's $r = -0.60$), a pattern which was even more evident amongst hardware manufacturers alone ($r = -0.65$, both relationships statistically significant at the 99%

level). These trends are entirely in line with recent employment trends by size and class in UK manufacturing industry as a whole (Frank, Miall & Rees, 1984).

6.5 Two contrasting regional case studies

The discussion thus far has concentrated on the locational dynamism of the computer industry at a national level. In this section attention focusses on two areas, Cambridgeshire/Hertfordshire and Scotland, which have both experienced recent computer employment growth. The nature of this growth and the character of the computer industry in the two areas is considered below.

6.5.1 Cambridgeshire/Hertfordshire

The growth of high technology industry in Hertfordshire and Cambridgeshire over the post-war period has been coincident with the process of decentralisation of jobs and population from London. During the 1950s, Hertfordshire had the fastest rate of growth of population of any county in the British Isles of 3.2% p.a., only one quarter of which was due to natural increase (Wray et al, 1974). Since the 1960s however, the locus of population growth has shifted further away from the metropolis to Cambridgeshire. Between 1971 and 1981, Cambridgeshire's population grew by 14.5% compared with an increase of only 0.6% in Great Britain as a whole (OPCS, 1984). Less than a third of this was due to natural increase. The influence of in-migration is shown by the fact that the fastest rate of increase was amongst the 25-44 age group (+27.2%). Following the completion of the M11 motorway between Cambridge and London in 1979, and the electrification of the Cambridge-Liverpool Street train line, due by 1987, it is likely that this above average rate of population increase will be sustained, not least by continuing growth of commuting to Greater London.

The population of Hertfordshire (957,000 in 1981) is distributed in a number of small towns and intervening rural areas with no single centre dominant. The county includes the former new towns of Stevenage, Welwyn, Hatfield and Hemel Hempstead plus the garden city of Letchworth. The population of Cambridgeshire (579,000 in 1981) is more focussed on the twin centres of Cambridge and Peterborough (designated as a new town in 1967) but the county also contains large tracts of rural areas, particularly in the Fenland.

The geography of the British computer industry

The computer industry in Hertfordshire dates from 1923 when British Tabulating Machines (BTM), one of the forerunners of ICL, was attracted from London to Letchworth by the encouragement of the Garden City company. In 1955, BTM opened a second site in Stevenage, though this is now involved purely in administrative functions rather than production. Despite job-shedding since 1979, STC ICL is still the major computer industry employer in Hertfordshire. The company's data centre is in Hitchin, and two former ITT subsidiaries (IDEC in Stevenage and STC's business systems division in Barnet) are now under the direct control of ICL. The second major computer firm in Hertfordshire, CASE, a specialist manufacturer of data communications equipment, also moved out from London in 1970 to its present HQ at Watford, and now employs over 1,300 worldwide.

Of the new towns in Hertfordshire, Hemel Hempstead has been the most successful in attracting internationally-mobile computer/telecoms companies including Honeywell, Northern Telecom and McDonnell Douglas as well as indigenous companies such as Information Technology Ltd. and Oberon International. Other major computer firms in the county include GEC Computers in Borehamwood which is involved mainly in defence subcontracting; and F International in Berkhamstead, a computer services firm which employs over 800 contract staff, 96% of whom are female, and which has pioneered the concept of home-working and a decentralised corporate structure.

In Cambridgeshire, with the notable exception of Peterborough Software, most computer employment is in the south of the county around Cambridge. The electronics industry in Cambridge dates from the formation in 1881 of the Cambridge Scientific Instruments company and in 1896 of W.G. Pye. Cambridge also gained an early lead in the nascent computer industry, through the establishment in 1946 of a research team under Professor Wilkes in what is now the university's computer laboratory. Much of the early work at Cambridge was sponsored by the J.Lyons catering company whose Lyons Electronic Office (LEO) computer was the first to be used in a commercial environment. Thus, while other university departments such as Manchester were involved in theoretical mathematics and defence work, in Cambridge an early link was forged between university and commerce.

In the post-war period, the prevalent planning ethos in Cambridge, expressed by the Holford report (1950), was to preserve the unique character of the city by limiting industrial development. One example of this policy was the refusal by the county council to allow IBM permission to establish its European research and development laboratories in Cambridge (Segal Quince & Partners, 1985, p18). The company chose instead to locate at Hursley in Hampshire. As a consequence, the growth of the computer industry in Cambridge before 1975 was largely restricted to research bodies such as the Computer-Assisted Design Centre (CADCentre) set up by the Ministry of Technology in 1969, as a 'centre of excellence' in the emerging technology of CAD/CAM. The university computer laboratory had already established a strong CAD group and a powerful Atlas 2 machine was also available to support the new centre. The CADCentre has subsequently been the source of founders of no less than 14 software/consultancy firms, and was itself privatised in 1983.

The change of direction in county policy towards industrial development is argued by Segal Quince and Partners (1985) to have followed the publication of the University-inspired Mott Committee report (1969). The report was directed towards the need to increase interaction between teaching and scientific research and its application in industry, medicine and agriculture, and recommended that limited growth of existing and new science-based industry and applied research units should be encourage in the Cambridge area. One specific proposal, for the setting up of a Science Park, was taken up by Trinity College in 1970 and the Cambridge Science Park, the first of its kind in Britain, was opened in 1975. There are now more than 50 high-technology tenants with a combined employment of 1,480 by April 1985 (Moore & Spires, 1983; Carter & Watts, 1984).

The expansion of the computer industry in Cambridge, which has taken place largely since 1975, has been associated with a remarkably high rate of new firm formation in high technology sectors in general. The 'Cambridge Phenomenon' of indigenous development of science-based industry has been studied by Segal Quince and Partners (1985). More recent work by the company estimates that by December 1985 there were around 400 currently surviving technology-based firms within a 15 mile radius of Cambridge. Some of these firms have grown to a considerable size. For instance, five of the computer firms founded since 1975, Acorn, Sinclair, CIS, Comart and Torch, now employ more than 100 workers. Most have remained small, but it is the sheer volume of new firms which has contributed to local employment. Segal Quince (1985, p24-32) estimate that technology-based firms in the area provide at least 13,700 jobs, or 17% of local employment in the Cambridge travel-to-work area. The characteristics of computer new firms around Cambridge and the particular role of the university are studied in chapter five.

Since 1980, two new trends have become apparent in the development of the computer industry around Cambridge. The first is the attraction of mobile firms to the area. There have also been a number of new openings of R&D units by major multinational companies such as Logica and Data General, and even IBM has established a 'listening post' on the Science Park. These firms have been drawn by the growing reputation of Cambridge as a high technology growth centre, by the availability in the area of specialised technical skills and by the potential for research collaboration with university departments. A second trend is the influx of overseas capital through the acquisition of local firms, including Acorn, taken over by Olivetti in 1985, CIS by Computervision, Shape Data by Evans and Sutherland, and ARCb y McDonnell Douglas. The motivation of the overseas multinationals in taking over local firms is to acquire in particular skills in Computer-Assisted Design (CAD) and microcomputer design. While the firms concerned have undoubtedly benefitted from the extra capital resources of their new parents, in the long-term it means that ultimate control over the local industry is passing out of the local area and consequently local sovereignty is reduced. Nevertheless, this greater integration with the world economy is probably an inevitable part of the maturing of the 'Cambridge Phenomenon'.

6.5.2 Scotland

The origins of electronics research in Scotland can be traced back through a long line of distinguished Scottish scientists and engineers including Maxwell and Kelvin. But the modern industry dates from the war-time establishment of a factory of the Manchester-based Ferranti company in Edinburgh to produce gyroscopic gunsights. Ferranti headed the Scottish Development Group set up by the Scottish Office in 1947 to spread the new electronics technology to local industry. The company has subsequently expanded its Scottish group and it is now the major electronics employer (7,700 jobs) in Scotland. Most of these jobs are in the defence sector, but one Ferranti subsidiary, Infographics in Livingston, which was set up as a joint venture with Cetec of the US in 1976, operates in the field of Computer-Assisted Engineering (CAE).

During the 1940s and early 1950s, four major US multinationals manufacturing electro-mechanical business machines established branch plants in Scotland, and these still provide the bulk of Scottish computer industry employment. The long term (nearly 40 years) stability of these foreign-owned branch plants is thus noteworthy. The IBM plants in Greenock make IBM the major single employer in the Scottish computer sector. The Honeywell plant set up at Newhouse, near Motherwell, initially manufactured industrial controls equipment, but since 1963 has also been involved in assembly of the parent company's minicomputer range on the same site. NCR chose Dundee for its operations and now designs and manufactures a range of Automatic Teller Machines (ATMs), and latterly the 'Tower' range of microcomputers. Burroughs initially located its Scottish manufacturing operations in Strathleven, but has subsequently chosen new town locations in Glenrothes and Cumbernauld (both now closed) and Livingston (since 1979). In addition to these four US multinationals, Timex, which is ultimately controlled from Norway, also came to Scotland in 1946 and since 1982 has been involved in subcontract work principally for Sinclair/Amstrad and IBM.

During the 1960s and early 1970s, when regional policy was once more in an 'active' phase (Moore, Rhodes & Tyler, 1983), a number of US and Japanese manufacturers of semiconductors were attracted to Scotland, including National Semiconductor, General Instruments, Motorola and NEC. A second 'wave' of US computer industry companies have come to Scotland following Britain's membership of the EEC in 1973 and the formation of the 'Scottish Development Agency' (SDA) in 1975 since when the area has been consciously marketed as Europe's 'Silicon Glen'. This second wave includes new starts by DEC in Ayr & South Queensferry, Wang in Stirling, Burroughs and Apollo in Livingston and SCI in Irvine plus expansion by IBM in Greenock. Also the Birmingham-based company Apricot has established a microcomputer manufacturing plant at Glenrothes.

The continuing importance of Scotland as a 'European' rather than a specifically British manufacturing base is shown by the fact that eight of the top ten US/Japanese information system companies now maintain a presence there. By contrast, only one (Ferranti) of the top ten European companies has facilities in Scotland (Scottish Development Agency, 1985). The EEC tariff structure for electronics, introduced in the late 1960s, is higher for semiconductors and other individual components (17%) than for electronic sub-assemblies (5%) (NEDO Electronics EDC, 1983, p2). Consequently, non-European computer manufacturers have been encouraged to set up plants to assemble computers in 'kit form' within the EEC tariff wall. Britain was the natural choice for the US multinationals because of its common language and cultural heritage. Within Britain, Scotland offered a ready supply of skilled labour and engineering expertise particularly during the immediate post-war years when labour was in short supply. Today Scotland claims to produce the highest number of graduates per capita of any country in Western Europe (SDA, 1985, p5). Its 8 universities and 70 colleges are also biased towards science and technology which account for 45% of student places.

The availability of regional policy incentives during the post-war period was seen as being a major locational influence by 80% of the overseas establishments surveyed in Scotland. The particular case of IBM in Greenock illustrates this point. While the relative importance of regional policy in the British economy is generally acknowledged to have declined since 1975 (Martin & Hodge, 1983; Oakey, 1983b), the co-ordination of regional economic initiatives has been greatly improved by the foundation of the Scottish Development Agency. In addition, the new town development corporations, and before them the Scottish Industrial Estates Corporation (SIEC) have offered favourable terms for leasing premises. It is notable, however, that in a number of cases, foreign-owned branch plants which were originally established in Scotland for assembly of kits imported from the parent firm have acquired other functions over time. This has been the case for DEC, for instance, which set up an assembly facility at Ayr in 1976. In 1980, it opened its European Business Centre for Quality Assurance and distribution and a European manufacturing applications software group. In 1984, the Ayr site acquired facilities for Printed Circuit Board (PCB) and VLSI test and assembly. Most recently in August 1985, DEC announced an £82m new semiconductor design and manufacturing plant at South Queensferry in Lothian. The evidence from DEC of the increasing technological sophistication of its Scottish operations over time and a highly contemporary product range can be repeated in a number of other multinational investors. This challenges the 'branch plant economy' stereotype of 'mature' products in a technological backwater. In recent years the percentage of the product range (weighted by employment size) designed in Scotland has risen to more than a third as several overseas firms, notably NCR and Burroughs, have also set up design facilities.

The geography of the British computer industry

The rising level of local R&D activity has also been prompted by a number of new starts by indigenous Scottish companies in the last decade, including two, Lattice Logic and Rodime, which have grown rapidly in employment. There is evidence of an above average rate of firm formation in the computer sector in Scotland and 26 firms founded since 1975 currently employ almost 1,000 workers. While the Scottish Development Agency identified the computing sector as its top priority in attracting foreign investment, the company of management consultants it hired to form its electronics strategy concluded that "There are no real opportunities for indigenous Scottish companies to enter the market" (Booz, Allen & Hamilton, 1979, p6). Perhaps as a consequence of this report, the SDA has had a poor record of investment in the indigenous computer sector. In 1983/4 disclosed investments in 4 out of a possible 34 indigenous computer companies amounted to only £0.8m compared with £41m given in two years in selective assistance to overseas companies (SDA, Annual Report, 1984). Ironically, Scottish-based firms like Rodime have had to go to America to raise funds. In some instances, the SDA has invested in overseas firms (for instance, Wang) in markets where an indigenous competitor was already operating (Fortronic). Many small firms are highly critical of what they term the 'Scottish Disaster Agency' for neglect of the home-based industry, and for being too easily misled by multinationals with promises of job creation that never fully materialise.

The electronics sector in Scotland now numbers some 43,000 jobs in 280 plants with additional employment in sub-contract, service and supply firms (Firn & Roberts, 1984). Employment in electronics currently exceeds the level in the shipbuilding (29,000), coal (26,000) and steel (19,500) sectors which have traditionally been the mainstays of the Scottish economy. Furthermore, following employment loss in the early 1970s, the electronics sector in Scotland has gained 8,700 (+25%) jobs between 1978 and 1984 while manufacturing employment generally has fallen by 172,600 (-28%), and electronics employment in Great Britain as a whole has fallen by 86,300 (-25%). The resilience of the Scottish electronics industry is even more remarkable in that it has coincided with a period of rundown in regional policy (Martin, 1985), which had been more active during earlier periods of expansion in the late 1940s and the 1960s. The explanation for Scotland's recent 'success' may lie in the fact that the local economy is more aligned to the international electronics market rather than the national market which has experienced deep recession since 1979. If this is true then it would imply that the Scottish electronics sector would suffer during any future downturn in the European market or contraction by the US multinationals under pressure in their home market. Thus the fact that cyclical activity in the 'branch plant economy' differs from the national economy should not be taken to mean that it is immune from cyclical downturns.

6.6 A comparison of the case-study areas

6.6.1 Technological change, legal status and employment

The evolution of the computer industry has followed different paths in Cambridgeshire/Hertfordshire and Scotland. In the former, high technology industry has grown through indigenous firm formation and through industrial movement within the core area. In Scotland, the electronics industry has expanded primarily through inward investment initially attracted by regional policy but latterly it has developed its own momentum through new openings in both the indigenous and externally-owned sectors. In Cambs/Herts, the locus of growth has shifted progressively away from London to the new towns of Hertfordshire in the 1950s and 1960s and to the university town of Cambridge since 1975. In Scotland, growth initially took place in the urban areas of Clydeside and Dundee, but latterly has shifted to the new towns of Glenrothes, Livingston and Irvine, the university towns of Edinburgh and Stirling, and rural areas such as Blairgowrie, Beith and the West Coast. In both areas therefore, the net effect of employment change has been an increase of employment in small towns and rural areas and a decrease in the level of spatial concentration.

Table 6.11 shows the current legal status of establishments and employment in the two regions compared with the average for Great Britain. Three major differences between the two areas may be highlighted. Firstly, the average size of establishments is much larger in Scotland (124 employees), particularly among foreign-controlled establishments (486), than in Cambs/Herts (75) or the rest of Great Britain (102). Secondly, the level of local control is much higher in Cambs/Herts (70% of employment) than Scotland (19%) or the rest of Great Britain (49%). Thirdly, foreign capital has entered the local economy through direct establishment of branch plants in Scotland, but through

Table 6.11: Computer industry establishments and employment, 1984 by
organisational type in Cambs/Herts, Scotland and Great
Britain

Subregion	Local control	UK external control	Foreign branches	Foreign acquired	All estabs 1984
Cambs/Herts					
Estabs. (No.)	115	6	3	13	137
(percentage)	(83.9%)	(4.4%)	(2.2%)	(9.5%)	(100.0%)
Employment (No.)	7,165	219	44	2,791	10,219
(percentage)	(70.1%)	(2.1%)	(0.4%)	(27.3%)	(100.0%)
Scotland					
Estabs. (No.)	47	9	13	0	69
(percentage)	(68.1%)	(13.0%)	(18.8%)	(0.0%)	(100.0%)
Employment (No.)	1,675	589	6,317	0	8,581
(percentage)	(19.5%)	(6.9%)	(73.6%)	(0.0%)	(100.0%)
Great Britain					
Estabs. (No.)	513	81	62	32	688
(percentage)	(74.6%)	(11.8%)	(9.0%)	(4.7%)	(100.0%)
Employment (No.)	33,934	11,827	18,561	5,592	69,914
(percentage)	(48.6%)	(16.9%)	(26.5%)	(3.0%)	(100.0%)

Source: Questionnaire survey data

Figure 6.10:   Cumulative percentage of employment by
                age of plant in Cambs/Herts and Scotland
                1945-84

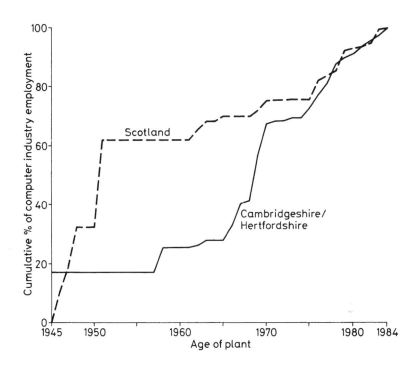

acquisition activity in Cambs/Herts. Figure 6.10 shows the contrast in the age profile of establishments in the two areas. In Scotland, some 62% of employment is in firms which have been in the area since 1951, whereas in Cambs/Herts only 18% of employment is in this category.

While these differences outlined above concerning legal status and average size and age of establishments are quite distinct, there is some evidence of recent convergence between the structure of the industry in the two subregions. Table 6.12 shows that in Cambs/Herts 80% of the net gain in employment between 1980 and 1984 has taken place in overseas establishments because in the locally-controlled sector job gains have been offset by job-shedding, particularly in ICL and GEC. Consequently, the level of overseas ownership in Cambs/Herts has increased recently, primarily through acquisitions. In 1980, only 20% of survey employment was foreign-controlled, but this has risen to 28% in 1984 with a particular increase in Cambridgeshire. In Scotland by contrast, 71% of the net gain in employment took place in the locally-controlled sector because of restructuring taking place in several of the overseas branch plants, including Burroughs and NCR. According to the questionnaire survey data, the number of foreign-owned establishments in Scotland had risen from 8 in 1980 to 13 by 1984, but their total employment in 1984 grew by only 2% to 6,317, which was 73% of total employment in the computer sector, down from 89% in 1980.

The arguments advanced in chapter two concerning changing skill requirements in the computer industry, and in chapter three on job-shedding in ICL apply equally well to employment change in Scotland. The key factor has been the impact of technological change, and in particular the transition from electro-mechanical to microprocessor-based products, which has enabled large-scale manufacturing capabilities to be maintained with a greatly reduced workforce. The current average size of manufacturing branch plants in Scotland (226) compares with McDermott's (1976, p321) estimate of an average size of 1,358 employees per establishment. Significantly, some 1,420 jobs, or 87% of the net expansion of computer industry employment in Scotland between 1980 and 1984 took place in new openings and new firms. The rate of formation of new establishments reached a peak in 1983, the last full year of the survey, when 16 new establishments (23% of those in the survey) were set up. Consequently, despite the fact that gross job creation was greater in Cambs/Herts, net increase was greater in Scotland.

The geography of the British computer industry

Table 6.12: Gross employment change by organisational type in
Cambs/Herts and Scotland, 1980-84

| Legal status | Employ. 1984 | Cambs/Herts (1980-84) | | | |
		Gains	Losses	Net Change	% Change[a]
Local control	7,165	+1,526	-1,290	+236	+3.3%
UK external control	219	+53	0	+53	+24.2%
Overseas branch	44	+33	0	+33	+75.0%
Overseas acquired	2,791	+1,129	0	+1,129	+40.5%
All establishments	10,219	+2,741	-1,290	+1,451	+14.2%

| Legal status | Employ. 1984 | Scotland (1980-84) | | | |
		Gains	Losses	Net Change	% Change[a]
Local control	1,675	+1,151	-4	+1,147	+68.4%
UK external control	589	+359	-10	+349	+59.2%
Overseas branch	6,317	+779	-655	+124	+2.0%
All establishments	8,581	+2,289	-669	+1,620	+18.9%

Note a — Data coverage = 71.3% of employment, 1984
        % Change is Net Change 1980-84 divided by total emp. 1984
        because only partial employment data is available for 1980

Source: Questionnaire survey data

Table 6.13: Employment by activity-type in Cambs/Herts,
             Scotland and Great Britain

Activity-type	Cambs/Herts	Scotland	Great Britain
Micro, mini & mainframe			
computer systems	43.3%	51.2%	30.8%
VDUs, disc drives, datacoms,			
& other peripherals	11.5%	35.4%	14.5%
'Custom' software, turnkey			
systems & consultancy	20.6%	9.3%	20.6%
'Package' software,			
computer bureaux	8.6%	1.6%	10.5%
Distribution, accessories			
and other	16.0%	2.5%	23.6%
All activities	100.0%	100.0%	100.0%
Employment	10,219	8,581	69,914

Note: Activity-type is derived from the percentage of sales
       (by value) in each establishment in each category
       weighted by its employment in 1984

Source: Questionnaire survey data

6.6.2 Functional and occupational divisions

Table 6.13 shows the division of employment by activity
in the two areas compared with the average for Great Britain.
More than 85% of employment in Scotland is engaged in hardware
manufacture but the local market is relatively small, and
consequently only 2.5% of employment is taken up in the
distribution of products not designed or manufactured on-
site. Software employment forms a relatively minor part of the
Scottish industry, particularly since the closure of ICL's

Dataskil subsidiary at Dalkeith in 1983. Much of the employment in software is in the design and development departments of the hardware manufacturers rather than computer services firms. Nationally, software provides almost a third of total employment, and a further quarter is taken up in distribution. In Hertfordshire there are also a number of major manufacturing plants, including ICL, GEC, CASE and ITL. In Cambridgeshire however, few firms have volume production facilities on site, preferring instead to subcontract manufacture to utilise excess capacity in the electronics industry elsewhere. Consequently, the rationalisation which has taken place in the home computer market during 1985 has had little direct effect on computer employment in the county where most employment is in design, sales and administrative occupations.

Activity-type divisions are also reflected in the breakdown of skill divisions shown in table 6.14. In Scotland, the ratio of white collar to blue collar workers is only 1.5:1 compared with 4:1 in Great Britain and 6:1 in Cambs/Herts. In Cambs/Herts, occupational divisions are oriented more towards technical, professional and administrative skills rather than production. However, there is a division within the subregion between Cambridgeshire, where R&D employment (43%) is more than three times the level of Hertfordshire (13%). In Scotland, the level of R&D employment (8.7%) is less than a half of the national average (21.7%). Nevertheless, this is much higher than that recorded in McDermott's (1979) survey (1.9%). Whereas McDermott found no significant variation in the level of R&D employment in Scotland between organisational types, in this survey R&D employment in the indigenous sector (15%) was more than twice that in the externally-controlled sector (7%).

While occupational divisions in Cambs/Herts and Scotland, especially the level of R&D, do correspond to the stereotype of a 'core' region and a 'peripheral region', no such differences are apparent in gender divisions. Indeed the level of female participation in Scotland (30%) is actually lower than in Cambs/Herts (37%) and part-time working, while being of little significance in either area, is also marginally higher in Cambs/Herts (4.5%) than Scotland (3.0%). Gender divisions in the workplace reflect the high level of administrative, sales and clerical staffing in the 'core' region which is increasing in relative terms. By contrast, in Scotland, unskilled assembly work, which also provides a high proportion of jobs for female workers, has declined in

Table 6.14: Occupational composition among establishments in
             Cambs/Herts, Scotland and Great Britain, 1984

Occupation	Cambs/Herts		Scotland		Great Britain	
Management, sales						
and clerical	3,271	(43.5%)	1,599	(19.2%)	16,729	(34.1%)
Research &						
Development	1,444	(19.2%)	721	(8.7%)	10,632	(21.7%)
Technicians, and other						
skilled	1,736	(23.1%)	2,639	(31.7%)	12,285	(25.0%)
Semi-skilled and unskilled						
manual	1,074	(14.3%)	3,357	(40.4%)	9,397	(19.1%)
Total	7,525	(100.0%)	8,316	(100.0%)	49,043	(100.0%)
Establishments	85		59		420	
Data coverage (emp.)	73.6%		96.9%		70.1%	
(establishments)	62.0%		85.5%		61.0%	

Source: Questionnaire survey data

relative importance.

6.6.3 Conclusions

This section has investigated differences in the 'character' of the computer industry in two contrasting regional environments. The key differences between the 'core' region of Cambridgeshire/Hertfordshire and the 'peripheral' region of Scotland lie in the legal and functional status of establishments and the historical evolution of the industry in the two areas. These differences are exemplified in the variations in activity-type, occupational composition and the level of technological dependency of establishments, though not so much in product modernity or absolute employment change. However, it has also been shown that differences within the core region between the stock of establishments in Hertfordshire and around Cambridge are equally as marked in terms of employment composition and function as between the core and the periphery. To return to the terminology developed earlier, it may be argued that Cambridge and Scotland represent two particular 'types' of 'Technology-Oriented Complex' (TOC). Cambridge is a Type I TOC in which a high rate of new firm formation has been stimulated by a research environment generated by a major university. In Scotland inward investment has been encouraged by government policy and initial successes in attracting major firms in the post-war period has created a skilled labour pool which has sustained further growth.

Evidence put forward in this chapter however shows convergence between the industry structures in the two areas over the last decade. In Scotland the major employment growth has taken place through new openings and new firms whereas in Cambridge, the maturing of the 'Cambridge Phenomenon' has attracted external capital into the area to finance expansion. The evolution of the industry in Hertfordshire fits neither pattern, but is more akin to that of Scotland in that most of the major employers have 'moved in' to the area, either from abroad or from elsewhere in the UK (London) rather than being founded in Hertfordshire. However the area differs from Scotland insofar as this inward investment has been lead by market forces rather than government-backed initiatives.

In both Cambs/Herts and Scotland the recent pattern of employment change has been underlain by technological change. Job-shedding has taken place in semi-skilled and unskilled manual occupations while job growth has occured in R&D, software, sales and management. The shift in the locational pattern of the industry in the two areas has reflected these changes. In the core region, job growth has shifted northwards, further away from London, and in Scotland eastwards from the conurbation of Strathclyde to the university town of Edinburgh and the new towns of Livingston and Glenrothes. The dominant theme in both areas has been deconcentration from larger to smaller and more numerous establishments and from larger settlements to small towns and rural areas.

Chapter Seven

CONCLUSIONS: CRISIS AND DEVELOPMENT

It has been argued in this book that the period since 1979 has witnessed a growing crisis in the British computer industry which has eclipsed that of the early 1960s discussed in chapters three and four. The dimensions of this crisis are international uncompetitiveness, and an accelerating trade imbalance; loss of sovereignty through acquisitions of UK firms by overseas multinationals; and the financial collapse, job-shedding and loss of market share of the UK's major computer manufacturer, ICL.

Several different approaches may be taken to interpreting this crisis. One alternative is to survey the major trends which have affected the industry over the last decade. The themes of corporate restructuring of the older, larger firms and dynamic growth in smaller newer firms have been developed throughout the book. It is clear that these two trends reflect overlapping product cycles associated with mainframe/minicomputer and microcomputer technology. The effects that technological change has wrought on the occupational composition and the geographical structure of the computer industry in Britain are surveyed in section 7.1. A second alternative is to evaluate the comparative performance of ICL and IBM over the last decade (section 7.2). It is evident that the financial crisis at ICL between 1979 and 1982 led to a weakened competitive position relative to IBM which may never be reversed. A third alternative is to examine the position of British firms in the international marketplace. In section 7.3 trade statistics from the Organisation for Economic Co-operation and Development (OECD) are used to show the deteriorating position of the British balance of trade particularly after 1979. Finally, in section 7.4 the impact of recent government policy is assessed. It is argued that the lack of a comprehensive industrial policy and an overcommitment to defence spending has had an adverse effect on the domestic computer industry.

Conclusions: Crisis and Development

7.1 A review of general trends

7.1.1 Competitive structure

In chapter two, it was shown that at least two major product cycles are evident in the computer industry. The first is associated with the market for mainframe computers in which IBM has been approaching a position of monopolistic domination for several decades. In the UK the transition from an oligopoly to a duopoly during the 1970s was traced in chapter three. Since the troubles of ICL in 1981, this duopoly has trended towards a monopoly. One spatial consequence of this trend has been the restructuring or closure of large branch plants manufacturing mainframe or minicomputers. These plants, typically established in the 1950s or early 1960s, have a skilled manual workforce and are geared towards batch production of high cost systems, and few have R&D or sales functions. Some of these plants have made a transition to high volume production such as IBM in Greenock or ICL at Letchworth. Others have gained R&D facilities (NCR in Dundee), or have used spare capacity for subcontract work for other manufacturers (Timex in Dundee). But the majority have reduced their workforce or closed completely.

A second product cycle based around innovation in microelectronics has been evident in the computer industry since the mid-1970s. This has given rise to an increased rate of new firm formation and opportunities for new market entrants in specialised fields such as home computers, data communications and package software. Evidence presented in chapter five shows that new firm formation peaked in computer hardware in the late 1970s and in software probably in 1982. In both sectors market rationalisation is now taking place, through acquisitions and liquidations.

In the period under study, the overlapping of these two product cycles has prompted a decline in the average size of operating units and a great increase in the volume of competing firms. Consequently, there has been a decrease in the level of spatial concentration in the computer industry. However, chapter six shows that this has taken place through an intra-regional rather than an inter-regional shift, and through the opening of new firms and new branches rather than through relocation. It seems probable that this process has now reached a peak, and while further movement out of urban areas may take place, it is likely to occur through acquisition and rationalisation rather than the opening of new productive capacity.

7.1.2 Skills balance

While much of the literature on the effects of technological change on skill requirements argues from a perspective of deskilling (Braverman, 1974; Conference of Socialist Economists, 1981; Massey, 1984), the evidence for the computer industry at least, points to the contrary experience of reskilling. It is evident from Figure 2.2 and Tables 2.10 and 2.14 that such employment growth which has taken place in the computer industry has been in non-manual, administrative, sales and particularly R&D occupations. The necessity for increasingly specialised skills has become the overriding locational factor for those parts of the industry which are expanding, particularly in software and R&D. In theory, this should act as a counter-balance to the process of decentralisation discussed in the previous section. In practice, new firms and other new units have opened up on the semi-rural fringe of the conurbations, principally in the South East; in areas of existing concentration such as the M4 corridor and Scotland; and in university towns such as Cambridge and Edinburgh.

The pattern of occupational change is reflected in the locational shifts shown in Figures 6.7 and 6.8 for computer hardware. The major employment growth has taken place in R&D occupations in the counties forming a crescent to the west and north of Greater London. The only exceptions to this general trend have been the new towns of Glenrothes, Livingston and Cwmbran where new productive capacity has been opened in computer peripherals manufacture leading to an increase in the level of demand for semi-skilled manual labour. In chapter three it was shown that the two major employers in the UK computer industry, IBM UK and STC ICL, had both located most of their software development and R&D facilities in the 'M4 corridor' area of the South East. As these operations have expanded in relative importance, they have effectively determined the labour market orientation for these highly specialised skills. Only latterly has an alternative growth pole emerged in the area around Cambridge.

Information regarding spatial trends in the computer services sector is more limited but data from the questionnaire survey indicates that some 73% of the 4,092 new jobs created in the software industry between 1980 and 1984 were in the 'core' regions of the South East, East Anglia and the South West. This compares with just 63% of existing software employment in these regions at the 1981 census of employment (table 6.4).

The evidence therefore points to an increasing dichotomy of occupational composition in the computer industry between R&D, software and non-manual occupations in the core regions and manual, hardware manufacturing jobs in the periphery. Whereas spatial deconcentration of aggregate employment may be occurring at an intra-regional scale through new firm formation, at an inter-regional scale there has been a polarisation in the 'quality' of employment and a strengthening of regional labour market 'stereotypes'. This has occurred to the detriment not only of the periphery but also of the intermediate areas and conurbations of the West Midlands and Greater Manchester. The spatial division of functions is especially apparent in the operation of the US multinationals which make use of investment grants and lower industrial costs to locate automated assembly and warehouse functions in the periphery while maintaining control, sales and R&D functions in the core region. However, in Scotland at least, the increasingly important new firms sector is also geared towards hardware manufacture rather than software. Perhaps this reflects the background and experience of local entrepreneurs or perhaps the opportunities for subcontract which the multinational branch plants provide. In either case it may be seen as a 'second round' effect of the spatial hierarchy of functions in the overseas manufacturing sector.

In the absence of planning controls what has occurred in the computer industry over the past decade is a pattern of uneven development. The effect of technological change, operating through the competitive structure of the industry, its skills balance and other locational factors, has been to create a spatial dislocation between areas of job growth and job loss. There has been a shift away from larger urban areas (apart from London) towards smaller towns and rural areas. At the regional level, there has been a loss of jobs in the Midlands and North West and a gain of skilled jobs in the core regions and of lesser skilled manual jobs in the periphery. The key factor in shaping these spatial trends has been the distribution of highly qualified personnel both as a source of potential entrepreneurs and as a pool of skilled labour. While scientists and engineers are theoretically highly mobile and can be recruited through national advertising, their importance to the modern computer industry is such that firms must come to where they want to live and work rather than vice versa. Insofar as these sorts of people will choose to live away from areas of urban and industrial decline, it is likely that future development of high technology industry will continue this pattern of uneven development.

7.2 IBM (UK) and STC ICL: A comparative evaluation

7.2.1 IBM (UK) and STC ICL in the UK market

In 1984, which is the most recent year to allow a comparison to be made between the published results of the UK's leading private sector companies (Allen, ed. 1985), IBM (UK) and ICL were ranked 61st and 116th in the UK on turnover, and 113th and 94th respectively on employment. The difference between the two companies is however more marked on profitability for which the companies ranked 22nd and 127th on operating profit before interest and tax. On export performance IBM (UK) was ranked 7th in the UK while ICL has declined to disclose direct exports since 1981.

Within the UK computer industry, IBM (UK) and ICL occupy first and second positions respectively in terms of turnover, a situation which has existed since the formation of ICL in 1968. The position is illustrated in table 7.1 which shows the year end 1984 results of the top 15 computer manufacturers in the UK. A direct comparison between companies is invalidated by the fact that not all the companies listed deal exclusively in computer electronics; because for several international companies it is difficult to separate UK-based and overseas activities; and because the companies have different dates for reporting their annual results. Nevertheless, the table provides an insight into the market dominance of IBM (UK) and ICL who command 42.2% and 16.9% respectively of the total turnover of the top 15 companies. By contrast, the share of the nearest rival involved solely with computer-related activities, Digital Equipment Corporation (DEC), was just 5.5% of this total.

An alternative measure of market share is provided by the figures for shipments and installed base given in chapter two. In 1963, the constituent parts of ICL had 82% of the installed base of mainframe computers in the UK. By 1968, this had fallen to 41%. In 1985, International Data Corporation (IDC) estimates show that ICL's share had slipped further to just 31% of the installed base and 15% of shipments of mainframe computers by value. In contrast, IBM's share had risen from a negligible amount in 1963 to 63% of mainframe shipments, by value, in 1985.

Conclusions: Crisis and Development

Table 7.1: Fifteen leading computer manufacturers in the UK,
financial results, 1984

Rank	Company	Origin	Year end	Turnover (£m)	Pre-tax profit (LOSS) (£m)	Emp.
1	IBM (UK)	US	12/84	2349	325	17,506
2	STC ICL	UK	12/84	942.6	40.3	21,656 [a]
3	Racal Electronics Datacoms division [b]	UK	03/84	309.0	n.a.	n.a. [a]
4	DEC	US	06/84	302.9	6.7	2,967
5	Hewlett-Packard [b]	US	10/84	293.1	17.6	2,783
6	Burroughs Machines Ltd. [b]	US	12/84	232.3	40.3	3,880
7	Control Data [c]	US	11/84	227.3	-3.9	2,972
8	Commodore	Bah	06/84	158.4	19.1	338
9	Ferranti Computer Systems Ltd. [b]	UK	03/84	152.2	13.1	4,800 [a]
10	NCR Ltd. [b]	US	11/84	141.8	27.9	3,313
11	Honeywell Info. Systems Ltd.	US	12/84	130.2	16.4	2,400
12	Acorn Computers	Italy	07/84	93	10.8	350 [a]
13	Sperry Computer Systems Division	US	03/84	78.5	7.7	1,000
14	Sinclair Research [b]	UK	03/84	77.7	14.2	125 [a]
15	Data Recording Instruments Co Ltd.	UK	03/84	74.7	3.4	1,400
	Top Fifteen			5,562.7	538.6	65,490 [a]

Notes

n.a. - Not available

a - Includes non computer-related activities

b - Includes company activity overseas

c - Includes Systime Computers (acquired 1985)

Bah - Bahamas

Sources: Extel Company Cards, Company Annual Reports

Figure 7.1: Annual turnover, pre-tax profits and employment for IBM (UK) and ICL, 1974-85

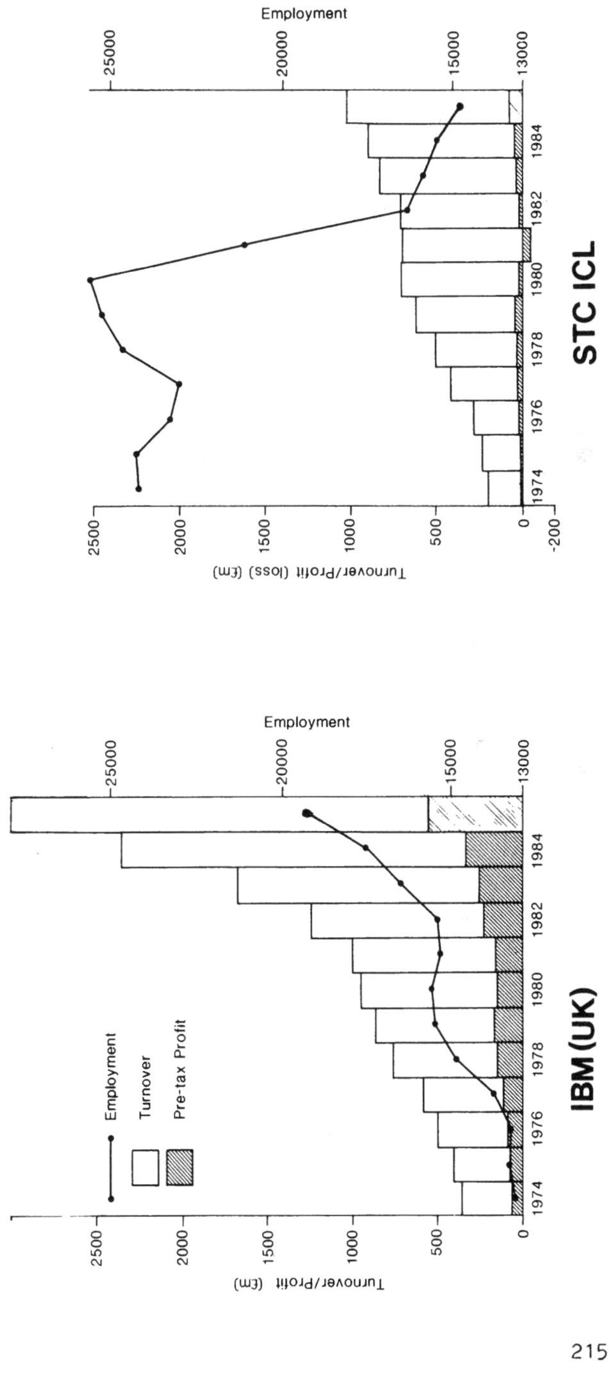

215

Conclusions: Crisis and Development

Table 7.2: Annual results of IBM (UK) 1975-1985

Year	Turnover (£m)	Pre-tax profit (£m)	Employment	Exports (£m)
1975	396.3	72.3	13,440	177.7
1976	493.9	86.8	13,391	239.0
1977	578.8	110.2	13,814	263.7
1978	758.5	146.5	14,905	334.0
1979	882.3	162.1	15,498	433.7
1980	954.4	153.3	15,590	452.4
1981	1,001.8	160.8	15,362	419.8
1982	1,240	225	15,454	522
1983	1,677	255	16,300	745
1984	2,349	325	17,506	1,175
1985	3,043	521	18,798	1,582

Source: Company Annual Reports

Table 7.3: Annual results of ICL PLC 1975-1985

Year	Turnover (£m)	Pre-tax profit (Loss) (£m)	Emp (world)	Emp (UK)
1975	239.8	16.2	28,069	24,312
1976	288.3	23.1	27,317	23,350
1977	418.7	30.3	32,156	23,054
1978	509.4	37.5	33,978	24,726
1979	624.1	45.7	34,401	25,313
1980	715.8	25.1	33,087	25,654
1981	711.1	(49.8)	25,564	21,114
1982	720.9	23.7	23,581	16,343
1983	845.6	45.6	22,573	15,879
1984	942.6	40.3	21,656	15,263
1985	1,037.8	53.8	21,528	14,379

Source: Company Annual Reports

Year on year change in turnover and profitability for
the two companies for the period 1975-85, which is shown in
Fig. 7.1 and Tables 7.2 & 7.3, reveals a contrasting picture.
ICL exhibited a 23.6% per annum compound growth rate in
turnover between 1973 and 1980 which was the peak year for its
UK employment. This was also the year in which profits
declined by 45%, precipitating a major crisis and threatening
the collapse of the company when it was followed by a £49.8m

loss in 1981. The rescue deal put together by the Government (detailed in chapter four) necessitated the loss of more than 10,000 jobs in the UK and a further 1,000 jobs abroad to bring the company back to profitability in 1982 and to restore growth in turnover of 12.9% between 1982 and 1985. IBM (UK) by contrast showed a slower compound growth rate of 18.5% p.a. between 1974 and 1980 (though from a higher base). Growth slumped to just 5% between 1980 and 1981 but thereafter turnover increased by 35% between 1982 and 1985, undoubtedly gaining market share from ICL during the latter's problems.

The latest year for which figures are available (year end Dec. 1985) was in many ways the most outstanding year of the past decade for IBM with a rise in profits of 60%, turnover up by 30% and exports up by 35% as the new 'Sierra' 3090 range of mainframes was introduced. The improvement in trading conditions was also reflected in the recruitment of 1,800 new employees in 1985 - the highest increase for ten years. The new recruits included the highest ever graduate intake by IBM (UK) of 420. UK employment in IBM had been at a lower level than ICL until 1982 but has risen slowly over the last decade. Indeed, during the height of the recession, 1981-2, only IBM (UK) increased employment at all among the top 30 manufacturing employers while ICL by contrast recorded the most severe percentage job loss among the top 30.

Tables 7.4 and 7.5 present an inter-firm comparison of the recent trading position of STC ICL and IBM (UK) (Ingham & Harrington, 1980). It must be noted that there are problems of compatibility in the two sets of figures: In particular, the IBM figures include sales of computers, peripherals and computer sub-assemblies not manufactured in this country. IBM does not disclose figures showing the value of these 'imports' but estimates that over the last decade 'imports' and 'exports' within the company have been approximately in balance. Thus it can be estimated that IBM 'imports' accounted for three-quarters of total goods and services purchased during 1984. ICL also puts its own name on finished products manufactured elsewhere, for instance in Japan by Fujitsu (e.g. ATLAS mainframes, and Electronic Point of Sale (EPOS) terminals); in Canada by Mitel (Private Automated Branch Exchanges (PABX)); and in America by Sun Microsystems (Professional workstations). Internal ICL estimates of the overseas component of goods and services purchased for manufacturing operations is around 40%, up from 15% in 1970 (ICL annual report, 1970, p7).

Conclusions: Crisis and Development

Table 7.4: Inter-firm Comparison I - Turnover, Profits,
           and Exports for STC ICL and IBM (UK)

	STC ICL	IBM (UK)
Turnover, 1985 (£m)	1,037.8m	3,043m
Turnover growth p.a. 1980-85	+7.7%	+26.1%
Pre-tax profit 1985 (£m)	54m	521m
Profitability growth p.a. 1980-85	+16.5%	+27.7%
Pre-tax profit 1985/Turnover 1985	5.2%	17.1%
Employment (UK) 1985	14,379	18,798
Employment change p.a. 1980-85	-10.9%	+3.8%
Exports 1985 (£m)	420.6 [a]	1,582
Exports growth p.a. 1980-85	+6.1% [a]	+28.4%
Exports 1985/Turnover 1985	40.5%	52.0%

Notes
  a - Turnover from sales of overseas subsidiaries

Source: Company Annual Reports

IBM has consistently maintained turnover and profitability at higher levels than ICL and during the period 1980-85 the rate of growth of pre-tax profits in IBM was almost twice that in ICL while the rate of growth of turnover was three times greater. ICL's activities have undergone a major restructuring since 1980 shedding 12,561 jobs worldwide and consequently it has reduced its labour cost:turnover ratio from 47.7% to 36.4%. Nevertheless a further 13,400 jobs would need to be lost if STC ICL were to match IBM (UK)'s labour cost:turnover ratio and 14,100 if the remaining staff were to be paid at the same average salary as IBM staff (£ 20,427).

STC ICL also fares badly in comparison to IBM on rate of capital investment as a percentage of turnover, though capital investment as a percentage of operating profit for ICL (100.2% 1985) is higher than for IBM (UK) (58.3% 1985). The composition of fixed assets in the two companies also varies considerably. In ICL only 15% by value of the fixed assets is taken up in land and buildings whereas the greater part is invested in plant and machinery and revenue-earning equipment on rental to customers, particularly overseas. The value of IBM property was almost ten times greater than ICL property constituting around 35% of fixed assets, because most IBM property is owned rather than leased. This is indicative of a

Conclusions: Crisis and Development

Table 7.5: Inter-firm Comparison II - Labour Costs, Investment,
Assets, Interest and Taxation for STC ICL and IBM (UK)

	STC ICL			:	IBM (UK)		
	1980	1982	1985	:	1980	1982	1985
Labour Costs (£m)	341.4	301.7	377.9	:	160	210	384
Labour Costs/Sales	47.7%	41.8%	36.4%	:	16.8%	16.9%	12.6%
Employees	33,087	23,581	20,528	:	15,590	15,454	13,798
Labour Costs/Emps.	£9,027	£10,983	£18,409	:	£10,263	£13,589	£20,427
Investment (£m)	80.4	61.5	53.9	:	131	119	304
Investment/Sales	11.2%	8.5%	5.2%	:	13.7%	9.6%	10.0%
Fixed Assets (£m)	128.8	161.9	142.3	:	285	339	636
Operating Profit/ Fixed Assets	0.44	0.29	0.38	:	0.85	0.93	0.82
Interest (£m)	28.1	30.7	17.8	:	-	-	-
Taxation (£m)	10.2	7.8	17.9	:	100	60	134

Source: Company Annual Reports

high commitment by IBM to prestige premises. Nevertheless,
return on assets for IBM is twice that of ICL.

Undoubtedly part of the structural weakness in ICL's
trading position is the accumulation of loans for which
interest payments are due. In 1982 for instance, almost two-
thirds of the company's operating profit was given over to
interest payments. By contrast, IBM (UK) has considerable cash
reserves which have been built up from £219m in 1980 to £597m
in 1985. This may well be used to underwrite a major
acquisition in the near future, possibly in the
telecommunications field into which IBM is moving. ICL has

also incurred major costs in the programme of rationalisation and redundancies which appeared in the accounts as 'one-off extraordinary item' of £78.1m in 1981. This was the same year in which the company announced losses of £49.8m before tax, and it marked an attempt by the company to make provision for further anticipated rationalisation costs while 'wiping the slate clean' for future shareholders reports. No such 'extraordinary items' have appeared in recent IBM annual reports. Other business costs do fall heavily on IBM however, and it is, for instance, one of the top ten corporate tax-payers in the UK, having paid £517m in the period from 1980 to 1985, almost ten times the contribution of ICL. Payments by IBM (UK) to its US parent in the form of dividends are not disclosed, but are likely to be substantial. The shareholders dividend, distributed to the mainly American shareholders, was worth £173m in 1985.

7.2.2 IBM Corp. and STC ICL in the European and world markets
In the context of the world market, the contrast between IBM and ICL is even more pronounced than in the UK. The worldwide sales of IBM Corp. in 1985 amounted to $50.1 billion, while ICL's turnover in that year was just $1,470, less than a seventh of IBM's pre-tax profit of $11.6 billion, and less than a third of IBM's worldwide expenditure on Research and Development of $4.7 billion. In international terms, IBM is the world's most profitable commercial company and, in terms of market capitalisation but not turnover, the world's largest company. In 1982, when the profits of the top 50 largest industrial companies declined by 23.4% according to a report in Fortune magazine (Times, 5/8/83), IBM's profits increased by the same margin. However, in 1985 profits remained stagnant as revenue from US hardware sales actually fell. IBM blamed this in problems of the data processing industry in general and on the 'softness' of the US economy. In the interim six-monthly results for 1986 there is no sign of a recovery and little evidence that IBM will be able to reach its publicly-stated target of a turnover of $100 billion in 1990.
A comparison of the worldwide activities of IBM and ICL is shown in the pie charts Fig. 7.2. From these it may be seen that ICL is in a competitive position with IBM only in Europe and the Commonwealth. The United States of America, where IBM has an estimated 65% share of the market for large mainframe computers (Golden, 1983), forms a relatively negligible part of the activities of ICL (less than 2%) though it formerly had a manufacturing plant at Utica in New York state which it

Figure 7.2:   Geographical spread of turnover for IBM Corp.
and STC ICL, 1983

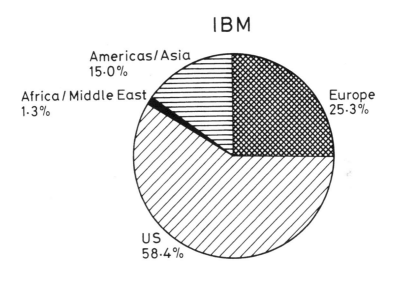

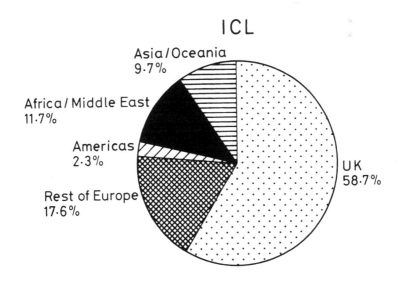

acquired from Singer Business Machines in 1976. This plant was closed down during rationalisation in 1985.

Table 7.6: Top 10 data-processing companies in the world in terms of revenue, 1985, plus selected UK companies

Rank	Company	Country	1985 DP Revenue ($m)	DP Revenue as % of total	Share of Top 100
1	IBM	US	50,056.0	97%	33.2%
2	DEC	US	7,029.4	100%	4.7%
3	Sperry	US	4,755.1	86%	3.2%
4	Burroughs	US	4,685.3	93%	3.1%
5	Fujitsu	Japan	4,309.5	66%	2.9%
6	NCR Corp.	US	3,885.5	90%	2.6%
7	NEC	Japan	3,761.8	38%	2.5%
8	Control Data	US	3,679.7	100%	2.4%
9	Hewlett-Packard	US	3,675.0	56%	2.4%
10	Siemens	FRG	3,265.0	18%	2.2%
24	STC PLC	UK	1,330.8	52%	0.9%
55	British Telecom	UK	455.1	4%	0.3%
61	Racal	UK	380.8	35%	0.3%
77	Ferranti	UK	282.1	38%	0.2%

Source: Datamation magazine, June 1986

The trade journal Datamation publishes an annual list of the top one hundred data processing companies worldwide (hardware and software). Table 7.6 shows the top ten companies in this list plus selected UK companies (Datamation, June 1986). IBM, which is ranked first, has a 33.2% share of the total revenue of the top 100, up from 33.1% in 1983. STC ICL, which is ranked 24th, has only a 0.9% share of this market, down from 1.2% in 1983. Part of the apparent weakening in ICL's market share is however due to currency fluctuations.

In Europe ICL is one of a group of indigenous national firms that attempt to compete with IBM. However, this is an unequal struggle. In 1984, for instance IBM's European data-processing revenues exceeded the combined turnover of its twelve closest European competitors (Datamation magazine, August 1985). ICL ranked tenth in European data processing revenues in 1984 behind Siemens (West Germany), Olivetti (Italy), CII-Honeywell Bull (France), Ericsson (Sweden),

Conclusions: Crisis and Development

Nixdorf (West Germany) and four US companies including IBM.
ICL's new management team appointed at the behest of the
Government in May 1981 following the company's collapse, have
adopted a far more European stance than hitherto, even to the
extent of holding their first major post-reorganisation press
conference in Paris on 14th September 1981 (de Jonquieres,
1981). ICL has also launched a series on European
collaborative ventures in addition to those made with
Japanese and North American firms detailed in section 3.2. In
particular, ICL is funding jointly with Siemens of West
Germany and Bull of France a research institute to be known as
the European computer industry research centre GmbH which
started operations in Munich in January 1984. The centre,
which is intended to carry out basic research on knowledge
processing and advanced information-handling techniques
rather than developing commercial projects, should employ 50
researchers when it is fully operational. In addition, ICL is
participating in the EEC-funded 'Esprit' research programme in
information technology.

In February 1984, ICL was among 12 leading European
computer manufacturers which signed an agreement to put into
effect the international standards for interface protocols
and networks for the industry currently being defined by the
International Standards Organisation (ISO). This is seen as an
important step in leading to 'Open Systems Interconnection'
(OSI) which would allow free international competition
between manufacturers. ICL has been particularly vigorous in
petitioning the government to adopt these international
standards and new product releases by the company have been
OSI-compatible. The European firms were joined in April 1984
by the American firms DEC and Burroughs, in an attempt to stop
the IBM 'System Network Architecture' (SNA) , which has been
operational since 1974, becoming the de facto standard in
Europe and thus suppressing competition.

The battle over what constitutes fair competition is
also being fought in the courts. Following an eight year
report, the EEC decided to take IBM to court over alleged
unfair trading practices. The case, which was settled out of
court in August 1984, was narrowed down from the original four
grievances to the fundamental complaint that IBM does not
disclose technical details about the interface requirements
of new products until they are actually shipped to customers,
instead of when they are first announced. This denies adequate
time for competing firms to develop 'plug compatible'
hardware. In the American courts a series of private law suits

initiated by the Greyhound Computer Corporation in 1969 and by six other companies in 1973 claiming damages for alleged violation of Federal antitrust law, had all been resolved either out of court or in favour of IBM by the early 1980s. A civil antitrust complaint initiated by the Department of Justice seeking to reorganise IBM into a series of independent competing organisations, was dropped by the U.S. Government in 1982 amid fears of Japanese competition in the vital computers and telecommunications industry. Ironically, while the US courts decreed that the local telephone operations of AT&T should be split off from the main organisation, IBM has been allowed to expand its operations into telecommunications through the takeover of the PBX manufacturer, Rolm Corp.

IBM has recently been following a policy of engaging in collaborative agreements with firms involved in complementary but not competitive technologies. In the US, IBM has acquired the data communications firm Rolm, plus stakes in the telecommunications supplier MCI and the microchip manufacturer Intel. In the field of Local Area Networking IBM has collaborated on research with Microsoft on the MS-Net operating system and software, has purchased product rights from Sytek for the broadband PC Net and has entered distribution agreements with Novell and Torus. In Europe IBM has recently been involved in talks about possible collaborative ventures with European public telecommunications companies (PTTs), and in the markets of banking, electronic funds transfer, and satellite technology. These moves are facilitated by convergence between the technologies of computing and telecommunications and by liberalisation of nationalised authorities such as British Telecom. However, they are also a response to competition from the newly-deregulated telecommunications giant AT & T which has initiated similar links with the Italian office automation firm, Olivetti.

7.2.3 ICL, IBM and the geography of the British computer industry

During the course of the last thirty years, the manufacturing, software and R&D activities of both ICL and IBM (UK) have become significantly more concentrated in the South Eastern region. For ICL, the growth of software and R&D facilities in Berkshire and administrative, sales and marketing functions in London since 1970 has produced a new geography of the company which now has a majority of its

employment (56%) in the South East. This contrasts with the
original Midlands/North West orientation of Ferranti and
English Electric. For IBM, UK manufacturing facilities were
originally concentrated in Scotland but since 1958, first R&D,
then high value manufacturing and finally administrative and
marketing functions for the company have been located in
Hampshire. IBM is now a major employer in Hampshire with
around 7,000 employees in the county in 1985 (IBM (UK) Ltd.,
n.d.). Elsewhere in the South East, educational, sales and
customer support facilities bring the proportion of IBM
employees within that region to more than two-thirds of the
total. Thus the increasing concentration of computer industry
employment in the South East generally noted in chapter six
can be seen to be principally a reflection of employment
change in the two major companies.

Table 7.7:   Selected socio-economic characteristics of
             Winchester, Bracknell and GB, 1981

Area	% Social Class I & II	% of men with higher education qualifications	% of males unemployed
Winchester, Hants	34.6%	22.1%	4.5%
Bracknell, Berks	34.9%	19.8%	5.2%
GB average	23.6%	13.7%	10.5%

Note   Social Class I = Managerial/professional occupations
       Social Class II = Intermediate skilled non-manual
                         occupations

Source: OPCS (1984) Key statistics for local authorities,
          Census 1981 Tables 5, 6 and 7A.

What are the factors underlying changing locational
determinants for the two companies? Undoubtedly the major
factor has been the need to recruit high-calibre staff.
Changing skill requirements in the computer industry have
placed a premium on highly-qualified personnel and IBM's
recruitment advertising budget, for instance, is over £1m per
annum. Table 7.7 shows selected socio-economic characteristics
of the resident population in the Local Authority districts
of Bracknell, Berks and Winchester, Hants where ICL and IBM
(UK) have their main R&D facilities. In comparison to the
national average, both areas have a higher proportion of the

resident population engaged in managerial and professional occupations (social classes I and II), and more males with higher educational qualifications, but less than half the national rate of male unemployment. Both areas have an attractive semi-rural residential environment, and are located in Britain's so-called 'M4 Corridor' - an area which has good access to London and international airports. The growth of this subregion as a centre for high-technology industry is traced by Breheny & McQuaid (1985). They identify the key role of military and civil research establishments and inward investors in promoting industrial growth in the area. Clearly the presence of ICL and IBM research units in the area has been influential in attracting other computer industry R&D units to the area including DEC in Reading, Hewlett-Packard in Wokingham and Information Technology Ltd. in Winchester. Poaching of staff between companies in the area is rife.

A second contributory factor to the changing 'geography' of the two firms is the effect of technological change on labour requirements. The level of labour intensity in the production process has declined significantly with electronics miniaturisation. The number of ICL employees involved in manufacturing has declined from 13,000 in the early 1970s to less than 4,000 now. Thus a substantial proportion of the ICL redundancies have been of manual employees, concentrated in areas with ICL manufacturing plants, chiefly the counties of Staffordshire, Cheshire, Greater Manchester and Hertfordshire all of which have declined in total computer industry employment since the mid-1970s (see Figs. 6.7 and 6.8). The increasing capital intensiveness of the manufacturing process is less immediately apparent in IBM as both manufacturing plants in Greenock and Havant have continued to increase in overall employment. However, this has been achieved through an internal shift from manual to non-manual occupations in keeping with IBM's policy of full employment. Almost three.out of every four IBM employees in the UK are now involved in non-manual occupations. One by-product of this is that the availability of regional development grants in assisted areas has had little influence on the location of new investment as software and R&D facilities have not until recently been eligible for assistance.

Table 7.8: Exports of computers and office machinery by
country of origin, 1974-84

Area	1974		1984		% Change p.a.
	Value ($m)	(%)	Value ($m)	(%)	1974-1984
US	2,525	(32.4%)	13,510	(31.2%)	+18.3%
Japan	655	(8.4%)	8,990	(20.8%)	+29.9%
W. Germany	1,192	(15.3%)	3,483	(8.0%)	+11.3%
United Kingdom	723	(9.3%)	2,927	(6.8%)	+15.0%
France	690	(8.9%)	1,838	(4.2%)	+10.3%
Italy	441	(5.7%)	1,283	(3.0%)	+11.3%
Benelux	363	(4.7%)	2,032	(4.7%)	+18.8%
Scandinavia	292	(3.8%)	956	(2.2%)	+12.6%
Rest of Europe	216	(2.8%)	2,033	(4.7%)	+25.1%
South America	224	(2.9%)	587	(1.3%)	+10.1%
Asia	210	(2.7%)	2,873	(6.6%)	+29.9%
Canada	207	(2.7%)	1,140	(2.6%)	+18.6%
Rest of World	48	(0.6%)	1,623	(3.7%)	+42.2%
TOTAL	7,786	(100.0%)	43,275	(100.0%)	+18.7%

Source: OECD

7.3 The international competitiveness of the British computer industry

7.3.1 International trade statistics

Trade statistics produced monthly and annually by the
Organisation for Economic Co-operation and Development (OECD)
provide a useful guide to the level of activity in computer

markets worldwide and the relative international balance of power. Because of the relative 'openness' of international markets, import statistics can be used as a surrogate for domestic demand in most nations except those with a strong manufacturing base or protectionist trade policies. Similarly export statistics can be used as a measure of international competitiveness among the domestic industries of computer exporting countries.

Table 7.8 uses OECD data to chart global trends in exports of computers and office machinery over the period from 1974 to 1984. The most notable change in the relative position of international competitors over this period is the rise of Japanese companies to take more than a fifth of world export markets in 1984. The main loser has been the European nations whose combined share of the world market fell from a half in 1974 to a third in 1984. Furthermore the cumulative trade deficit in Europe had grown to almost $10 billion in 1984 compared with trade surpluses of $5 billion in the United States and $8 billion in Japan. Of the European nations only Eire, which is used as a manufacturing base by multinational corporations, maintains a trade surplus.

The UK's share of the world market for computers and office machinery fell by more than a quarter between 1974 and 1984. However, it is evident that there has been a marked deterioration since 1979. Between 1974 and 1979, the rate of growth of computer exports from the UK was 21% p.a., but since 1979 this has fallen to just 9% p.a., around half the rate of growth in world market demand. This deterioration since 1979 is entirely in line with arguments advanced earlier concerning the crisis in the domestic computer sector. Imports of computers into the UK have continued to grow at a consistently higher rate than exports. Since 1979, imports of computers have grown by 17% p.a., equivalent to the international average. Thus it can be inferred that it is not true that the general industrial recession in British industry has reduced home demand for computers. Rather it is the specific failure of the domestic computer industry to compete with foreign manufacturers in the home and overseas markets.

7.3.2 British firms in the international and domestic markets

Tables 7.9 and 7.10 show the position of UK firms in 1985 in the world market (calculated from the Datamation top 100 data processing firms – see also Table 7.6) and in the UK market (calculated from sales of the top 20 data processing

Conclusions: Crisis and Development

Table 7.9: The Datamation top 100 data-processing firms, 1985,
by nationality

Nation	No. of companies in top 100	Combined 1985 DP revenue ($m)	Percent of top 100	% Change 1984-85
US/Canada	68	115,311	(76.5%)	+8.8%
Japan	12	18,517	(12.3%)	+8.7%
West Germany	5	5,771	(3.8%)	+16.1%
United Kingdom	7	3,128	(2.1%)	-0.8%
France	3	2,519	(1.7%)	+14.1%
Italy	1	2,518	(1.7%)	+18.7%
Netherlands	1	1,366	(0.9%)	+9.6%
Sweden	1	1,233	(0.8%)	+9.8%
Others	2	437	(0.3%)	+25.8%
Top 100	100	150,800	(100.0%)	+9.2%

Source: Datamation magazine, June 15 1986, p56-59
NB DP = Data processing

Table 7.10: The top 20 data processing firms in the UK, 1984
by nationality

Nation	No. of companies in top 20	Combined 1984 DP revenue (£m)	Percent. of top 20	% Change 1983-84
United States	9	3,504.5	(58.5%)	+36.6%
United Kingdom	9	2,233.5	(37.3%)	+9.0%
Others	2	251.4	(4.2%)	+426.7%
Top 20	20	5,989.4	(100.0%)	+28.5%

Source: Extel Company Cards
NB DP = Data processing

firms in 1984). In both markets there has been a marked
deterioration in the relative position of UK-owned firms
though the reasons for this differed. In the world market, the
falling value of sterling relative to the dollar produced an
apparent fall in the sales of the seven UK firms included in
the top 100. In sterling values however sales increased by 3%,
though this was still below the international average for the
industry. In the UK market, the declining market share
attributable to indigenous firms is partly due to the
acquisition by overseas companies of Acorn, and Systime.
However, the remaining nine indigenous companies in the top 20
grew only by 14% which again was less than the industry
average in the UK. In short, there has been a serious slippage
in the competitive position of the top UK-owned computer
firms which has been compounded by currency fluctuations and
acquisitions.

7.4 Industrial policy and the crisis in the British computer industry

Finally, a comment must be made on the 'success' or
otherwise of the government's intervention in the computer
industry during the 1960s through the creation of ICL as a
'flag carrier' for the domestic computer industry. During the
1970s, ICL experienced much faster rates of growth than IBM
(UK) and even managed to narrow the gap in market share for a
short time. Equally, there is no evidence that ICL lost its
technological progressiveness relative to IBM during this
period (Stoneman, 1977). Perhaps the best defence for the
government's policy lies in the fact that the UK is the only
country in Europe where IBM has less than a 50% market share
(De Jong, 1981, p266). The creation of ICL managed to stabilise
in the short term the slide towards US domination of the
industry that was occurring during the 1960s. The defence of
the UK computer industry during the 1960s had been based on
'nationalistic' preferential procurement policy and single-
tender contracting. However, the withdrawal of preferential
treatment for ICL after 1980, combined with the lack of
foresight on the part of management of the implications of
technological change, precipitated ICL's 1979-82 financial
crisis.

It is by no means clear that STC's takeover of ICL has
done anything to improve ICL's competitiveness. Certainly the
merger of the two companies has correctly anticipated
the direction of technological convergence between

telecommunications and computing. However, the financial base of the new company remains weak and there is little evidence so far of 'synergy' between the two companies. In comparison to IBM the joint company is overstaffed and further job shedding seems inevitable. In many ways it is unrealistic to talk of 'competing with IBM'. As one ICL manager commented, "IBM shapes the market environment of the computer industry within which other firms compete". Since 1981 ICL has moved towards a position of manufacturing only selected products and 'buying-in' other parts of the range from other manufacturers. Thus the original argument advanced in 1968 for supporting a domestic manufacturer able to compete internationally is somewhat weakened. However, ICL is now one of the few European-owned manufacturers of mainframe computers, and the 'strategic' argument for supporting ICL against US domination of the industry is as strong as ever. IBM's monopolistic position in the supply of mainframe computers has allowed it to impose its pricing policy and its proprietary interface protocols on the industry. Thus any moves by overseas firms to acquire STC following its recent trading difficulties and thereby to acquire ICL should be strongly resisted.

It is clear that a new direction in government policy has been required since 1980 to stem the growing balance of payments deficit in information technology goods. When the policy of preferential treatment for ICL ended in 1980 there was an opportunity to develop an EEC-wide computer policy. For instance, it might have been possible to use import restrictions and tariffs to give the European data processing firms the same protection afforded to their US and Japanese competitors. Similarly, European-wide funding of computer R&D could have supplemented or replaced individual country's efforts, as has occurred in the aerospace industry. In other research-intensive industries such as aerospace, European collaboration has become of major importance. Individual national markets are too limited to support volume production and individual companies are too small to fund the necessary R&D costs. There is also an opportunity for collaboration in data communications particularly if international interface standards (Open Standards Interconnection - OSI) can be agreed upon and insisted upon in government purchasing policy. The precedents for European cooperation are not good following the collapse of the UNIDATA project in the early 1970s. Nevertheless, at the mainframe/mini end of the computer industry collaborations is essential if a viable European R&D and manufacturing capability is to be maintained. European link-ups on research have been limited thus far to pre-competitive basic research (for instance the Esprit and Eureka programmes). Consequently European firms have formulated collaborative ventures mainly with North American and Japanese firms. ICL (UK), Siemens (West Germany) and Secoinsa (Spain) have links with Fujitsu of Japan; Bull (France) has links with Honeywell (US) and NEC (Japan); and Philips (Netherlands) and Olivetti (Italy) have links with AT&T of the US. In the data processing world therefore European unity has been a non-starter, but in the absence of such co-operation it is likely that the European trade deficit in electronics will continue to grow.

At the microcomputer/software end of the computer industry the situation is very different. Here it is small and often new firms which have thrived and the larger firms which have been slow to respond to the demands of rapid technological change. New firms are the seedcorn of future industrial competitiveness and it was shown in chapter five that the computer new firms sector in Britain is currently in a very healthy state. Government policy towards the computer industry needs to recognise the importance of small firms. Better provision for their needs should be made in public purchasing, venture capital provision and regional development agencies. It should be appreciated too that management buy-outs and spin-offs are also a source of new firms and enhanced competitiveness. There is scope for encouraging sponsored spin-outs from larger organisations through changes in the tax law and through improved provision of venture capital finance.

At first sight, these policy recommendations may seem contradictory: European co-operation and consolidation at the top end of the industry; diversification and the encouragement of new firms at the bottom end. However, it is the contention of this book that it is no longer possible to treat the computer industry as a single entity. Rather policy should reflect the way in which technological change has transformed the industry. Policy prescription needs to be relevant to the stage of the product cycle, and the computer industry is now sufficiently mature to accommodate several overlapping product cycles.

The position of the present government towards high technology could, at best, be described as 'ambivalent', at worst as 'hypocritical'. Despite the extension of loan guarantee facilities to ICL in 1981 to prevent financial collapse, the government's policy towards the computer industry has largely been non-interventionist (see chapter four). The government's support for the information technology industry has consisted more of 'gestures' (such as IT year in 1982, or the practice of giving visiting dignitaries a British-designed home computer) than of material help. More positive moves, such as the Alvey programme or the 'bail out' of ICL in 1981, have come on the initiative of individual ministers, but on the whole industrial policy has been neglected and uncoordinated (House of Lords, 1985, p60-81). The Department of Trade and Industry (DTI) has had more than its share of misfortune with two ministerial resignations and a further minister being the victim of an IRA bombing campaign. Even so, the run-down in its operations has been unmatched by any other governmental department. Under the current Conservative administration, DTI expenditure has been cut by 56% in real terms (1979-86; cf overall rise of 9%, HM Treasury, 1986, table 2.2). DTI spending is projected to fall from 5.1% of the total governmental budget in 1978-9 to just 1.0% in 1988-9 (HM Treasury, 1986, Chart 1.11). While it is true that some of this 'saving' has been achieved through the privatisation of formerly nationalised industries, there is no evidence that the revenue gained from these sales of public assets has been reinvested. The sale of British Telecom in particular diverted considerable amounts of potential private sector investment from industry to the reduction of the Public Sector Borrowing Requirement (PSBR).

By contrast defence spending has risen by 30% between 1979 and 1986. In chapter four it was shown that the proportion of the R&D budget spent on defence has progressively risen and following the signing of the agreement to collaborate with the American government on the Strategic Defence Initiative (SDI), this imbalance towards defence can only increase. It is hard to escape the conclusion that under the current administration there has been a significant shift of human and material resources from commercial industry to the defence sector. If it is true, as certain free market ideologues have suggested, that the cause of Britain's industrial demise is because private enterprise has been 'crowded out', then it is because of a defence sector which is out of all proportion to Britain's current international status. It is the contention of this book that if the current neglect of industrial policy at the expense of defence spending continues then in ten years' time it will no longer be possible to write of a British computer industry.

Bibliography

ACARD (1980) Information Technology, HMSO, London, 55pp

ACARD with ABRC (1983) Improving the research links between higher education and industry, HMSO, London, 79pp

Allen, M. (ed. 1985) The Times 1000, 1985-6, Times Books, London

Allesch, J. (1985) The role of the universities in the development of the HTBNF sector: The example of Berlin, FRG, Anglo-German Symposium, Cambridge, April 9-10, 1985

Alvey Committee Report (1982) A Programme for Advanced Information Technology, Dept. of Industry, HMSO, London, 71pp

Anthony, D. (1983) 'Japan' in Storey, D.J. (ed. 1983) The small firm: An international survey, Croom Helm, London, 274pp

Augarten, S. (1985) Bit by bit: an illustrated history of computers, Allen & Unwin, London, 324pp

Aydalot, P. (1984) 'Questions for regional economy', Tidjschrift voor Economische en Sociale Geografie, 75.1, 4-13

Aydalot, P. (1985) 'The location of new firm creation: the French case', Forthcoming in Keeble, D.E. & Wever, E. (eds 1986) New firms and regional development in Europe, Croom Helm, London, 336pp

Barron, I. & Curnow, R. (1979) The future with microelectronics: Forecasting the future of information technology, Frances Pinter, London, 243pp

Beaumont, J. (1982a) 'The location, mobility and finance of new high-technology companies in the UK electronics industry', Unpublished MSS, Dept. Trade & Industry, South East Regional Office, 28pp

Beaumont, J. (1982b) 'The finance of new high-technology companies in the UK electronics industry', Unpublished MSS, Dept. Trade & Industry, South East Regional Office, 9pp

Bellringer, B. (1973) The grass roots of ICL, Unpublished MSS, ICL History Archives, Stevenage, 2pp

Benn, Rt. Hon A.W. (1967) The Government's policy for Technology, Lecture given at Imperial College, London, 17/10/67, Mintech, London, 15pp

Beresford, P. (1985a) 'MoD cash targeted at electronics', Sunday Times, 5/5/85 p66

Beresford, P. (1985b) 'Sliding scale of British industry', Sunday Times, 21/7/85 p63

Binks, M. & Coyne, J. (1983) 'The birth of enterprise: An analytical and empirical study of the growth of small firms', Hobart Paper, no.98, Institute of Economic Affairs, London, 83pp

Binks, M. & Jennings, A. (1983) New firms as a source of industrial regeneration, Paper delivered at 6th National Small Firms Policy and Research Conference, University of Durham, Sept. 1-3, 1983, 17pp

Birch, D.L. (1979) The job generation process, MIT Working Paper, Programme on neighbourhood and regional change

Blackaby, F. (ed. 1979) 'Deindustrialisation', National Institute of Economic and Social Research Economic Policy Papers, no. 2, Heinemann Educational, London, 274pp

Boddy, M. & Lovering, J. (1985) 'High technology industry in Bristol: The aerospace/defence nexus', p45-82 in Gripaios, P. (ed. 1985) The South West economy, Plymouth Polytechnic, Plymouth, 121pp

Bolton Committee (1971) Committee of Inquiry on Small Firms, Parliamentary session 1971, vol.IX, p47, Cmnd 4811

Booz, Allen & Hamilton (1979) The electronics industry in Scotland: A proposal strategy, Scottish Development Agency, Glasgow, 96pp

Bosworth, D.L. (ed. 1983) The employment consequences of technological change, Macmillan, 1983, 256pp

Bowles, J.R. (1981) 'Research & Development Expenditure: expenditure and employment in the seventies', Economic Trends, 334, Aug. 1981 p94-111

Bowles, J.R. (1984) 'Research & Development in the UK in 1981', Economic Trends, 370, Aug. 1984 p81-96

Braun, E. & MacDonald, S. (1978) Revolution in miniature: The history and impact of semiconductor electronics, CUP, London, 231pp

Braverman, H. (1974) Labour and Monopoly Capitalism: The degradation of work in the twentieth century, Monthly Review Press, New York and London

Brayshaw, P. & Lawson, G. (1982) 'Manpower training in the electronics industry', EITB Reference Paper, RP/5/82

Breheny, M. (1986) Defence procurement and regional development: The case of the M4 corridor, Unpublished paper given at the IBG Conference, Univ of Reading, Jan. 6-9, 1986

Breheny, M., Cheshire, P. & Langridge, R. (1983) 'The Anatomy of Job Creation? Industrial Change in Britain's M4 Corridor', Built Environment, 9.1, 61-71

Breheny, M.J. & McQuaid, R.W. (1985) 'The M4 Corridor: Patterns and Causes of Growth in High Technology Industry', Univ. of Reading, Dept. of Geography, Geographical Papers, 87, 41pp

Bibliography

British Business (1985) 'Industrial R&D in the UK in 1983', British Business, Jan. 18-25, p130-2

British Business (1985) 'Computer services: Turnover up 22% in 1984', British Business, 27 Sept.-3 Oct., p618-9

British Technology Group (1985) BTG Review

Britton, J.N.H. (1985) 'Research and development in the Canadian economy: sectoral, ownership, locational and policy issues', p67-114 in Thwaites, A.T. & Oakey, R.P. (eds 1985) The regional impact of technological change, Frances Pinter, London

Brock, G.W. (1975) The US Computer Industry: A Study of Market Power, Ballinger, Cambridge, Mass., 250pp

Brusco, S. (1982) 'The Emilian model: productive decentralisation and social integration', Cambridge Journal of Economics, 6, 167-84

Bullock, M. (1983) Academic enterprise, industrial innovation and the development of high technology financing in the US, Brand Bros. & Co., London, 44pp

Burgess, J.A. (1982) 'Selling places: Environmental images for the executive', Regional Studies, 16.1, 1-17

Business Statistics Office (Trienially) 'Expenditure and employment in industrial research and development' Business Monitor, MO14

Business Statistics Office (Annually) 'Analyses of UK manufacturing (local) units by employment size', Business Monitor, PA 1003

Business Statistics Office (Annually) 'Report on the Census of Production', Business Monitor, PA1002

Business Statistics Office (Quarterly) 'Computer Services', Business Monitor, SDQ9

Business Statistics Office (Quarterly) 'Import penetration and export sales ratios for manufacturing industry', Business Monitor, MQ12

Business Statistics Office (Quarterly) 'Office machinery and electronic data-processing equipment', Business Monitor, PQ3302 (formerly PQ366 - 'Electronic data-processing equipment')

Business Statistics Office (Quarterly) 'Overseas trade analysed in terms of industries', Business Monitor, MQ10

Business Statistics Office (1977) 'Statistics of Product Concentration of UK Manufacturers', Business Monitor, PO1006

Business Statistics Office (1978) Historical record of the Census of Production, 1908-70, Business Statistics Office, Gwent

Bibliography

Business Statistics Office (1979) 'Directory of Businesses', Business Monitor, PA1007

Buswell, R.J. (1983) 'Research and development and regional development: A review', p9-22 in Gillespie, A. (ed. 1983) London papers in regional science, 12

Buswell, R.J., Easterbrook, R.P. & Morphet, C.S. (1985) 'Geography, Regions and R&D activity: The case of the UK', p33-66 in Oakey, R.P. & Thwaites, A.T. (ed. 1985) The regional impact of technological change, Frances Pinter, London, 249pp

Buswell, R.J. & Lewis, E.W. (1970) 'The geographical distribution of industrial research activity in the UK', Regional Studies, 4.3, 297-306

Butcher Committee (1985) 'Signposts for the future', Final Report of the IT Skills Shortages Committee, Dept. of Trade and Industry, London

Butler, E.B. & Williams, B.R. (1983) 'Research & Development expenditure in the UK', Technical Change Centre, Working Paper, No. 83-002

Cabinet Office (Annually since 1983) Annual Review of Government-funded Research & Development, HMSO, London

Cameron, G.C. (1979) 'The national industrial strategy and regional policy', p297-322 in Maclennan, D. & Parr, J.B. (eds 1979) Regional Policy: Past experience and new directions, Martin Robertson, Oxford, 334pp

Cane, A. (1982) 'Annual Computer Census: IBM grip tightens on UK market', Financial Times, 20/9/82 p20

Carter, C. (ed. 1981) Industrial policy and innovation, Heinemann, London, 241pp

Central Statistical Office, (Annually) Annual Abstract of statistics, HMSO, London

Central Statistical Office, (Annually) Regional Trends, HMSO, London

Central Statistical Office, (Annually) Social Trends, HMSO, London

Central Statistical Office, (1976) Guide to official statistics, HMSO, London, 391pp

Central Statistical Office (1979) Standard Industrial Classification, revised 1980, HMSO, London, 69pp

Central Statistical Office (1981) Indexes to the Standard Industrial Classification, revised 1980 HMSO, London

Charles, D. (1985) Corporate strategy and R&D location, Unpublished postgraduate research paper, IBG Annual Conference, Leeds, Jan. 1985

Checkland, S.G. (1981) The upas tree: Glasgow 1875-78, Univ. of Glasgow Press, Glasgow

Cheshire, P. (1979) 'Inner areas as spatial labour markets: a critique of the inner area studies', Urban studies, 16, 29-43

Chisholm, M.D.I. (1976) 'Regional policies in an era of slow population growth and higher unemployment', Regional Studies, 10, 201-13

Civil Service Department (Annually) Civil Service Statistics, HMSO, London

Clark, J. (1983) 'Employment projections and structural change', p110-125 in Bosworth, D. (ed. 1983) The employment consequences of technological change, Macmillan, London, 256pp

Clark, J., Freeman, C. & Soete, L. (1981) 'Long Waves, Inventions and Innovations', p63-77 in Freeman, C. (ed. 1983) Long Waves in the World Economy, Butterworths, London, 245pp

Clark, U.G. (1976) 'The cyclical sensitivity of employment in branch and parent plants', Regional Studies, 10.3, 293-8

Clarke, I. (1985) The Spatial Organisation of Multinational Corporations, Croom Helm, London, 287pp

Clarke, Sir R. (1973) 'Mintech in retrospect, Parts I & II', Omega, 1, p25-38 & p137-163

Coates, R. (1985) 'A new broom in the house that Robb built', Computer News, 14/3/85 p28-9

Collins, N. & Williams, I. (1985) 'Switch Off: The crisis in STC and Thorn-EMI', Sunday Times, 7/7/85 p61

Computer News (1984a) 'Government kills off BT-IBM network plan', Computer News, 18/10/84 p1

Computer News (1984b) 'IBM head retaliates over JOVE rejection', Computer News, 8/11/84 p1

Computer News (1985) 'ICL slips down league table', Computer News, 29/8/85 p6-7

Conference of Socialist Economics - Microelectronics Group (1980) Microelectronics, capitalist technology and the working class, CSE Books, London, 148pp

Congdon, T. (1985) 'And now the high-tech deficit', The Times, 16/4/85

Connolly, J. (1968) History of computing in Europe, IBM World Trade Corp.

Cooke, P. (1985) 'Regional innovation policy: Problems and strategies in Britain and France', Environment & Planning C: Government & Policy, 3.3, 253-67

Cooke, P., Morgan, K. & Jackson, D. (1984) 'New technology and regional development in austerity Britain: the case of the semiconductor industry', Regional Studies, 18.4, 277-289

Cooper, C.M. & Clark, J. (1982) Employment, economics and technology: the impact of technological change on the labour market, Wheatsheaf, Brighton, 146pp

Coopers & Lybrand Associates, Drivas Jonas (1980), Provision of small industrial premises, Small Firms Division, Dept. of Trade and Industry, London

Crisp, J. (1982) 'IBM plans £20m factory expansion at Havant', Financial Times, 15/9/84

Crisp, J. (1983) 'A slimming course helps to revive ICL', Financial Times, 25/5/83 p 7

Crisp, J. (1985) 'Final connection in the ICL recovery plan', Financial Times, 25/4/85 p8

Cross, M. (1981) New firm formation and regional development, Gower, Farnborough, Hants, 342pp

Cross, M. (1982) 'Science in the Park', New Scientist, 18/2/82 p432-4

Cross, M. (1983) 'The United Kingdom', p84-119 in Storey, D.J. (ed. 1983) The small firm: an international survey, Croom Helm, London, 274pp

Crum, R. & Gudgin, G. (1978) Non-production activities in UK manufacturing industry, Commission of the European Communities, Brussels, 176pp

Dale, R. (1979) From Ram Yard to Milton Hilton: A history of Cambridge Consultants, Cambridge Consultants Ltd., Cambridge, 37pp

Dalyell, T. (1983) A Science Policy for Britain, Longman, London 135pp

Danson, M.W. (1982) 'The industrial structure and labour market segmentation: Urban and regional implications', Regional Studies, 16.4, 255-65

Datamation (1986) 'The Datamation 100', Datamation magazine, June 1986, p50-53

Davies, S. (1979) The diffusion of new processes, CUP, New York

Davis, J. (1985) 'Foreign investors given Government promise on free choice of regions', The Times, 27/3/85 p2

Dawkins, W. (1985) 'Small business aid shake-up', Financial Times, 13/3/85

De Jonquieres, G. (1981a) 'ICL's dash to make up for lost time', Financial Times, 16/9/81 p25

De Jonquieres, G. (1981b) 'ICL and Sinclair to collaborate on design of telephone terminal', Financial Times, 8/12/81 p32

De Jonquieres, G. (1984a) 'Nimble giant throws all competitors on defensive', Financial Times, Electronics in Europe

Bibliography

Survey, 28/3/84 pIV

De Jonquieres, G. (1984b) 'ICL fights for a place in the sun', Financial Times, 30/3/84 p24

DeGrasse, R. W. Jnr. (1983) Military expansion: Economic decline. The impact of US military spending on US economic performance, M.E. Sharpe Inc., Armonk, New York, 247pp

Delapierre, M., Gerard-Varet, L.A., & Zimmermann, J.B. (1981) 'The computer and data-processing industry', p257-88 in de Jong, H.W. (ed. 1981) The structure of European industry, Martinus Nijhoff, The Hague, 322pp

Dept. of Employment Gazette (1983) 'Final report on the September 1981 Census of Employment', Dept. of Employment Gazette, Occasional Supplement No. 2, Dec. 1983

Dept. of Employment Gazette (1985) 'Employment statistics', Dept. of Employment Gazette, Historical Supplement No. 1, April 1985

Dept. of Industry (1974) The regeneration of British Industry, HMSO, London, Cmnd. 5710

Dept. of Trade & Industry (1984) Companies in 1983, HMSO, London

Diamond, D. & Spence, N. (1983) Regional policy evaluation: A methodological review and the Scottish example, Gower, Aldershot, 170pp

Dorfman, N.S. (1983) 'Route 128: The development of a regional high-technology economy', Research Policy, 12.6, p299-316

Dosi, G. (1983) 'Technological paradigms and technological trajectories', p78-101 in Freeman, C. (ed. 1983) Long Waves in the World Economy, Butterworths, London, 245pp

Dosi, G. (1984) Technical change and industrial transformation: The theory and an application to the semiconductor industry, Macmillan, London, 338pp

Duncan, M. (1981) 'The Information Technology Industry in 1981', Capital & Class, 17, p78-113

The Economist (1983) 'Living by their wits: a survey of the Scottish economy', The Economist, 19/9/83

The Economist (1985) 'Privatisation in Britain: Making the modern dinosaur extinct', The Economist, 23/2/85 p72-4

Economist Intelligence Unit (1982) Chips in industry, The Economist, London

Eglin, R., Barber, L. & Brooks, R. (1983) 'Ivory Towers Ltd.', Sunday Times, 13/2/83 p63

Elias, P. & Keogh, G. (1982) 'Industrial decline and unemployment in Inner city areas of Great Britain: a review of the evidence', Urban studies, 19, 1-15

Bibliography

Electronics Location File (1984) 'UK Electronics Survey',
    Electronics Location File, 8, Feb. 1984
Elton, C.J. (1983) 'The impact of the Rayner review on
    unemployment and employment statistics', Regional Studies,
    17, p143-6 policy' Regional Studies, 14.3, pp 161-79
Faux, R. (1984) 'How the SDA Nurtured High Technology in
    Silicon Glen', The Times, 27/4/84
Feldman, M.A. (1985) 'Biotechnology and Local Economic Growth:
    The American Pattern', p65-79 in Hall, P. & Markusen, A.
    (eds 1985) Silicon Landscapes, Allen & Unwin, Boston,
    160pp
Fidgett, A. (1984) 'The engineering industry: its manpower and
    training', EITB Reference Paper, RP/1/84, 18pp
Financial Times (1981a) 'A last chance for ICL', Financial
    Times, 12/5/81 Editorial p22
Financial Times (1981b) 'ICL to axe 5,200 more jobs: warning of
    big losses', Financial Times, 6/6/81 p1
Firn, J.R. (1975) 'External control and regional development:
    The case of Scotland', Environment & Planning, A, 393-414
Firn, J.R. & Roberts, D. (1984) 'High technology industries', in
    Hood, N. & Young, S. (eds 1984) Industry, policy and the
    Scottish economy, Edinburgh Univ. Press, Edinburgh, 421pp
Forrester, J.W. (1977) 'Growth Cycles', De Economist, 4, 525-43
Forsyth, D.J.C. (1972) US investment in Scotland, Praeger,
    London
Fothergill, S. & Gudgin, G. (1979) 'The job generation process
    in Britain', Centre for Environmental Studies, Research
    Series no.32, CES, London
Fothergill, S. & Gudgin, G. (1982) Unequal growth: Urban and
    regional employment change in the UK, Heinemann, London,
    210pp
Fothergill, S., Kitson, M. & Monk, S. (1984) Urban industrial
    decline: The causes of the urban-rural contrast in
    manufacturing employment change, Final Report - June 1984,
    Cambridge University Dept. of Land Economy
Fox, B. (1982) 'Electronics sweeps the Emerald Isle', New
    Scientist, 4/2/82, p302-4
Frank, C.E.J., Miall, R.H.C, & Rees, R.D. (1984) 'Issues in small
    firms research of relevance to policy-making', Regional
    Studies, (Policy Review Section), 18.3, p257-66
Freeman, C. (1971) 'The role of small firms in innovations in
    the UK since 1945', in Bolton Committee of Inquiry on
    Small Firms, Research Report no.6, HMSO, London
Freeman, C. (1974, 2nd ed. 1982) The economics of industrial
    innovation, Frances Pinter, London, 250pp

Freeman, C. (1979) 'The kondratiev long waves, technical change and unemployment', in OECD (1979) Structural determinants of employment and unemployment, Vol. 2, OECD, Paris

Freeman, C. (1980) 'Government Policy', p310-25 in Pavitt, K. (ed. 1980) Technical Innovation and British economic performance, Macmillan, London, 353pp

Freeman, C. (1983) Long Waves in the World Economy, Butterworths, London, 245pp

Freeman, C. (1984) The Role of Technical Change in National Economic Development, Unpublished MSS, Science Policy Research Unit, University of Sussex

Freeman, C., Clark, J. & Soete, L. (1982) Unemployment and technical innovation: A study of long waves and economic development', Frances Pinter, London, 214pp

Froebel, F., Heinrichs, J. & Kreye, O. (1980) The new international division of labour, CUP, Cambridge, 406pp

Frost, M. & Spence, N. (1981) 'Policy responses to urban and regional economic change in Britain', Geographical Journal, 147, 321-49

Galbraith, J.K. (1967) The New Industrial State, Hamish Hamilton, London

Ganguly, A. (1983a) 'Lifespan analysis of businesses in the UK 1973-82', British Business, 12-19 Aug. 1983, p838-845

Ganguly, A. (1983b) 'Year of birth/year of death analyses of businesses in the UK', British Business, 7-13 Oct. 1983, p306-10

Ganguly, A. (1984) 'Business Starts and Stops: Regional Analyses by Turnover Size and Sector 1980-83', British Business, 15-22 Sept., p350-3

Ganguly, A. (1985a) 'Business starts and stops: UK county analysis 1980-83', British Business, 18-25 Jan. 1985, p106-110

Ganguly, A. (1985b) 'Jobs, high-tech and small firms - more lessons from US experience', British Business, 12-19 April 1985, p10-11

Ganguly, A. (1985c) 'UK firms grow by 11% per cent in five years', British Business, 23-30 Aug. 1985, p354-6

Ganguly, A. & Povey, D. (1982) 'Small firms: The international scene', British Business, 19-26 Nov. 1982, p486-91

Gillespie, A. (ed. 1983) 'Technological change and regional development', London Papers in Regional Science, 12, Pion, London, 171pp

Glasmeier, A., Markusen, A. & Hall, P. (1983a) 'Defining high technology industries', IURDS Working Paper no.407, Univ. of California, Berkeley, 24pp

Bibliography

Glasmeier, A., Markusen, A. & Hall, P. (1983b) 'Recent evidence
   on high technology industries' spatial tendencies: a
   preliminary investigation', IURDS Working Paper no.417,
   Univ. of California, Berkeley
Goddard, J.B. (1980) The mobilisation of indigenous potential
   in the UK: A report to the regional policy directorate of
   the European Community, CURDS, Newcastle-upon-Tyne
Goddard, J. Coombes, M. & Owen, D. (1984) 'Residential
   unemployment   rates: Regional   and   Urban   policy
   perspectives', CURDS Functional Regions Factsheet, 8,
   5/1/84
Goddard, J.B. & Thwaites, A.T. (1984) 'Unemployment in the North;
   Jobs in the South - the regional dimensions to the
   introduction of new technology', Centre for Urban and
   Regional Development Studies, Discussion Paper, No. 54,
   University of Newcastle-upon-Tyne
Golden, F. (1983) 'John Opel: Shaking up the giant', Time
   Magazine, 3/1/83 p18
Goldsmith, M. (ed. 1984) UK Science Policy: A Critical Review
   of Policies for Publicly-funded Research, Longman, Harlow,
   Essex
Gould, A.J. & Keeble, D.E. (1984) 'New firms and rural
   industrialisation in East Anglia', Regional Studies, 18.3,
   189-201
Grant, W. (1982) The political economy of industrial policy,
   Butterworths, London, 160pp
Greater London Council (1985) London Industrial Strategy, GLC,
   London, 633pp
Green, S. (1982) Location and Mobility of Computer Service
   Companies, Unpublished MSS, Dept. of Trade and Industry, SE
   Regional Office, 13pp
Gudgin, G. & Fothergill, S. (1984) 'Geographical variation in
   the rate of formation of new manufacturing firms',
   Regional Studies, 18.3, 203-6
Hall, P. (1981) 'The Geography of the Fifth Kondratiev Cycle',
   New Society, March 26, 535-7
Hall, P. (1985) 'The geography of the fifth Kondratiev' p 1-19
   in Hall, P. & Markusen, A. (eds 1985) Silicon Landscapes,
   Allen & Unwin, Boston, 160pp
Hall, P. & Markusen, A. (eds 1985) Silicon Landscapes, Allen &
   Unwin, Boston, 160pp
Hall, P., Markusen, A., Osborn, R. & Wachsman, R. (1983) 'The
   computer software industry: prospects and policy issues',
   IURDS Working Paper no. 410, Univ. Of California, Berkeley

Bibliography

Hannah, L. (1976) The rise of the corporate economy, Methuen, London, 243pp

Hanson, D. (1982) The new alchemists: Silicon Valley and the microelectronics revolution, Little & Brown, Boston

Harris, F. & McArthur, R. (1985) 'The issue of high technology: An alternative view', NWIRU, Univ. of Manchester, School of Geography, Working Paper Series no.16, 42pp

Haug, P., Hood, N. & Young, S. (1983) 'R&D intensity in the affiliates of US-owned electronics companies manufacturing in Scotland', Regional Studies, 17.6, 383-392

Hawkins, K. (1979, 2nd ed. 1984) Unemployment, Penguin, Harmondsworth, 152pp

Heaford, G. (1985) 'Chips cubed - The ICL-Fujitsu link-up', British Business, 12-19 July, p60-62

Henry, M. (1983) 'The UK Electronics Industry: A qualified success', Barclays Review, 58.3, Aug. 1983, p56-61

Henwood, F.H. with Thomas, G. (1982) Science, technology and innovation: a research bibliography, Wheatsheaf books, Brighton, 250pp

HM Govt. (1972) Framework for Government Research & Development, HMSO, London, Cmnd. 5046

HM Treasury (1983) Changing employment patterns: Where will the new jobs be?, Unpublished memorandum by the Chancellor of the Exchequer, NEDO, London

HM Treasury (1986) The Government's expenditure plans 1986/7 to 1988/9, 2 Vols. Cmnd. 9702, HMSO, London

Hewer, A. (1980) 'Manufacturing industry in the Seventies: An assessment of import penetration and export performance', Economic Trends, June 1980, p97-109

Hillier, J. (1985) 'Multinational control in the Bristol economy', Area, 17.2, 123-7

Hirsch, S. (1967) Location of Industry and International Competitiveness, OUP, Oxford, 133pp

Hoare, A.G. (1974) International airports as growth poles: a case study of Heathrow airport, IBG Transactions & Papers, No. 63

Holford Committee (1950) Cambridge planning proposals: A report to the town and country planning committee of the Cambridgeshire County Council, Cambridgeshire County Council, Cambridge, 2 vols.

Holland, S. (1976) The regional problem, Macmillan, London

Hood, N. & Young, S. (1977) 'The long-term impact of multinational enterprise on industrial geography: The Scottish case', Scottish Geographical Magazine, 33, p279-94

244

Hood, N. & Young, S. (1983) Multinational investment strategies in the British Isles: A study of multinational enterprises in the Assisted Areas and in the Republic of Ireland, HMSO, London, 389pp

Hood, N. & Young, S. (eds 1984) Industry, policy and the Scottish economy, Edinburgh Univ. Press, Edinburgh, 421pp

House of Commons (1970) 'Reports, Accounts & Papers of the Select Committee on Science & Technology, Sub-Committee D', House of Commons Memoranda, Session 1969-70, vol. 137; House of Commons Appendices, Session 1969-70, vol. 272

House of Commons Public Accounts Committee (1978) '8th report from the Committee of Public Accounts', House of Commons Papers, 26, Session 1977-78

House of Commons Public Accounts Committee (1984) '15th report from the Committee of Public Accounts', House of Commons Papers, Session 1983-84, vol. 144

House of Lords (1985) Report from the Select Committee on Overseas Trade, Vol. 1, Session 1984-5, HMSO, London

Howells, J.R.L. (1984) 'The location of Research & Development: some observations and evidence from Britain', Regional Studies, 18.1, 13-29

IBM (UK Holdings) Ltd. (Not dated) IBM in Hampshire, IBM (UK) Ltd., Portsmouth, 14pp

IBM (UK Holdings) Ltd. (Not dated) IBM UK, IBM (UK) Ltd., Portsmouth, 36pp

IBM (UK Holdings) Ltd. (Annually since 1981) Annual review of operations

IBM Europe (Not dated) IBM in Europe, IBM Europe, Paris, 34pp

IBM Europe (1983) IBM in the European Community, IBM Europe, Paris, 7pp

IBM Europe (1984a) Facts about IBM operations in Europe, the Middle East, and Africa, IBM Europe, Paris, 9pp

IBM Europe (1984b) Facts about IBM's corporate responsibility programs in Europe, the Middle East and Africa, IBM Europe, Paris, 17pp

ICL (Not dated) ICL Distributed office systems, ICL PLC, London

ICL Public Limited Company (Annually since 1968) Annual Reports and Accounts

Illeris, S. (1985) 'New firm creation in Denmark: The importance of the cultural background' p141-50 in Keeble, D.E. & Wever, E. (eds 1986) New firms and regional development in Europe, Croom Helm, London, 322pp

Ingham, H. & Harrington, L.T. (1980) Inter-firm comparison, Heinemann, London, 150pp

Irvine, J. & Martin, B. (1984) Foresight in Science: Picking the winners, Frances Pinter, London, 166pp

Johnson, P.S. (1983) 'New manufacturing firms in the UK regions', Scottish Journal of Political Economy, 30, 25-9

Johnson, P.S. & Cathcart, D.G. (1979) 'New manufacturing firms and regional development: Some evidence from the Northern region', Regional Studies, 13.3, 269-80

Johnston, R.J. (ed. 1981) The dictionary of human geography, Basil Blackwell, Oxford, 411pp

Johnstone, W. (1982) 'No room in the middle for skilled men', The Times, 16/8/82

Johnstone, W. (1984) 'Financial Support needs to begin at home', The Times, 27/3/84 p17

Jordans & Sons (Surveys) (1981) The British Defence Industry, Jordans & Sons (Surveys) Ltd., London

Katz, B.A. & Phillips, A. (1981) 'Government, technological opportunities and the emergence of the computer industry', p419-46 in Giersch, H. (ed. 1982) Conference on Emerging Technology, Mohr, Tubingen, 480pp

Keeble, D.E. (1976) Industrial Location and Planning in the UK, Methuen, London, 317pp

Keeble, D.E. (1980) 'Industrial decline, regional policy and the urban-rural manufacturing shift in the UK', Environment & Planning, A, 12, 945-62

Keeble, D.E. (1986a) 'Industrial Change in the United Kingdom', Chapter 1 in Lever, W.F. (ed. 1986) Industrial Change in the United Kingdom, Longman, Harlow

Keeble, D.E. (1986b) 'The Changing Spatial Structure of Economic Activity and Metropolitan Decline in the United Kingdom', in Ewers H.-J., Matzerath, H., & Goddard, J.B. (eds 1986) The Future of the Metropolis: Economic aspects, de Gruyter, Berlin, New York

Keeble, D.E. & Gould, A. (1985) 'Entrepreneurship and manufacturing firm formation in rural regions: the East Anglian case', in Healey, M.J. and Ilbery B.W. (eds 1985), Industrialisation of the Countryside, Geobooks, Norwich

Keeble, D.E. & Kelly, T.J.C. (1985a) 'New firms and high technology industry in the UK: the case of computer electronics', p75-104 in Keeble, D.E. & Wever, E. (eds 1986) New firms and regional development in Europe, Croom Helm, London, 322pp

Keeble, D.E. & Kelly, T.J.C. (1985b) The regional distribution of new technology-based firms in the UK, Paper delivered at the Anglo-German symposium on HTBNFs in Britain and Germany, Cambridge, April 9-10, 1985

Bibliography

Keeble, D.E. & Wever, E. (1986) 'Introduction', p1-34 in Keeble, D.E. & Wever, E. (eds 1986) New firms and regional development in Europe, Croom Helm, London

Kelly, R. (1979) 'Technological innovation: International Trade Patterns', p41-56 in Gerstenfeld, A. & Brainard, R. (eds 1979) Technological innovation: Government/Industry Co-operation, 277pp

Kelly, T.J.C. (1986a) The location and spatial organisation of high technology industry in Great Britain: Computer electronics, Unpublished Ph.D, Dept. of Geography, Univ. of Cambridge

Kelly, T.J.C. (1986b) The anatomy of job creation: The case of the computer electronics industry, Unpublished paper given at the IBG conference, Jan 6-9, 1986, Univ. of Reading

Kondratiev, N.D. (1926) 'Die langen wellen der Konjunktur', Archiv fur Sozialwissenschaft, 56, 573-609 (tr.1935) 'The Long Waves of Economic Life', Review of Economic Statistics, 105-115

Kuhn, T.S. (1962, 2nd ed. 1970) The structure of scientific revolutions, International encyclopaedia of United Science, 2.2, Univ. of Chicago Press, 210pp

Lamb, J. (1982) 'IT82 - a critical year for Britain', New Scientist, 28/1/82, p221-4

Lamont, N. MP (1981) 'Innovation, technical change and regional development', Opening address of the Regional Studies Association Conference, 13/11/81, reprinted in Regional Studies, 16.5 (1982) 389-90

Langridge, R.J. (1984) 'Defining 'high-tech' for locational analysis', Discussion Paper in Urban and Regional Economics, Series C, no.22, Univ. of Reading, Dept. of Economics

Larsen, J.K. & Rogers, E.M. (1984) Silicon valley fever: Growth of high technology culture, Allen & Unwin, Hemel Hempstead, Herts., 302pp

Lavington, S. (1980) Early British Computers, Manchester University Press, Manchester, 139pp

Law, C. (1983) 'The defence sector in British Regional Development', Geoforum, 14, p169-84

Lawson, G. (1984) 'Electronic data processing equipment', EITB Sector Profile

Lawson, G. (1985) 'Manpower in the electronics industry', EITB Sector Profile, RM 8501, 25pp

Leigh, R., North, D. & Steinberg, L. (1984) Restructuring and locational change in London's electronics industries, Paper presented to 'The Future of the Metropolis'

Conference, Technical Univ. of Berlin, Oct 25-6, 1984

Levi, P. (1982) 'Cambridge: The place where success breeds growth', Financial Times, 30/11/82, p13

Lipietz, A. (1977) 'Le capital et son espace', Maspero: Economie et socialisme, 34

Little, A.D. (1977) New technology-based firms in the UK and the Federal Republic of Germany, Anglo-German foundation for the study of industrial society, Wilton House Publications Ltd., London, 323pp

Lloyd, P.E. & Mason, C.M. (1984) 'Spatial variations in new firm formation in the United Kingdom: Comparative evidence from Merseyside, Greater Manchester and South Hampshire', Regional Studies, 18.3, 207-220

Lovering, J. (1985) 'Regional intervention, defence industries, and the structuring of space in Britain: The case of Bristol and South Wales', Environment & Planning D: Society & Space, 3, p87-107

McDermott, P.J. (1976) 'Ownership, organisation and regional dependence in the Scottish electronics industry', Regional Studies, 10, 319-335

McDermott, P.J. (1977a) 'Overseas investment and the industrial geography of the UK', Area, 9, 200-207

McDermott, P.J. (1978) 'Changing Manufacturing Enterprises in the Metropolitan Environment: The case of electronics firms in London', Regional Studies, 12.5, 541-50

McDermott, P.J. (1979) 'Multinational manufacturing firms and regional development: external control in the Scottish electronics industry', Scottish Journal of Political Economy, 26.3, 287-306

McDermott, P.J. & Taylor, M. (1982) Industrial Organisation and Location, CUP, Cambridge, 226pp

MacGregor, B.D., Langridge, R.J., Adley, J. & Chapman, B. (1985) New firms and high-technology industry in Newbury district, Unpublished MSS, Dept. of Geography, Univ. of Reading

Macmillan Committee (1931) Report of the Committee on Finance and Industry, London, HMSO

McQuaid, R. (1985) 'The role of defence procurement in Regional Development in the UK', M4 Working Note 14, Dept. of Geography, Univ. of Reading

Macrae, N. (1985) 'Into entrepreneurial Britain: 25 ways to create employment/entrepreneurialism', The Economist, 16/2/85

Maddock, Sir I. (1983) Civil exploitation of defence technology, Report to the Electronics EDC, NEDO, London

Bibliography

Malecki, E.J. (1980) 'Corporate organisation of R&D and the location of technological activities', Regional Studies, 14, 219-34

Malecki, E.J. (1981) 'Science, technology and regional economic development: Review and prospects', Research Policy, 10.4, 312-334

Malecki, E.J. (1984a) 'High technology and local economic development', Journal of American Planning Association, 50.3, 262-69

Malecki, E.J. (1984b) 'Military spending and the US defense industry: regional patterns of military contracts and subcontracts', Environment & Planning C: Government & Policy, 2, p31-44

Malecki, E.J. & Rees, J. (1982) 'Technological change: a research agenda', p27-45 in Robson, B.T. & Rees, J. (eds 1982) Geographical agenda for a changing world, SSRC, London

Mandel, E. (1972 tr. 1975; 2nd ed. 1980) Late Capitalism, (Der SpatKapitalismus), Verso, London, 618pp

Mandel, E. (1978) The second slump, Verso Books, London

Mandel, E. (1980) Long Waves of Capitalist Development: The Marxist Interpretation, CUP, Cambridge, 151pp

Mandel, E. (1981) 'Explaining Long Waves of Capitalist Development', p195-201 in Freeman, C. (ed. 1983) Long Waves in the World Economy, Butterworths, London, 245pp

Markusen, A. (1983) 'High tech jobs, markets and economic development prospects', IURDS Working Paper No. 403, Univ. of California, Berkeley, 27pp

Markusen, A. (1985) Profit cycles, oligopoly and regional development, MIT Press, Cambridge, Mass. 357pp

Marsh, P. (1983) 'Britain's high technology entrepreneurs', New Scientist, 10/11/83, p427-32

Marsh, P. (1985a) 'Hi-tech Growth Companies: City Where Dreams Come True', Financial Times, 5/1/85

Marsh, P. (1985b) 'A hard-nosed breed of academics moves into commerce', Financial Times, 13/3/85

Martin, R.L. (1982) 'Job loss and the regional incidence of redundancies in the current recession', Cambridge Journal of Economics, 6, 375-95

Martin, R.L. (1985) 'Monetarism masquerading as regional policy? The Government's new system of regional aid', Regional Studies, 19.4, 379-88

Martin, R.L. (1986) 'Industrial restructuring, labour shake-out and the geography of recession', chapter 1 in Danson, M. (ed. 1986) Recession and redundancy: Restructuring the regions, Geobooks, Norwich

Martin, R.L. & Hodge, J.S.C. (1983) 'The reconstruction of British regional policy: The crisis of conventional practice', Environment & Planning C: Government & Policy, 1.2, 133-52

Martin, W.E. (ed. 1981) The Economics of the Profits Crisis, Dept. of Industry seminar proceedings, 1/4/80, HMSO, London, 226pp

Mason, C.M. (1983) 'Some definitional difficulties in new firms research', Area, 15.1, 53-60

Mason, C.M. (1985) 'The geography of 'successful' small firms in the United Kingdom', Environment & Planning A, 17.11, 1429-1566

Mason, C.M. (1986) 'The small firm sector', in Lever, W. (ed. 1986), Industrial change in the UK, Longman, Harlow, Essex

Mason, C.M. & Harrison, R.T. (1985a) The regional impact of public policy towards small firms in the UK, Paper presented to 'New firms and Area Development in the European Community', conference, Utrecht, March 21-2, 1985

Mason, C.M. & Harrison, R.T. (1985b) 'The geography of small firms in the UK: Towards a research agenda', Progress in Human Geography, 9.1, 1-37

Massey, D. (1979) 'In what sense a Regional Problem?', Regional Studies, 13.2, 231-241

Massey, D. (1984) Spatial divisions of labour: social structures and the geography of production, Macmillan, London, 339pp

Massey, D. & Meegan, R.A. (1978) 'Industrial restructuring versus the cities', Urban studies, 15, 273-88

Massey, D. & Meegan, R.A. (1979) 'The geography of industrial organisation: the spatial effects of the restructuring of the Electrical engineering sector under the Industrial Reorganisation Corporation', Progress in Planning, 10.3, 155-237

Massey, D. & Meegan, R.A. (1982) The anatomy of job loss: The how, why and where of unemployment, Methuen, London, 258pp

Matthews, R.C.O. (1982) Slower growth in the western world, Heinemann, London, 176pp

Matthews, T. (1984) 'Ireland: Where the greenbacks meet the green', Computer News, 6/9/84, p34-5

Mensch, G. (1975 tr. 1979) Stalemate in Technology: Innovations Overcome the Depression, Ballinger, New York, 241pp

Monopolies & Mergers Commission Report (1982) The Hong Kong and Shanghai banking corporation: Standard Chartered Bank Ltd., The Royal Bank of Scotland Group: A report of the

Bibliography

proposed merger, HMSO, London, Cmnd 8472

Moonman, E. (1971) British computers and industrial innovation: The implications of the Parliamentary Select Committee, Allen & Unwin, London, 126pp

Moore, B., Rhodes, J. & Tyler, P. (1983) 'The effects of government regional economic policy', Dept. of Land Economy Discussion Paper no.11, Univ. of Cambridge, 184pp

Moore, B. & Spires, R. (1983) The experience of the Cambridge Science Park, Unpublished paper given at OECD Workshop on Research Technology and Regional Policy, Paris, 24-7 Oct. 1983, 33pp

Moralee, D. (1981) 'The ICL story', Electronics & Power, 27, 11, p788-95

Morgan, K. (1983) 'The politics of Industrial Innovation in Britain', Government & Opposition, 18.3

Morgan, K. & Sayer, A. (1983) 'The International Electronics Industry and Regional Development in Britain', Urban and Regional Studies Working Paper, no. 34, Univ. of Sussex

Morgan, K. & Sayer, A. (1984) 'A 'modern' industry in a 'mature' region - the remaking of management-labour relations', Urban and Regional Studies Working Paper, no. 39, Univ. of Sussex

The Mott Committee (1969) 'Relationship between the university and science-based industry', Cambridge University Reporter, 22/10/69, p370-376

Murray, P. & Wickham, J. (1982) 'Technocratic ideology and the reproduction of inequality: The case of the electronics industry in the Republic of Ireland', p179-210 in Day, G. et al (eds 1982) Diversity and decomposition in the labour market

Nasbeth, L. & Ray, G.F. (1974) The diffusion of new industrial processes: An international study, CUP, Cambridge

NEDO (1981) Industrial performance: R&D and innovation, NEDO, London

NEDO (1982) Innovation in the UK, NEDO, London, 16pp

NEDO Electronic Capital Equipment SWP (1982) Real-time software R&D in the UK: A Survey and Recommendations for Action, NEDO, London, 12pp

NEDO Electronic Capital Equipment SWP (1984) Software engineering and CADMAT, NEDO, London, 21pp

NEDO Electronics EDC (1982) Policy for the UK electronics industry, NEDO, London, 32pp

NEDO Electronics EDC (1983) EEC tariff structure for electronic components and assemblies, NEDO Report EDC/ELEC(83)34, London, 27pp

Bibliography

NEDO Information Technology SWP (1983) <u>Policy for the UK</u>
    <u>Information Technology Industry</u>, NEDO, London
NEDO Information Technology SWP (1984) <u>Crisis facing UK</u>
    <u>Information Technology</u>, NEDO, London, 32pp
Northcott, J. & Rogers, P. (1984) 'Microelectronics in British
    industry: The pattern of change', <u>Policy Studies Institute</u>
Norton, R.D. & Rees, J. (1979) 'The product cycle and the
    spatial decentralisation of American manufacturing
    industry', <u>Regional Studies</u>, <u>13.2</u>, 141-51
Oakey, R.P. (1981) <u>High Technology Industry and Industrial</u>
    <u>Location</u>, Gower, Aldershot, Hants, 134pp
Oakey, R.P. (1983a) 'High-technology industry, industrial
    location and regional development: The British case',
    p279-95 in Hamilton, F.E.I. & Linge, G.J.R. (eds 1985)
    <u>Spatial analysis, industry and the industrial environment:</u>
    <u>Progress in research and applications</u>, Vol. 3, Wiley,
    Chichester, 652pp
Oakey, R.P. (1983b) 'New technology, government policy and
    regional manufacturing employment', <u>Area</u>, <u>15.1</u>, 61-5
Oakey, R.P. (1983c) 'Research and development cycles,
    investment cycles and regional growth in British and
    American small high-technology firms', <u>CURDS Discussion</u>
    <u>Paper</u>, <u>48</u>, Univ. of Newcastle-upon-Tyne
Oakey, R.P. (1984a) <u>High technology small firms: regional</u>
    <u>development in Britain and the United States</u>, Frances
    Pinter, London 179pp
Oakey, R.P. (1984b) 'Innovation and Regional Growth in Small
    High Technology Firms: Evidence from Britain and the USA',
    <u>Regional Studies</u>, <u>18.3</u>, 237-51
Oakey, R.P. & Thwaites, A.T. (1985) <u>The regional impact of</u>
    <u>technological change</u>, Frances Pinter, London, 249pp
Oakey, R.P., Thwaites, A.T. & Nash, P.A. (1980) 'The Regional
    Distribution of Innovative Manufacturing Establishments
    in Britain', <u>Regional Studies</u>, <u>14.3</u>, 235-53
Oakey, R.P., Thwaites, A.T. & Nash, P.A. (1982) 'Technological
    change and regional development: Some evidence on
    regional variations in product and process innovation',
    <u>Environment & Planning</u>, <u>A</u>, <u>14</u>, 1073-86
OECD (1979) <u>Structural determinants of employment and</u>
    <u>unemployment</u>, vols. I & II, OECD, Paris
OECD (1981) 'Information activities, electronics and
    telecommunications technologies: Impact on employment,
    growth and trade, vol.1', <u>Information Computer</u>
    <u>Communications Policy</u>, <u>no.6</u>

Bibliography

OECD (1984) OECD Science & Technology indicators: Resources devoted to R&D, OECD, Paris, 377pp

Office of Population, Censuses and Services (1984) Census 1981: Key statistics for Local Authorities, Great Britain, HMSO, London, 172pp

Pasinetti, L.L. (1981) Structural change and economic growth: A theoretical essay on the dynamics of the wealth, CUP, Cambridge, 281pp

Pavitt, K. (ed. 1980) Technical Innovation and British Economic Performance, Macmillan, London, 353pp

Pite, C. (1980) 'Employment and Defence', Statistical News, 51, p15-20

Pollard, S. (1982) The wasting of the British economy, Croom Helm, London, 197pp

Prais, S.J. (1976) The evolution of giant firms in Britain: A study of the growth of concentration in manufacturing industry in Britain 1909-70, CUP, Cambridge, 321pp

Premus, R. (1982) Location of high technology firms and regional economic development, Staff study for Joint Economic Committee, USGPO, Washington DC

Preston, P., Hall, P. & Bevan, N. (1985) 'Innovation in information technology industries in Great Britain', Dept. of Geography, Geographical Papers, no.89 Univ. of Reading

Rayner, Sir D. (1980) Review of government statistical services, Central Statistical Office, HMSO, London

Reed, C. (1985) 'Silicon Valley feels the pinch', The Guardian, 22/7/85, p23

Rees, J. (1979) 'Technological change and regional shifts in American manufacturing', Professional Geographer, 31.1, 45-54

Rees, J., Briggs, R. & Oakey, R.P. (1984) 'The adoption of new technology in the American machinery industry', Regional Studies, 18.6, 489-504

Rich, D.C. (1983) 'The Scottish Development Agency and the industrial regeneration of Scotland', Geographical Review, 73.3, 271-83

Robson, B.T. & Rees, J. (1982) Geographical agenda for a changing world, Report commissioned by SSRC Human Geography Committee, London

Ronayne, J. (1984) Science in government: A review of the principles and practice of science policy, Edward Arnold, London, 250pp

Rothschild, Lord (1971) A framework for Government Research & Development, HMSO, London, Cmnd. 4814

Rothwell, R. (1982) 'The role of technology in industrial change: Implications for regional policy', Regional Studies, 16.5, 361-9

Rothwell, R. (1984) 'The role of small firms in the emergence of new technology', Omega, 12.1, 19-29

Rothwell, R. & Zegveld, W. (1979) Technical change and employment, Frances Pinter, London, 178pp

Rothwell, R. & Zegveld, W. (1981) Industrial innovation and public policy: preparing for the 1990s, Frances Pinter, London, 251pp

Rothwell, R. & Zegveld, W. (1982) Innovation in the Small and Medium-Sized Firm: Their Role in Employment and Economic Change, Frances Pinter, London, 268pp

Rowlinson, F. (1985) A Geographical investigation into the Unlisted Securities Market, Unpublished B.A. Dissertation, University of Cambridge, Dept. of Geography

Saxenian, A. (1983a) 'The genesis of Silicon Valley', Built Environment, 9.1, p7-17

Saxenian, A. (1983b) 'The urban contradiction of Silicon Valley', International Journal of Urban and Regional Research, 7.2, 237-62

Sayer, A. (1983) 'Theoretical problems in the analysis of technological change and regional development', p59-73 in Hamilton, F.E.I. & Linge, G.J.R. (eds 1983) Spatial analysis, industry and the industrial environment Regional economies and industrial systems, Vol. 3, Wiley, Chichester, 652pp

Schumpeter, J.A. (1939) Business cycles: a theoretical, historical and statistical analysis of the capitalist process, (2 volumes), McGraw-Hill, New York

Schumpeter, J.A. (1942) Capitalism, socialism and democracy, Harper & Row, New York

Sciberras, E. (1977) Multinational electronics companies and national economic policies, JAI Press, Greenwich, Conn.

Sciberras, E., Swords-Isherwood, N.K. & Senker, P. (1978) 'Competition, technical change and manpower in electronic capital equipment: A study of the UK minicomputer industry', SPRU Occasional Paper Series, no.8, SPRU, Univ. of Sussex

Scottish Development Agency (1982a) Electronics in Scotland: Industry profile, Scottish Development Agency, Glasgow

Scottish Development Agency (1982b) Labour performance of US plants in Scotland, SDA, Glasgow, 24pp

Scottish Development Agency (1984a) Electronics companies in Scotland, SDA, Glasgow

Bibliography

Scottish Development Agency (1984b) <u>Annual report 1984: The agency in partnership</u>, SDA, Glasgow, 90pp

Scottish Development Agency (1985) <u>The information systems industry in Scotland: Programmed for growth</u>, SDA, Glasgow, 75pp

Scottish Education and Action for Development (1985) <u>Electronics and Development: Scotland and Malaysia in the international electronics industry</u>, SEAD, Edinburgh

Segal Quince & Partners, (1985) <u>The Cambridge Phenomenon: the growth of high-technology industry in a university town</u>, Segal Quince & Partners, Cambridge, 102pp

Short, J. (1981) 'Defence spending in the UK regions', <u>Regional Studies</u>, <u>15.2</u>, 101-110

Shutt, J. and Whittington, R. (1984) 'Large firm strategies and the rise of small units: the illusion of small firm job generation', <u>University of Manchester, School of Geography, Working Paper no. 15.</u>

Smith, K. (1985) 'Europe's computer demand undiminished', p73 in <u>Electronics Week</u>, 1/1/85

Sobel, R. (1981) <u>IBM – Colossus in transition</u>, Truman Talley Books, Times Books, New York, 360pp

Soete, L. (ed. 1985) <u>Technological trends and employment. Vol 3 – Electronics and Communications</u>, Gower, Aldershot, 255pp

Soete, L. & Dosi, G. (1983) <u>Technology and employment in the electronics industry</u>, Frances Pinter, London, 110pp

Solow, R.M. (1957) 'Technical change and the aggregate production function' <u>Review of Economics and Statistics</u>, <u>39</u>, p312-20 <u>vol.49</u>, p8-30

STC PLC (Annually) <u>Annual report and accounts</u>

STC/ICL (1984) <u>Recommended offer document to shareholders</u>, 27pp

Steed, G.P.F. (1982) 'Threshold Firms: Backing Canada's Winners', <u>Science Council of Canada: Background Study no. 48</u>, Ministry of Supply & Services, 173pp

Steed, G.P.F. and DeGenova, D. (1983) 'Ottawa's technology-oriented complex', <u>Canadian Geographer</u>, <u>27</u>, 263-278

Stoneman, P. (1977) 'Technological diffusion and the computer revolution: the UK experience', <u>Univ. of Cambridge, Dept. of Applied Economics Monograph no.25</u>, CUP, Cambridge, 219pp

Stoneman, P. (1983) <u>The economic analysis of technological change</u>, OUP, Oxford, 272pp

Storey, D.J. (1981) 'Finance for the new firm', <u>CURDS Discussion Paper no.36</u>, 37pp

Storey, D.J. (1982) <u>Entrepreneurship and the new firm</u>, Croom Helm, London, 223pp

Bibliography

Storey, D.J. (ed. 1983a) The small firm: An international survey, Croom Helm, London, 274pp

Storey, D. (1983b) 'Indigenising a regional economy: the importance of management buy-outs', Regional Studies, 17.6, Policy Review Section, 471-5

Storey, D.J. (1984) Business competitiveness: the role of small firms, Unpublished MSS, University of Newcastle-upon-Tyne, Centre for Urban and Regional Development Studies

Tank, A. (1984) 'DTI dismantling aid to industry', New Technology, 8/10/84 p25-30

Taylor, A. (1985) 'High technology industry and the development of science parks', p134-143 in Hall, P. & Markusen, A. (eds 1985) Silicon Landscapes, Allen & Unwin, Boston, 160pp

Thompson, C. (1978) Crumbs from the Ivory Tower: An informal survey of spin-off firms from the Univ. of Berkeley, Unpublished Master of City Planning thesis, Univ. of California, Berkeley, 65pp

Thwaites, A.T. (1978) 'Technological change, mobile plants and regional development', Regional Studies, 12, 445-61

Thwaites, A.T. (1982) 'Some evidence of regional variations in the introduction and diffusion of industrial products and processes within British manufacturing industry', Regional Studies, 16.5, 371-81

Thwaites, A.T. (1983) 'The employment implications of technological change in a regional context', p36-53 in Gillespie, A. (ed. 1983), London papers in regional science, Pion, London

Thwaites, A.T., Oakey, R.P. & Nash, P. (1981) 'Industrial innovation and regional development', Final Report to the Dept. of the Environment, vol.1, CURDS,

The Times (1983) 'Top 50 down in Fortune', The Times, 5/8/83

Tinbergen, J. (1981) 'Kondratiev cycles and so-called long waves: The early research', p13-18 in Freeman, C. (ed. 1983), Long waves in the world economy, Butterworths, London, 245pp

Townsend, J., Henwood, F., Thomas, G., Pavitt, K. & Wyatt, S. (1981) 'Science and technology indicators for the UK: Innovations in Britain since 1945', SPRU Occasional Papers, no. 16, Univ. of Sussex

TUC (1983) Where are the new jobs coming from?, Unpublished memorandum by the TUC, NEDO, London, 28pp

Turing, A.M. (1936) 'On compatible numbers, with an application to the Entscheidungs problem', Proceedings of the London Mathematical Society, Series no.2, 42, 230-65

256

Bibliography

Tyler, P. (1982) 'The growth of male and female manufacturing employment across the regions of the UK, 1952-76', Dept. of Land Economy, Discussion Paper no.6, Univ. of Cambridge

Tyler, P., Moore, B. & Rhodes, J. (1984) 'Geographical variations in industrial costs', Dept. of Land Economy, Discussion Paper no.12, Univ. of Cambridge, 122pp

Vernon, R. (1966) 'International investment and international trade in the product cycle', Quarterly Journal of Economics, 80, 190-207

Watts, D.H. (1981) The branch plant economy: A study of external control, Topics in Applied Geography Series, Longman, London, 104pp

Weiss, M.A. (1983) 'High technology industries and the future of employment', Built Environment, 9.1, 51-60

Westaway, J. (1974) 'The spatial hierarchy of business organisations and its implications for the British urban system', Regional Studies, 8.1, 145-55

Whittington, R.C. (1984) 'Regional bias in new firm formation in the UK', Regional Studies, 18.3, 253-6

Wiener, M.J. (1981) English culture and the decline of the industrial spirit 1850-1980, CUP, Cambridge, 217pp

Williams, R. (1984) 'British Technology Policy', Government & Opposition, 19.1, p30-51

Willott, W.B. (1981) 'The NEB involvement in electronics and information technology', p203-212 in Carter, C. (ed. 1981) Industrial Policy and Innovation, Heinemann, London, 241pp

Wilson, Rt. Hon J.H. (1971) The Labour Government, 1964-70 Weidenfeld & Nicholson, & Michael Joseph, London

Wilson Committee Report (1979) The financing of small firms: Interim Report of the Committee to review the functioning of financial institutions, HMSO, London, Cmnd. 7503. Final Report (1980) Cmnd. 7937

Wragg, R. & Robertson, T. (1978) 'Post-war trends in employment, productivity, output, labour costs and prices by industry in the UK', Research Paper no.3, Dept. of Employment, London

Wray, M., Markham, R. & Watts, D.R. (1974) Location of industry in Hertfordshire: Planning and industry in the post-war period, Hatfield Polytechnic, Hertfordshire, 312pp

Young, P. (1983) The power of speech: A history of Standard Telephones and Cables, 1883-1983, Allen & Unwin, London, 221pp

Young, S. (1984) 'The foreign-owned manufacturing sector', p93-127 in Hood, N. & Young, S. (eds 1984) Industry, policy and the Scottish economy, Edinburgh Univ. Press, Edinburgh, 421pp

INDEX

Index

Index

Index